Nutrition Almanac Cookbook

NUTRITION ALMANAC COOKBOOK

Nutrition Search, Inc.
John D. Kirschmann, Director
with
Lavin J. Dunne

McGraw-Hill Book Company

New York   St. Louis   San Francisco   Auckland
Bogotá   Guatemala   Hamburg   Johannesburg
Lisbon   London   Madrid   Mexico   Montreal
New Delhi   Panama   Paris   San Juan   São Paulo
Singapore   Sydney   Tokyo   Toronto

1 2 3 4 5 6 7 8 9 SEM SEM 8 7 6 5 4 3

ISBN 0-07-034846-4

First McGraw-Hill Edition

Library of Congress Cataloging in Publication Data

Main entry under title:
Nutrition almanac cookbook.
Bibliography: p.
Includes index.
1. Cookery.   2. Menus.   I. Nutrition Search, Inc.
TX651.N87   1983   641.5'63   82-25898
ISBN: 0-07-034846-4

Book design by Sharkey Design

CONTENTS

FOREWORD

Nutrition Search has taken a giant step forward with this system for balancing meals. We feel it is a breakthrough in foods and nutrition. For the first time, all the nutrients known to be essential to good health have been included in meal planning and in specific menus. The levels of five vitamins, six minerals, calories, proteins, carbohydrates, and fats have been carefully balanced in every menu to supply the Recommended Dietary Allowances (RDA) as prescribed by the National Research Council of the National Academy of Sciences. The key is the balance or proper proportion of all the recommended nutrients.

A great deal of ingenuity and thousands of hours of research made it possible to come up with a complete analysis of food. Then, with the use of a computer, we were able to balance and proportion all the meals included in this book.

It is apparent that we are what we eat. If we compute the nutrient value of the average American diet, we find that meals considered balanced are actually lacking in adequate nutrient levels. It is nearly impossible to obtain a nutritionally balanced meal without intensive programming.

We think the *Nutrition Almanac Cookbook* will fill that need. It will help people look better, feel better and live longer, healthier lives.

John D. Kirschmann,
Director,
Nutrition Search, Inc.

INTRODUCTION:
THE NUTRITION ALMANAC
PROGRAM

Years of research compiling the *Nutrition Almanac* have led us to realize the necessity of preparing this cookbook. With the use of a food composition computerized program, we have developed menus to provide the Recommended Daily Allowance (RDA) requirement of all nutrients including five vitamins, six minerals, calories, proteins, carbohydrates and fats.[1] The *Nutrition Almanac Cookbook* is the first cookbook ever compiled in this way.

Many people who have tried this program find that it is a safe, effective plan for weight control—for losing weight, for gaining weight, for maintaining weight. When the body receives all of its essential nutrients, calories are effectively utilized.

To use the book, calculate the number of calories required per day for your individual height, body frame, and activity level. Simply eat the number of calories you need, based on these menus, and your nutrition requirements should be met. To determine your individual calorie needs:

1. Decide on your desired weight. The Height and Weight Chart on page 175 will help you make a realistic determination.
2. Turn to page 173 and determine your level of activity. Using the Metabolic Rate Chart,

calculate the appropriate number of calories for your desired weight.

Now you are ready to plan your daily meals. If you need 2,050 calories, for example, you might plan:

Breakfast: Cornmeal Griddle Cakes (page 163) . . . . 612 calories
Lunch: Chef's Salad (page 128) . . . . 698 calories
Dinner: Rolled Halibut (page 95) . . . . 743 calories
Total: 2053 calories

Each menu lists the number of calories per serving. Each recipe serves four people. Many recipes can be halved or quartered and all can be doubled, depending on your needs. You can apply your calorie intake to one, two or three meals a day. One hundred calories more or less daily is allowable.

If you are cooking for a family or group with varying caloric needs, you will have to devise methods for dividing the menus proportionately. Forms A and B on pages 221 and 222 can help you estimate how much to serve to each person. Make copies of Form C so that each person who wishes to keep track of his or her calorie intake may do so. To maintain the proper nutrient balance, participants should be served plates with properly estimated portions, rather than helping themselves to as much of each food as they wish.

---

[1] Other nutrients, such as B_6, B_{12}, folic acid, vitamins D and E, are not listed, because either adequate data is not yet available or the requirements have not been established.

This ensures that each person will receive the recommended portion of each food rather than limited amounts of some and excesses of others.

Since the menus in this book have been calculated and balanced to provide adequate amounts of all recommended nutrients, it is essential that you follow the menu. Use the food substitution list below each menu nutrient table. Each substitute will provide the same nutritional balance as the food it replaces.

There are notable advantages to this system. Principally, it provides equal proportions of all nutrients at each meal, as well as *complete protein* at each meal. Complete protein, which has all eight essential amino acids, is essential to growth and development. In order to be accepted by the body as complete protein, all eight amino acids must be consumed together at the same meal and not at intervals throughout the day. Any excess protein is used as a carbohydrate by the body. The B complex vitamins and vitamin C are water-soluble and are not retained in the body. They must be replenished daily and will be provided at each meal by these menus. More importantly, all the nutrients interact, and lack of one may affect the requirements or functions of others. An adequate intake of all of these in everyday foods is essential to good health.*

These menus take the guesswork out of planning nutritious meals. And adequate nutrition may be obtained at a relatively low calorie level, a notable advantage in today's sedentary, overweight society.

* Individual requirements are influenced by age, sex, body size, activity level and state of health. Illness, undue stress, or a notably warmer or colder climate can affect requirements. Any illness or nutrient deficiency will interfere with the proper utilization of the nutrients in the food you eat. We strongly urge you to read the NUTRITION ALMANAC (McGraw-Hill) for information on all nutrients and specific illnesses and their possible correction by the use of supplements. Consult a physician who is familiar with nutritional therapy before taking large quantities of vitamins and minerals.

Children ages 6–18 require extra calcium (from 100 to 600 mgs). Refer to the Food Composition Chart for foods providing calcium and add to diet; or take needed supplements.

THE FUNCTION OF CALORIES

Calories are made up of carbohydrates, fats and proteins; the energy and building-block nutrients that supply fuel for body heat and work. Their fuel potential is expressed in calories, a term that signifies the amount of chemical energy that may be released as heat when food is metabolized. *Carbohydrates and protein yield four calories of energy per gram, while fats yield nine calories per gram.* Foods high in energy are high in calories, while foods low in energy are low in calories.

THE FUNCTIONS OF PROTEIN

Protein is the major source of building material for the muscles, blood, skin, hair, nails and internal organs, including the brain and heart. Protein is of primary importance in the growth and development of body tissues, and it is needed to rebuild worn-out or destroyed tissues. It is also needed for the formation of hormones, antibodies and enzymes. Adequate protein prevents reduction of muscle tone, prevents blood and tissues from becoming too acid or alkaline, and helps in blood clotting and regulation of water balance.

During digestion, the protein is broken up into smaller units called amino acids. Eight of the amino acids are essential in adults, ten in children. Food containing all the essential amino acids is termed complete protein. If essential amino acids are missing, it is termed incomplete protein. To obtain a complete protein meal from incomplete proteins, foods must be carefully combined so that food weak in an essential amino acid will be balanced by foods adequate in the same amino acid. The foods must also be eaten at the same time, or the body will consider the foods as separate, incomplete protein (i.e., have macaroni and cheese for lunch, not macaroni for lunch and cheese a couple of hours later). Protein is the only caloric nutrient that can build muscle, hair, nails, renew cells, etc., and use the rest for energy. However, the eight essential amino acids have to be present. The rest is then used for energy or stored as fat.

PROTEIN DEFICIENCIES

Protein deficiencies may lead to abnormalities of growth and tissue development. The hair, nails and skin will especially be affected, and muscle and bone development will be poor. A child whose diet is deficient in protein may not attain his potential physical stature. Extreme protein deficiency in children results in the disease Kwashiorkor. It is characterized by stunted mental and physical growth, loss of hair pigment, and swelling of joints. In adults, protein deficiency may result in a lack of vigor and stamina, mental depression, and weakness, accompanied by poor resistance to infection, impaired healing of wounds, and slow recovery from disease.

THE FUNCTION OF CARBOHYDRATES

Carbohydrates function chiefly to provide energy for body functions and muscular exertion, and to assist in digestion and assimilation of other foods. They provide immediate energy, so the body can save protein for the building and repair of tissues. Carbohydrates help regulate protein and fat metabolism. The three forms of carbohydrates are sugars, starches, and cellulose.

All sugars and starches are converted by the digestive juices to a simple sugar called glucose, or "blood sugar." Some is used for immediate energy to support the basic functions of breathing, heartbeat and cell activity; and some is used as fuel for tissues of the brain, nervous system, and muscles. A small amount is converted to glycogen and stored in the liver and muscles, and the excess is converted to fat and stored throughout the body as a reserve source of energy. An individual begins to lose weight when his fat reserves are reconverted to glucose and used for body fuel.

The eating of sweet carbohydrate snacks provides the body with almost instant energy, because it brings on a sudden rise in the blood sugar level. However, the blood sugar level drops again rapidly, bringing on a craving for more of the sweet food, and possibly fatigue, dizziness, nervousness, and headache. The craving for more sugar can lead to an individual consuming more. The result is a pattern of craving, snacking, and low blood sugar.

THE FUNCTION OF FATS

Fats are the most concentrated source of energy in the diet. In addition to providing energy, they are a carrier for the fat-soluble vitamins A, D, E, and K. Fat deposits surround and protect body organs and insulate the body. A deficiency in fats leads to a deficiency in fat-soluble vitamins and produces eczema or other skin disorders. Excessive fats in the diet may lead to abnormal weight gain and abnormally slow digestion and absorption. Abnormal amounts of cholesterol may also be stored throughout the body if fat intake is excessive.

No RDA has been set for fats. However, linoleic acid should provide about 2% of the calories in the diet. Vegetable fats such as corn, safflower and soybean oils are high in linoleic acid.

THE FUNCTION OF WATER

It is essential that adequate water be consumed each day—it transports all the foodstuffs to the cells, and the operations within the cells occur in a watery medium. Substances in the body have to be maintained in solution, and secretions and waste must be carried out of the cells by water. Water helps regulate body temperature and is necessary for all building functions in the body.

THE FUNCTION OF VITAMINS

Vitamins are organic compounds that occur in foods and are essential for life and growth processes. As constituents of enzymes, vitamins function as catalysts in many metabolic reactions. Enzyme action within body cells is necessary to maintain life. The body must constantly manufacture enzymes because most enzymes decompose after performing their functions. If a vitamin needed to produce a specific enzyme is not present, the chemical reactions controlled by that enzyme cannot take place. Growth and development are then impaired.

Vitamins are of two types: fat-soluble and water-soluble. The fat-soluble vitamins, A, D, E, and K, can be stored within the body for future use. Hypervitaminosis, or vitamin toxicity, is a possibility for A, D, and K if excessive amounts are taken. Symptoms of toxicity may be headache, nausea, weakness, and drowsiness.

Water-soluble vitamins, the B complex and C, are not retained in the body but are excreted in the urine. Daily intake is essential.

Vitamin A is most important for good eyesight and a healthy complexion. It also fights bacteria and infection. Deficiency symptoms are night blindness; photophobia; rough, dry, scaly, skin; and increased susceptibility to infections.

Vitamin D improves absorption and utilization of calcium and phosphorus, which are required for bone formation. Deficiency symptoms are poor bone and tooth formation, and softening of bones and teeth.

Vitamin E protects fat-soluble vitamins and the red blood cells, since it functions as an antioxidant. Many claims have been made as to the therapeutic values of vitamin E, but they have not yet been substantiated. One deficiency symptom is the rupturing of red blood cells.

Vitamin K is necessary for formation of prothrombin, which is needed for blood to clot. A lack of prothrombin increases the tendency to hemorrhage.

The B complex contains eleven separate vitamins. Since they are water-soluble, they must be replaced daily. The B vitamins are active in carbohydrate, protein, and fat metabolism; are necessary for normal functioning of the nervous system; help maintain muscle tone in the gastrointestinal tract; and are necessary for health of the skin, hair, eyes, mouth, and liver.

An important point to remember about the B vitamins is that they should all be taken together. They are so interlaced in function that large doses of any of them may be therapeutically valueless or may cause a deficiency in others. It's therefore preferable to obtain all of them in a natural food source such as whole grains, green leafy vegetables, brewer's yeast, or organ meats, rather than individually or in synthetic sources.

Symptoms of general B complex deficiency may include dry, rough, or cracked, scaly skin; dull, dry hair; fatigue, headache, poor appetite, nervousness, mental depression, and gastrointestinal tract disorders.

Vitamin C is a water-soluble vitamin also known as ascorbic acid. Although essential to overall body health, it is especially important for maintaining healthy skin. It maintains the protein collagen; helps heal wounds, scar tissue, and fractures; gives strength to blood vessels; may provide resistance to infection; and aids in the absorption of iron.

Deficiency symptoms include bleeding gums, swollen or painful joints, slow healing of wounds and fractures, and bruising.

THE FUNCTION OF MINERALS

Minerals are also vital to overall mental and physical well-being. They are constituents of the bones, teeth, soft tissue, muscle, blood, and nerve cells. They act as catalysts for many biological reactions in the body, including muscle response, transmission of messages through the nervous system, digestion, and metabolism. They are important in producing hormones. Minerals' actions are interrelated, and their efficiency is increased by the presence of proper amounts of other nutrients. Minerals help to maintain the internal water balance, acid-alkaline balance, and draw chemical substances into and out of cells.

Calcium acts in cooperation with phosphorus to build and maintain healthy teeth and bones. It assists in blood clotting and maintains muscle tone. Deficiency symptoms include tetany, softening bones, back and leg pains, and brittle bones.

Iron is necessary for hemoglobin, the coloring of red blood cells. Hemoglobin transports oxygen in the blood from the lungs to the tissues which need oxygen as a form of energy. Iron is also necessary for formation of myoglobin, which transports oxygen to the muscles. Deficiency symptoms are weakness, paleness of skin, dizziness, and anemia.

Magnesium helps form bones, acts as a catalyst in utilization of other nutrients, and is necessary for proper functioning of nerves and muscles. Deficiency symptoms are nervousness and muscular excitability.

Potassium helps in transportation of fluids to the cells, and works to control the activity of the heart muscles, nervous system and kidneys. Deficiency symptoms include apathy, muscle weakness, poor gastrointestinal tone, respiratory failure, and cardiac arrest.

Sodium maintains normal fluid levels in the cells, and maintains the health of the nervous, blood, muscular, and lymph systems. Chloride, copper, fluoride, iodine, manganese, sulphur, and zinc also must be present in the body for proper balance.

Protein, carbohydrates, fats, vitamins, and minerals must all be present in the body, in proper proportions, for good health.

——— WHY YOU'RE NOT ———
GETTING WHAT
YOU NEED

The National Research Council has established the RDA for basic nutrients. Their suggestions on how to meet these levels comprise the "Basic 4"—a simplified system that says to eat two meat group foods, two milk group foods, four bread or cereal servings, and four vegetable and fruit servings.

DAILY FOOD GUIDE

1. Protein foods—2 or more servings
2. Milk and milk products
   - children: 2–4 cups
   - teenagers: 3–4 cups
   - adults: 2 or more cups
3. Vegetables and fruits—4 or more servings
   - dark green or deep yellow every other day
   - leafy green vegetables freely
   - citrus fruit or juice, tomato juice, or food high in vitamin C daily
4. Breads and cereals—4 or more servings

Any average day's diet, if it actually contained all these foods, might still prove lacking in B vitamins, magnesium, or other nutrients, while oversupplying others.

However, few people organize their daily food intake this carefully, and consequently most don't get the nutrients they need daily. Breakfast is frequently skipped, snacks consumed rather than meals, fresh fruits and vegetables missed, or milk, potatoes, bread, etc., omitted because they're "fattening."

More than one-half the subjects surveyed in some twenty-five different studies had food intakes which gave them less than RDA levels of calcium, iron, thiamine, and vitamin C. Almost half were lacking in niacin. Over 40% get too little riboflavin. And about a third were missing RDA levels of vitamin A.[1]

Generally, these were the only nutrients studied—possibly other deficiencies occur as well.

Women are most likely to have an intake inadequate in iron. In fact, it is virtually impossible to obtain the recommended 18 mg. of iron

[1] Deutsch, Ronald M., *The Family Guide To Better Food and Better Health* (Des Moines: Meredith Corp., 1971), p. 21.

on a diet of less than 3000 calories, which is considerably more energy than is required.[1]

Americans are much more sedentary than a generation ago and require fewer calories to maintain their weight. This makes it doubly hard to ensure adequate nutrition when people simply eat the foods that appeal to them.

Conclusion: *It is very difficult to meet the RDA with typical food patterns; or if RDA is met, the caloric levels are likely to be overly high.*

CONSUMING LESS FOOD

First, our taste buds have gradually been trained to want and "like" many manufactured foods which are often lacking in nutrients. The natural tastes of unprocessed foods have become foreign to our bodies. We are also ignorant victims when it comes to knowledge about nutrition. We simply don't know what good nutrition is, much less how to achieve it. And consuming too much food and food poor in nutrients is but one sign of our common, rather thorough ignorance.

By using the research done for this book, we can practice properly balanced nutrition even though we don't know everything about it.

The important fact is that our bodies demand adequate nutrients. Often we don't even know it. But if we eat the popular, manufactured foods in our everyday lives, we are most likely overeating in order to supply our bodies' natural demands for nutrients.

HOW THESE MENUS WERE COMPILED

Each menu has been carefully tested several times in home and test kitchen situations to assure pleasant taste. The entire book of recipes has also been formed to include ample variety.

[1] Guthrie, Helen A., *Introductory Nutrition*. 2nd ed. (St. Louis: C. V. Mosby Co., 1971), p. 296.

Our primary consideration in compiling these menus was accuracy or reliable research. Beginning with a reliable source, the Recommended Dietary Allowances of nutrients in the National Science Foundation's publication, was, of course, essential. But achieving those daily amounts in actual menu planning and subsequent preparation is the key. We have included, therefore, charts showing substitute foods and calorie and nutrient breakdowns for each menu.

Simplicity is the other remaining guideline by which these menus were originated.

VITAMIN LOSS WHILE COOKING

Water-soluble vitamins: B vitamins and vitamin C. Water-soluble means just what it implies: that these vitamins will readily leave the food substance they are in and filter (leach) into the cooking or soaking water. All the B vitamins are generally together in foods. The three B vitamins which our diet seems to be lacking in will be dealt with most extensively. These are thiamine, riboflavin, and niacin. All these vitamins are alike in that they are water-soluble, destroyed by alkaline conditions, and stable in acid conditions. Thiamine is sensitive as well to oxygen and to heat over 120 degrees Centigrade. Riboflavin is extremely sensitive as well to light; and niacin, being the most stable, is sensitive only to those two areas which all the B vitamins have in common.

Vitamin C is probably the most highly sensitive vitamin. It is destroyed by oxygen from the air, especially in the presence of heat. The oxygen activates an enzyme which destroys this vitamin. Vitamin C is easily lost in alkaline conditions, such as baking soda, in the presence of light, copper, and iron. It is not as easily lost in the presence of acid.

Fat-soluble vitamins: these include vitamins A, D, E, K, and are not soluble in water, only in fat. They can only be absorbed by the body in the presence of fat in the diet. All fat-soluble vitamins are damaged by ultraviolet light. Vitamin A is peculiar to all other vitamins in the fact that carotene, the form in which vitamin A occurs in foods, can be utilized more efficiently by the body in the cooked rather than the raw form. Vitamin A, like C, also is sensitive to exposure to air, especially in the presence of heat.

Fruits and vegetables contain mainly vitamins A, B, and C; and should be handled according to their properties, keeping in mind the main characteristics of these vitamins.

FRUITS AND VEGETABLES

Storage of fruits and vegetables is important in preserving the nutrients. Do not wash before storage, only just before using. Fruits and vegetables should be stored in a cool, moist compartment of the refrigerator as soon as possible. The longer the storage time the greater the nutrient loss. If ripe fruits are left at room temperature their vitamins A, B, and C are gradually destroyed.

Storage should be in covered containers or plastic bags (with holes cut in them) designed to fit the item stored. Vitamins are volatile to air so the container used to store juice should not allow a lot of air space.

Fruits and vegetables should not be exposed to sunlight. Thick-skinned vegetables such as winter squash, potatoes, and onions should be stored in a cool, dry place.

Just before preparing, rinse rather than wash produce carefully, drain, and dry thoroughly—this prevents loss to water.

In most cases it is best to eat fruits and vegetables raw rather than cooked.

When cooking fresh fruits and vegetables, cook with skin on whenever possible to prevent leaching of vitamins into the water.

Boil water before placing fruits or vegetables in the pan (this drives the air out and replaces it with steam), and cook in the smallest quantity necessary, just sufficient to cover the bottom of the pan (approximately ½ inch). Boiling also inactivates enzymes which destroy nutrients. Steaming is a preferable method, which avoids any loss of nutrients into the liquid. Cover the pan when steaming.

Save the cooking water for soups, stock, gravies, sauces, drinks, or freeze into cubes for later use. It has been estimated that approximately one-third of the vitamin and mineral content is lost when vegetable liquid is discarded.

Cook in the shortest time possible. Don't cook in soda water, as it destroys the vitamin B_1 (thiamine) content. After vegetables begin to boil, reduce heat and simmer on medium or low heat.

Cooking in milk, baking, steaming, and frying are alternative methods of cooking which help retain nutrients.

Cook foods whole whenever possible, as less surface area is exposed to water. The smaller and thinner the pieces, the greater the loss. Avoid cooking in copper or iron utensils as they destroy vitamin C.

Oil on fruits and vegetables (salads) prevents oxidation of vitamin C.

Avoid leftovers. Each time they are reheated they lose more nutrients. If necessary, use them as soon as possible or in a salad.

GRAINS, BREADS, AND CEREALS

Breads and cereals or grain products are important mainly as a source of B vitamins. This group includes cereals, bread, pasta, and macaroni.

Whole grains require different storage conditions than do non-whole-grain products. Whole-grain flours should be refrigerated to avoid rancidity. Keep whole-grain bread in the refrigerator in a light-proof container. Vitamin B_2, or riboflavin, is destroyed when exposed to light.

EXAMPLE OF THE VALUE OF A SEED

If a person is accustomed to eating white bread he may have to get used to eating whole wheat bread, but once used to whole wheat bread he will notice it has a better taste.

TOTAL NUTRIENTS IN A KERNEL OF WHEAT

GERM IS 2½% OF KERNEL   BRAN IS 14% OF KERNEL   ENDOSPERM IS 83% OF KERNEL

Of the whole kernel
the germ contains:
64% Thiamine
26% Riboflavin
21% Pyridoxine
8% Protein
7% Pantothenic Acid
2% Niacin

Of the whole kernel
the bran contains:
73% Pyridoxine
50% Pantothenic Acid
42% Riboflavin
33% Thiamine
19% Protein

Of the whole kernel
the endosperm contains:
70–75% Protein
43% Pantothenic Acid
32% Riboflavin
12% Niacin
6% Pyridoxine
3% Thiamine

ENDOSPERM

BRAN

GERM

KERNEL
(magnification)

* Other Nutrients Found in the Whole Wheat
Grain are:

Calcium	Chlorine
Iron	Sodium
Phosphorus	Silicon
Magnesium	Boron
Potassium	Barium
Manganese	Silver
Copper	Inositol
Sulphur	Folic Acid
Iodine	Choline
Fluorine	Vitamin E
And other trace minerals	

Here is one example of the importance of the nutrients in a seed. In white bread the germ and bran have been removed; in whole wheat they have not. Therefore it is more nutritious to consume whole wheat bread than white bread. White enriched bread has only three of the eleven vitamin B complex added: thiamine, riboflavin, and niacin, as well as iron.

STORAGE AND COOKING OF MEATS AND FISH

With the exception of pork, meats served rare are nutritionally superior to well-done meats.

Never salt meat before cooking; it draws out the juices full of vitamins and minerals.

Save left-over cooking liquid from stewing meats; it contains iron, copper, and B vitamins. Skim the fat from the top and freeze the stock for soup.

Use tongs rather than a fork to turn meat.

Puncturing with a fork allows juices to seep out.

Juices which separate from meat during thawing should be used in gravy or added to soup stock.

Lowest temperatures and shortest cooking times consistent with other requirements should be used for maximum nutrient retention.

Canned meats are generally less nutritious than fresh or frozen because of the long cooking times and temperatures.

Cooking fish with the bones left in adds calcium and phosphorus.

STORAGE AND COOKING OF DAIRY PRODUCTS

Dairy products: this group contains eggs, milk, and cheese and is important for vitamin B_2, vitamin A, iron, calcium, and phosphorus.

Milk and cheese and its products should be stored in lightproof containers to minimize destruction of vitamin B_2. Brown glass milk bottles or cartons are superior to clear glass bottles.

Cook milk in a covered container over low heat, and watch carefully so it won't scorch or boil over.

The longer the time used in the heating process of milk, the greater is the destruction of calcium and phosphorus. Since the precipitate which settles to the bottom of the pan is made up largely of calcium phosphates, it is wise to stir the product as it heats to incorporate these salts.

Store eggs with the large end up to maintain quality, and keep away from strong-smelling foods.

Overcooked eggs lose their bright color, becoming grayish and dull. Appearance and nutritive value are both lost, since loss of color means loss of carotene, or vitamin A.

To reduce light destruction of vitamin B_2, cook eggs in a covered pan, and cover casseroles which contain cheese.

It is essential that you preserve nutrients in cooking. The menus in this book are balanced, nutritious meals—*if* you prepare them properly. Their success hinges on how well they are prepared, how consciously you protect and preserve the nutrients. No diet is balanced unless cooking is properly done.

"If nutrition is to be successfully applied, good cooking becomes a necessity."[1]

SUBSTITUTIONS

The following substitutions may be made at any time:

> *Salad dressing:* Any low-calorie or other dressing.
> *Butter:* Margarine or vegetable oil when feasible.
> *Seasonings:* Use any other herbs and spices you might prefer, and use them to replace salt if you wish; or decrease the amount of salt used in the recipes.

Anyone allergic to any particular food used in the menus or substitutions can obtain the food's nutrient value by taking supplements along with the meal. Refer to the Table of Food Composition on page 185 for food values.

We recommend at least a daily multivitamin and mineral supplement be taken with a meal.

[1] Davis, Adelle, *Let's Cook it Right* (New York: The New American Library, Inc., 1970), p. 25.

MEAT

Armenian Lamb on Rice
Broccoli with Buttermilk Sauce
Spiced Apple Juice
Cherries

Calories: 809 per serving   Protein: 33 grams per serving

Armenian Lamb

12 oz. lean lamb, cut into cubes
1 T. safflower oil
½ C. chopped onion
1 clove garlic, minced
1 C. canned tomatoes
1 green pepper, quartered
2 carrots, sliced lengthwise
1 medium eggplant, cut into
  cubes (2 C.)
1 small zucchini, cut into cubes
  (1 C.)
½ lemon, sliced
½ C. okra (optional)
½ t. paprika
⅛ t. ground cumin
1½ t. salt
½ t. pepper
1½ C. raw brown rice

In a large, heavy skillet, brown the lamb in the oil; add the onion and garlic. Stir until slightly browned. Add the tomatoes. Reduce heat, cover, and cook over low heat for 1 hour. Add a small amount of water if necessary.

Preheat oven to 350° F.

Transfer the meat mixture to a large casserole and add the remaining ingredients except the rice. Stir well. Cover tightly and place in the oven for 1 hour or until the vegetables are tender.

In the meantime, drop the rice into 3 C. boiling salted (1 t.) water and simmer covered 45–60 minutes, until all the water is absorbed. Serve equal portions of lamb over ¾ C. cooked rice.

Yields: 4 servings

Broccoli with Buttermilk Sauce

4 C. broccoli
1 C. buttermilk
½ C. lowfat yogurt
2 T. cornstarch
¼ t. onion salt
⅛ t. garlic salt
2 T. sour cream

Steam or boil the broccoli in ½" water just until crisp-tender.

In a small, heavy saucepan, heat the buttermilk, yogurt, and cornstarch. Add the onion salt and garlic salt. Stir until the mixture thickens. Add the sour cream and blend well, but do not allow to boil. Spoon over the cooked broccoli.

Yields: 4 servings

Spiced Apple Juice

4 C. unsweetened apple juice
Spices to taste, such as allspice,
  cinnamon, nutmeg, and
  cloves

Heat the apple juice and spices in a medium-size saucepan. Simmer for a few minutes. Cool to warm and serve.

Yields: 4 servings

■ Serve each person 1 C. cherries for dessert.

	CALORIES	PROTEIN GMS	CARBOHYDRATES GMS	FAT GMS	CALCIUM MGS	IRON MGS	MAGNESIUM MGS	PHOSPHORUS MGS	POTASSIUM MGS	SODIUM MGS	VITAMIN A I.U.	VITAMIN B₁ MGS	VITAMIN B₂ MGS	NIACIN MGS	VITAMIN C MGS
Armenian Lamb	378	21	18	26	59	2.7	61	215	859	874	6,296	.25	.33	5.5	59
Brown Rice, ¾ C.	134	3	29	.9	14	.6	34	83	79	317	0	.1	.02	1.5	0
Broccoli with Buttermilk Sauce	98	9	12	3	267	1.2	48	197	584	236	3,896	.18	.47	1.3	141
Spiced Apple Juice, 1 C.	117	.2	30	t	15	1.5	10	22	250	2		.02	.05	.2	2
Cherries, 1 C.	82		20	.3	26	.5	18	22	223	2	130	.06	.07	.5	12
TOTAL	809	33	109	30	381	6.5	171	539	1995	1431	10,322	.6	.94	9	214

Substitutions
Broccoli: 1 C. cooked spinach; 1 C. raw kale or collards
Spiced Apple Juice: Fruit Juice Soda (½ C. unsweetened fruit
    juice mixed with ½ C. club soda or sparkling mineral water)
Cherries: fruit of choice

MENU

Barbecued Short Ribs
Vegetable Salad with Sauce Vinaigrette
Baked Potatoes with Sour Cream
Skim Milk

Calories: 985 per serving   Protein: 38 grams per serving

Barbecued Short Ribs

2 lbs. short ribs
salt and pepper to taste
1 lemon, sliced
½ C. sliced onion
½ C. catsup
¼ C. chili sauce

Preheat oven to 350° F.

Place the short ribs on a rack in a shallow roasting pan, meaty side up. Season with salt and pepper and top with alternating slices of lemon and onion. Cover with aluminum foil and bake for 1 hour. After 1 hour of cooking, drain fat from ribs. Increase oven temperature to 400°F.

1 t. Tabasco sauce
1½ T. honey
1 t. safflower oil
3 T. cider vinegar
1 t. Worcestershire sauce

Combine the remaining ingredients in a blender until smooth. Brush the sauce on the ribs and continue baking for 30 minutes, basting at 15-minute intervals. After 30 minutes, turn the ribs over and bake 30 minutes more, basting as before.

Yield: 4 servings

Vegetable Salad

4 C. lettuce torn into bite-size
   pieces
2 C. chopped broccoli, steamed
1 large carrot, grated
1 T. chopped chives
¼ C. celery, cut diagonally
2 scallions, chopped
½ C. sliced green or red pepper
1 medium tomato, sliced
1 C. sliced mushrooms

Toss all ingredients together gently. Serve with 1 T. Sauce Vinaigrette per person.

Yields: 4 servings

Sauce Vinaigrette

⅓ C. cider vinegar or lemon
   juice
½ t. dry mustard
½ t. crushed tarragon
1 clove garlic, crushed
1 t. capers (optional)
1 scallion, minced
¼ t. salt or to taste
pepper to taste
⅔ C. safflower or olive oil

In a blender combine all ingredients except the oil. Add one-quarter of the oil and blend 1 minute. Repeat until all oil has been added.

Yields: 1 cup

■ Serve each person a baked potato with 1 T. sour cream, and 1 cup skim milk.

	CALORIES	PROTEIN GMS	CARBOHYDRATES GMS	FAT GMS	CALCIUM MGS	IRON MGS	MAGNESIUM MGS	PHOSPHORUS MGS	POTASSIUM MGS	SODIUM MGS	VITAMIN A I.U.	VITAMIN B₁ MGS	VITAMIN B₂ MGS	NIACIN MGS	VITAMIN C MGS
Barbecued Short Ribs	578	21	23	45	26	3	46	232	528	350	639	1	.25	6	10
Vegetable Salad	60	4	12	.6	106	1.7	40	112	650	42	5528	.19	.3	2	102
Sauce Vinaigrette, 1 T.	86		5	9.6	t	t	t	t	4.7	36					
Baked Potato, 1	145	4	33	.2	14	1	75	101	782	6	t	.15	.07	2.7	31
Sour Cream, 1 T.	30	.5	.5	3	17	.01	1.5	12	20	7	113	.005	.02	.01	t
Skim Milk, 1 C.	86	8	12	.4	302	.1	28	247	406	126	500	.09	.34	.22	2
TOTAL	985	38	86	59	465	5.8	191	704	2391	567	6780	1.4	.98	11	145

Substitutions
Baked Potato: French-fried, pan-fried, or steamed potatoes
Skim Milk: ½ C. yogurt or 1 oz. natural cheese

MENU

Batter Franks
Carrot Sticks
Green Peas
Skim Milk

Calories: 609 per serving   Protein: 30 grams per serving

Batter Franks

8 frankfurters
safflower oil for deep-fat frying
¾ C. whole wheat flour
½ t. salt
2 T. cornmeal
2 T. butter
1 egg, beaten
½ C. skim milk

Fry frankfurters. Heat oil for deep-fat frying.

Measure all the dry ingredients into a medium-size mixing bowl; cut in the butter thoroughly. Stir in the egg and milk and beat until smooth.

Dip the frankfurters in the batter, and fry in the oil until brown, approximately 6 minutes. Drain and serve.

Yields: 4 servings

Suggestion: For ease the batter may be mixed in blender to make smooth.

■ Serve ½ large carrot, ½ C. cooked green peas, and 1 C. skim milk per person.

	CALORIES	PROTEIN GMS	CARBOHYDRATES GMS	FAT GMS	CALCIUM MGS	IRON MGS	MAGNESIUM MGS	PHOSPHORUS MGS	POTASSIUM MGS	SODIUM MGS	VITAMIN A I.U.	VITAMIN B₁ MGS	VITAMIN B₂ MGS	NIACIN MGS	VITAMIN C MGS
Batter Franks	445	17	22	35	62	2.9	35	270	360	1100	463	.3	.28	3.5	.3
Raw Carrot, ½	21	.5	5	.1	19	.4	12	18	171	24	5500	.03	.03	.3	4
Green Peas, ½ C.	57	4	10	.3	19	1.4	25	79	157	1	430	.22	.09	1.9	16
Skim Milk, 1 C.	86	8	12	.4	302	.1	28	247	406	126	500	.09	.34	.22	2
TOTAL	609	30	49	36	402	4.8	100	614	1094	1251	6893	.64	.74	5.9	22

Substitutions
Raw Carrot: ½ C. cooked carrots
Peas: ½ C. asparagus; 1 C. broccoli, brussels sprouts, eggplant,
   or summer squash; 1 medium tomato
Skim Milk: ½ C. yogurt

═══ MENU ═══

Beef Pot Roast with Vegetables
Whole Wheat Dinner Rolls
Skim Milk
Boysenberries

Calories: 706 per serving   Protein: 35 grams per serving

Beef Pot Roast with Vegetables

1 lb. rump beef roast
3 large carrots, sliced
   lengthwise
1 C. sliced celery
1 C. chopped onion
3 med. potatoes, sliced (with
   skins)
1 t. salt
1 C. sliced mushrooms
beef stock

Preheat oven to 300° F.

Combine all the ingredients in a large casserole with beef stock to cover. Cover the casserole and bake 2 hours. Serve equal portions of meat and vegetables.

Yields: 4 servings

Suggestion: A large 2–3 lb. roast may be used if meat is bony or if leftovers are desired.

Whole Wheat Dinner Rolls

1 T. dry baking yeast
2 T. honey
¼ C. warm water
1½ C. skim milk
2 T. safflower oil
1 t. salt
1 egg, beaten
4 C. whole wheat flour

Ingredients should be at room temperature. Combine yeast and honey in warm water and set in a warm place.

Heat the milk to scalding (just to the point of boiling). Pour it into a mixing bowl and add the oil and salt. Cool until just warm. Add the egg. Add the yeast mixture. Stir in 2 C. flour and beat 100 strokes, or 7 minutes by electric mixer on low speed. Add the remaining flour, or enough flour until the dough is no longer sticky. Turn it onto a floured board and knead until smooth and elastic, approximately 10 minutes. Place the dough in an oiled bowl, turn the dough in the bowl to coat it with oil, cover the bowl with a damp cloth, and let dough rise in a warm place until double in size, approximately 1–1½ hours. (You can heat the oven to warm, then turn it off and place the dough in the oven.)

When double in bulk, knead the dough to original size. Allow to rise as before. (Rising time will be shorter.) When double in bulk, knead down again. Pull off plum-size pieces of dough, shape them into balls and place them on a greased baking sheet. Allow to rise in a warm place until double in bulk. Bake in a 350° F. oven for 20–30 minutes or until browned.

Yields: 24 rolls

■ Serve each person 1 whole wheat dinner roll with 1 t. butter, 1 C. skim milk, and for dessert ⅔ C. boysenberries. Freeze remaining rolls.

	CALORIES	PROTEIN GMS	CARBOHYDRATES GMS	FAT GMS	CALCIUM MGS	IRON MGS	MAGNESIUM MGS	PHOSPHORUS MGS	POTASSIUM MGS	SODIUM MGS	VITAMIN A I.U.	VITAMIN B₁ MGS	VITAMIN B₂ MGS	NIACIN MGS	VITAMIN C MGS
Beef Pot Roast	458	22	38	25	72	4	99	301	1352	676	8395	.27	.35	7	37
Whole Wheat Roll, 1	86	4	18	1.7	29	.75	25	94	103	100	56	.13	.05	1	t
Butter, 1 t.	34	t	t	3.8	1	0	.09	.66	1	47	157	t	t		0
Skim Milk, 1 C.	86	8	12	.4	302	.1	28	247	406	126	500	.09	.34	.22	2
Boysenberries, ⅔ C.	42	1	10	.27	17	.6	12	17	105	1	141	.02	.1	.9	11
TOTAL	706	35	78	31	421	5.5	164	660	1967	950	9249	.51	.84	9	50

Substitutions
Whole Wheat Roll: any whole grain bread; optional
Skim Milk: ½ C. yogurt or ice cream
Boysenberries: fruit of choice

Beef Stroganoff over Noodles
Buttered Green Beans
Orange-Date Salad

Calories: 763 per serving   Protein: 30 grams per serving

Beef Stroganoff

12 oz. round steak
2 T. butter
1½ C. sliced mushrooms
½ C. chopped onion
2 beef bouillon cubes
½ C. boiling water
1 T. tomato paste
½ t. dry mustard
¼ t. salt
1 T. whole wheat flour
¼ C. water
¾ C. sour cream
2 C. noodles

Cut meat into ¼″ strips. In a large skillet, brown the meat in the butter. Add the mushrooms and onion and sauté about 8 minutes.

Dissolve the bouillon cubes in the boiling water and add to the meat. Stir in the tomato paste, mustard, and salt. Cover, bring to a boil, reduce heat, and simmer until tender (approximately 15 minutes).

In a small bowl combine the flour and water; then slowly stir this into the meat mixture. Cook over medium heat, stirring constantly, until mixture comes to a boil. Reduce heat. Add the sour cream, stir, and continue to heat, but do not boil.

Prepare noodles according to package instructions. Serve proportionately among 4 persons.

Yields: 4 servings

Orange-Date Salad

4 oranges
2 C. endive
1 C. pitted dates
¼ C. honey
2 T. lemon juice
1½ T. safflower oil
⅛ t. salt
2 T. canned crushed pineapple
  (optional)

Peel and slice the oranges. Clean the endive. On 4 dishes arrange equal portions of the oranges and dates on endive leaves. In a shaker, combine the honey, lemon juice, oil, salt, and pineapple. Shake well. Spoon some over each salad.

Yields: 4 servings

■ Serve each person 1 C. cooked green beans with 1 t. butter.

	CALORIES	PROTEIN GMS	CARBOHYDRATES GMS	FAT GMS	CALCIUM MGS	IRON MGS	MAGNESIUM MGS	PHOSPHORUS MGS	POTASSIUM MGS	SODIUM MGS	VITAMIN A I.U.	VITAMIN B₁ MGS	VITAMIN B₂ MGS	NIACIN MGS	VITAMIN C MGS
Beef Stroganoff	342	22	7	26	71	3	30	271	607	685	741	.14	.4	5.7	6
Noodles, ½ C.	100	3	19	1	8	.7		47	35		56	.11	.07	1	0
Green Beans, 1 C.	31	2	7	.3	63	.8	40	46	189	5	680	.09	.11	.6	15
Butter, 1 t.	34	t	t	3.8	1	0	.09	.66	1	47	157	t	t		0
Orange-Date Salad	256	3	66	5.5	102	2.4	49	58	515	143	1107	.19	.14	1.7	70
TOTAL	763	30	99	37	245	6.9	119	423	1347	880	2741	.53	.72	9	91

Substitutions

Noodles: ½ C. cooked brown rice

Green Beans: ½ C. collards; 1 C. broccoli, brussels sprouts, kale, or spinach

Orange-Date Salad: substitute spinach or lettuce for the endive

MENU

Beef-Vegetable Bake
Whole Wheat Dinner Rolls
Skim Milk
Strawberries

Calories: 522 per serving   Protein: 30 grams per serving

Beef-Vegetable Bake

8 oz. lean ground beef
1 green pepper, cut in rings
1 C. sliced onions
3 large carrots, cut in strips
2 medium tomatoes, sliced
2 medium potatoes, cubed
½ package dry onion soup mix

Brown the ground beef and drain. Preheat oven to 375° F.

Arrange the vegetables in layers on the bottom of greased casserole; crumble the beef on top. Sprinkle the soup mix over the beef. Cover loosely with foil and bake for 40–50 minutes.

Yields: 4 servings

■ Serve each person 1 Whole Wheat Dinner Roll (see page 16) with 1 t. butter, 1 C. skim milk, and for dessert 1 C. strawberries

	CALORIES	PROTEIN GMS	CARBOHYDRATES GMS	FAT GMS	CALCIUM MGS	IRON MGS	MAGNESIUM MGS	PHOSPHORUS MGS	POTASSIUM MGS	SODIUM MGS	VITAMIN A I.U.	VITAMIN B₁ MGS	VITAMIN B₂ MGS	NIACIN MGS	VITAMIN C MGS
Beef-Vegetable Bake	260	17	34	8	69	4	73	237	1077	84*	9045	.35	.38	5	70
Whole Wheat Roll, 1	86	4	18	1.7	29	.75	25	94	103	100	56	.13	.05	1	t
Butter, 1 t.	34	t	t	3.8	1	0	.09	.66	1	47	157	t	t		0
Skim Milk, 1 C.	86	8	12	.4	302	.1	28	247	406	126	500	.09	.34	.22	2
Strawberries, 1 C.	56	1	13	.8	32	1.5	18	32	246	2	90	.04	.1	.9	88
TOTAL	522	30	77	15	433	6.4	144	611	1833	359	9848	.59	.87	7	160

Substitutions

Whole Wheat Roll: any whole grain bread; optional
Skim Milk: ½ C. yogurt or ice cream, or 1 oz. natural cheese
Strawberries: fruit of choice

* Sodium value for dry onion mix not available.

MENU

Vegetable Juice Cocktail
Boiled Dinner
Anadama Bread
Skim Milk

Calories: 877 per serving   Protein: 45 grams per serving

Vegetable Juice Cocktail

4 celery stalks
4 scallions
¼ C. parsley
1⅓ T. lemon juice
4 drops Tabasco sauce
  (optional)
4 C. tomato juice

Chop the vegetables into small pieces. Place the tomato juice in a blender and add all the other ingredients; blend until smooth.

Suggestion: If you chill before serving, place a cover over the juice to prevent loss of nutrients. Stir before serving.

Yields: 4 servings

Boiled Dinner

1½ lbs. corned beef, uncooked
2 small onions, quartered

Place corned beef in a heavy kettle and add hot water to cover. Bring to a boil and simmer 2½–3 hours or until tender.

4 large carrots, halved
2 potatoes, quartered
1 turnip, cubed
1½ C. cabbage wedges

Skim off excess fat from cooking liquid. Add the onions, carrots, potatoes, and turnip. Cover, bring to a boil, and simmer 15 minutes. Add cabbage and cook for another 10 minutes.

Serve with horseradish sauce if desired.

Yields: 4 servings

Anadama Bread

¾ C. boiling water
½ C. yellow cornmeal
¼ C. safflower oil
2 T. blackstrap molasses
1 t. salt
1 T. dry yeast
1 T. honey
½ C. lukewarm water
1 egg, beaten
2½ C. whole wheat flour
½ T. melted butter

In a large mixing bowl, combine the boiling water, cornmeal, oil, molasses, and salt. Cool to lukewarm.

Dissolve the yeast and honey in the lukewarm water. Add the egg and half the flour. Add the yeast mixture to the cornmeal mixture and beat for 2 minutes or 300 strokes. Add the remaining flour and mix with a spoon until thoroughly blended.

Spread the dough into an 8½" × 4½" loaf pan, shaping it with your floured hand. Let the dough rise to the top of the pan in a warm place. Sprinkle the top with extra cornmeal.

Bake in a 350° F. oven for 50–55 minutes. Remove the loaf from the pan. Brush the top with melted butter and allow to cool.

Suggestion: If the bread becomes too brown before baking time is up, cover with foil.

Yields: 18 slices

■ Serve each person 1 slice anadama bread with 1 t. butter, and 1 C. skim milk.

	CALORIES	PROTEIN GMS	CARBOHYDRATES GMS	FAT GMS	CALCIUM MGS	IRON MGS	MAGNESIUM MGS	PHOSPHORUS MGS	POTASSIUM MGS	SODIUM MGS	VITAMIN A I.U.	VITAMIN B₁ MGS	VITAMIN B₂ MGS	NIACIN MGS	VITAMIN C MGS
Vegetable Juice Cocktail, 1 C.	61	3	13	.45	46	3	31	62	757	544	2546	.15	.1	2	54
Boiled Dinner	594	31	33	35	93	5	60	225	957	1148	11054	.2	.3	4	48
Anadama Bread, 1 slice	102	3	16	4	25	1	28	76	138	125	45	.1	.03	.8	t
Butter, 1 t.	34	t	t	3.8	1	0	.09	.66	1	47	157	t	t		0
Skim Milk, 1 C.	86	8	12	.4	302	.1	28	247	406	126	500	.09	.34	.22	2
TOTAL	877	45	74	44	467	9	147	611	2259	1864	14302	.54	.77	7	104

Substitutions
Vegetable Juice Cocktail: 1 C. vegetable or tomato juice
Anadama Bread: any whole grain bread
Skim Milk: ½ C. yogurt

MENU

Chili Con Carne
Carrot Sticks
Buttermilk Biscuits
Skim Milk

Calories: 648 per serving   Protein: 44 grams per serving

Chili Con Carne

12 oz. lean ground beef
2 T. safflower oil
1 C. chopped onion
1 clove garlic, minced
½ C. chopped green pepper
2 C. canned tomatoes
2 C. kidney or pinto beans,
  cooked
1 C. tomato sauce or purée
1 t. salt
2 t. chili powder
1 t. ground cumin
½ t. crushed oregano
1 bay leaf

In a large, heavy saucepan, brown the beef in the oil. Add the onion, garlic, and green peppers and sauté until tender. Stir in the tomatoes, beans, tomato sauce, salt, and spices. Bring to a boil, cover, and simmer for 1 hour.

Yields: 4 servings

Buttermilk Biscuits

2 C. whole wheat pastry flour
1 T. baking powder
½ t. baking soda
½ t. salt
4 T. melted butter
¾ C. buttermilk

Preheat oven to 450° F.

Sift together the flour, baking powder, baking soda, and salt. Add the butter and buttermilk. Stir. Turn onto a floured board and knead briefly until smooth. Add more flour if the dough is too sticky. Pat dough out until 1″ thick and cut out biscuits with a knife or biscuit cutter. Place rounds close together on a greased baking sheet and bake 12–15 minutes. Serve warm.

Yields: 16 biscuits

■ Serve each person ½ large carrot, 1 biscuit with 1 t. butter, and 1 C. skim milk. Freeze remaining biscuits.

	CALORIES	PROTEIN GMS	CARBOHYDRATES GMS	FAT GMS	CALCIUM MGS	IRON MGS	MAGNESIUM MGS	PHOSPHORUS MGS	POTASSIUM MGS	SODIUM MGS	VITAMIN A I.U.	VITAMIN B_1 MGS	VITAMIN B_2 MGS	NIACIN MGS	VITAMIN C MGS
Chili Con Carne	423	32	45	17	106	7.6	49	442	1288	850	2164	.6	.35	7	58
Raw Carrot, ½	21	.5	5	.1	19	.4	12	18	171	24	5500	.03	.03	.3	4
Buttermilk Biscuit, 1	84	2.8	13	3.7	22	.58	19	73	78	118	158	.09	.04	.6	t
Butter, 1 t.	34	t	t	3.8	1	0	.09	.66	1	47	157	t	t		0
Skim Milk, 1 C.	86	8	12	.4	302	.1	28	247	406	126	500	.09	.34	.22	2
TOTAL	648	44	75	25	450	8.9	108	781	1944	1165	8476	.81	.76	8	64

Substitutions
Raw Carrot: tossed salad, vegetable, or vegetable juice of choice
Buttermilk Biscuit: any whole grain bread
Skim Milk: ½ C. yogurt

MENU

Chinese Pepper Steak
Brown Rice
Brussels Sprouts with Oil
Skim Milk

Calories: 685 per serving   Protein: 41 grams per serving

Chinese Pepper Steak

1 lb. round steak
¼ C. butter
1 clove garlic, minced
¼ t. salt
¼ t. pepper
¼ C. soy sauce
½ t. honey

Slice the steak thinly across the grain.

In a large, heavy saucepan, melt the butter; add the garlic, salt, and pepper. Add the beef, and brown. Stir in the soy sauce and honey. Cover and cook for 5 minutes over high heat. Lower heat. Add the sprouts, tomatoes, mushrooms, and green pepper. Lower heat to medium and cover and cook 4 minutes.

1 C. bean sprouts
2 medium tomatoes, sliced
1 C. sliced mushrooms
2 C. sliced green pepper
½ T. cornstarch
2 T. water
4 scallions, chopped

Dissolve the cornstarch in the water; add this to the meat mixture, and cook until thickened, stirring constantly.

Serve pepper steak over ¾ C. cooked rice per person and sprinkle with chopped scallions.

Yields: 4 servings

Brown Rice

1½ C. raw brown rice
1 t. salt
3 C. boiling water

Drop rice into boiling salted water. Cover, bring back to a boil, and simmer about 45 minutes or until rice is tender.

Yields: 3 cups

Brussels Sprouts with Oil

4 C. brussels sprouts
2 T. safflower oil
¼ t. salt

Steam or boil sprouts in ½" water just until tender. Immediately toss with oil and salt.

Yields: 4 servings·

■ Serve each person 1 C. skim milk.

	CALORIES	PROTEIN GMS	CARBOHYDRATES GMS	FAT GMS	CALCIUM MGS	IRON MGS	MAGNESIUM MGS	PHOSPHORUS MGS	POTASSIUM MGS	SODIUM MGS	VITAMIN A I.U.	VITAMIN B₁ MGS	VITAMIN B₂ MGS	NIACIN MGS	VITAMIN C MGS
Chinese Pepper Steak	375	27	10	26	55	5.8	44	320	868	1682	1447	.24	.48	7.4	63
Brown Rice, ¾ C.	134	3	29	.9	14	.6	34	83	79	317	0	.1	.02	1.5	0
Brussels Sprouts with Oil, ½ C.	90	3	5	7.3	25	.85	19	56	212	141	405	.06	.11	.6	68
Skim Milk, 1 C.	86	8	12	.4	302	.1	28	247	406	126	500	.09	.34	.22	2
TOTAL	685	41	56	35	396	7.4	125	706	1565	2266	2352	.49	.95	9.7	133

Substitutions
Brussels Sprouts: tossed salad or vegetable of choice
Skim Milk: ½ C. yogurt or 1 oz. natural cheese

MENU

Corned Beef Hash
Whole Wheat Dinner Rolls
Apple Juice Soda
Yogurt Dessert

Calories: 690 per serving   Protein: 30 grams per serving

Corned Beef Hash

12 oz. cooked corned beef
2 potatoes, boiled, with skin
1 T. butter
⅓ C. chopped onion
1 large green pepper, sliced
1 C. sliced celery
1 C. sliced carrots
2 C. sliced mushrooms
2 cloves garlic
2 t. Worcestershire sauce
⅛ C. chopped parsley
⅓ C. beef stock
2 C. tomato juice

Grind or dice the corned beef. Dice the boiled potatoes.

Melt the butter in a large, heavy pan. Add the vegetables (except the potatoes) and the garlic, and cook until tender. Stir frequently to prevent sticking. Remove the garlic. Add the beef, potatoes, and seasonings, cooking and stirring lightly over medium heat. Gradually add the beef stock and tomato juice while stirring, and add more water if necessary. Stir and cook until ingredients are well blended and thoroughly heated.

Yields: 4 servings

Apple Juice Soda

2 C. unsweetened apple juice
2 C. club soda or sparkling
  mineral water

Just before serving, combine juice and soda in a pitcher and stir. Serve over ice, if desired.

Yields: 4 servings

Yogurt Dessert

2 C. low-fat yogurt
⅔ C. fresh or frozen, thawed
  blueberries
⅔ C. fresh or canned cherries,
  pitted and halved
2 T. maple syrup or honey
¼ t. vanilla extract

Combine all the ingredients carefully. Spoon into individual dishes and chill.

Suggestion: Peaches and strawberries or apples may be used in place of the blueberries or cherries.

Yields: 4 servings

■ Serve each person 1 whole wheat roll with 1 t. butter (see page 16).

	CALORIES	PROTEIN GMS	CARBOHYDRATES GMS	FAT GMS	CALCIUM MGS	IRON MGS	MAGNESIUM MGS	PHOSPHORUS MGS	POTASSIUM MGS	SODIUM MGS	VITAMIN A I.U.	VITAMIN B₁ MGS	VITAMIN B₂ MGS	NIACIN MGS	VITAMIN C MGS
Corned Beef Hash	378	19	22	25	57	4.5	55	238	981	1448	5358	.23	.43	5	65
Whole Wheat Roll, 1	86	4	18	1.7	29	.75	25	94	103	100	56	.13	.05	1	t
Butter, 1 t.	34	t	t	3.8	1	0	.09	.66	1	47	157	t	t		0
Apple Juice Soda, 1 C.	59	.1	15	t	8	.08	5	11	125	1		.01	.03	.1	1
Yogurt Dessert	133	7	24	2	216	.5	25	171	328	80	122	.07	.25	.4	6
TOTAL	690	30	79	33	311	5.8	110	515	1538	1676	5693	.44	.76	6.5	72

Substitutions
Whole Wheat Roll: any whole grain bread
Yogurt Dessert: 1 C. skim milk and fruit of choice

MENU

Hamburgers on Buns
Spinach, Avocado, and Tomato Salad with Sauce Vinaigrette
Ambrosia Shake

Calories: 815 per serving   Protein: 46 grams per serving

Hamburgers on Buns

4 hamburger buns
1 t. salt
¼ t. pepper
4 T. catsup
1 lb. lean ground beef

Following the recipe on page 16, make 12 (double-size) Whole Wheat Dinner Rolls to use for hamburger buns. Freeze remaining buns.

Blend the seasonings into the ground beef. Shape into ¾"-thick patties and broil or fry in a skillet. Turn the patties until done to taste. Split the buns and serve each hamburger on a bun with 1 T. catsup.

Yields: 4 servings

Spinach, Avocado, and Tomato Salad

4 C. raw spinach torn into bite-size pieces
1 medium avocado, cut in cubes
2 medium tomatoes, cut in chunks

Very gently toss the spinach with the avocado and tomatoes. Serve with 1 T. Sauce Vinaigrette per person (see page 14).

Yields: 4 servings

Ambrosia Shake

3 bananas, cut into pieces
¼ C. orange juice
¼ C. honey
2⅔ C. skim milk

Blend all the ingredients in a blender until smooth. Chill. Reblend and serve.

Yields: 4 servings

	CALORIES	PROTEIN GMS	CARBOHYDRATES GMS	FAT GMS	CALCIUM MGS	IRON MGS	MAGNESIUM MGS	PHOSPHORUS MGS	POTASSIUM MGS	SODIUM MGS	VITAMIN A I.U.	VITAMIN B₁ MGS	VITAMIN B₂ MGS	NIACIN MGS	VITAMIN C MGS
Hamburger on a Bun	391	32	40	15	78	6	74	407	510	963	345	.36	.3	8	2
Spinach, Avocado, and Tomato Salad	114	3.5	9	8.5	66	2.4	77	69	744	43	5280	.16	.24	1.6	52
Vinaigrette Dressing, 1 T.	86	3	5	9.6	t	t	t	t	4.7	36					
Ambrosia Shake	224	7	52	.6	213	1	59	197	725	87	566	.14	.3	1	21
TOTAL	815	46	106	34	357	9.4	210	673	1984	1129	6191	.66	.84	10.6	75

Substitutions
Hamburger Bun: any whole grain bun; optional
Spinach Salad: avocado may be omitted
Ambrosia Shake: 1 C. skim milk or ½ C. yogurt and fruit of choice

Harvest Home Casserole
Fresh Buttermilk Oaten Bread
Bananas and Cream

Calories: 651 per serving   Protein: 25 grams per serving

Harvest Home Casserole

1 C. chopped onion
½ C. diced green pepper
1 large carrot, sliced
4 oz. lean ground beef
2 C. baked beans, or canned or
   cooked pinto beans, drained
1 C. cream-style corn
¼ t. salt
¼ t. chili powder

Preheat oven to 400° F.

Brown the onion, green pepper, carrot, and beef in oil in a medium skillet. Add the beans, corn, and seasonings.

Place in a casserole and bake 20 minutes.

Yields: 4 servings

Fresh Buttermilk Oaten Bread

1½ C. raw oatmeal
½ C. raisins
1½ C. buttermilk or sour milk
2½–3 C. whole wheat flour
1 t. salt
1½ t. baking soda
1 T. honey

One day before making the bread, soak the oatmeal and raisins in the buttermilk. Cover and refrigerate overnight.

The next day, preheat the oven to 350° F.

Sift the dry ingredients into a bowl.

Add the honey to the oatmeal mixture and stir. Add 2½ C. flour to the oatmeal mixture and knead to make a soft dough. Add more flour if dough is sticky. On a floured surface, roll the dough out into a rectangular shape, approximately 1½″ thick, and place it on a lightly floured baking sheet. Bake for 55 minutes or until well browned.

Note: This is a heavy bread.

Yields: 16 slices

■ Serve each person 1 slice of bread with 1 t. butter, and for dessert 1 medium sliced banana with ¼ C. half and half.

	CALORIES	PROTEIN GMS	CARBOHYDRATES GMS	FAT GMS	CALCIUM MGS	IRON MGS	MAGNESIUM MGS	PHOSPHORUS MGS	POTASSIUM MGS	SODIUM MGS	VITAMIN A I.U.	VITAMIN B₁ MGS	VITAMIN B₂ MGS	NIACIN MGS	VITAMIN C MGS
Harvest Home Casserole	284	16	77	6.5	97	4	69	232	561	986	3189	.18	.14	3	24
Fresh Buttermilk Oaten Bread, 1 slice	126	4.7	26	1	43	1.2	39	133	178	160	8.4	.17	.07	.99	t
Butter, 1 t.	34	t	t	3.8	1	0	.09	.66	1	47	157	t	t		0
Banana, 1	127	2	33	.3	12	1	49	39	550	2	270	.08	.09	1	15
Half and Half, ¼ C.	80	2	2	7	64	.04	8	56	76	24	260	.02	.08	.05	t
TOTAL	651	25	138	19	217	6.2	165	461	1366	1219	3884	.45	.38	5	39

Substitutions

Bananas and Cream: 1 C. raspberries, strawberries, or blueberries for the banana; ½ C. milk or yogurt for the cream

MENU

Tomato Juice with Lime
Hawaiian Ham on Rice
Tossed Salad with Sauce Vinaigrette
Skim Milk

Calories: 732 per serving   Protein: 25 grams per serving

Hawaiian Ham

10 oz. cooked ham, diced
½ C. sliced onion
1 large carrot, sliced
1 C. sliced mushrooms, sautéed in butter
1 green pepper, cut in rings
¾ C. canned unsweetened pineapple cubes, drained (reserve liquid)

Preheat oven to 350° F.

Place the diced ham in a 2-quart casserole and arrange the onion, carrot, mushrooms, and pepper rings on top.

Combine the pineapple and peach liquids in a measuring cup and add enough water to make 1 cup. Place the fruit over the vegetables and sprinkle with the raisins.

In a saucepan, blend the mustard, honey, cornstarch, and salt;

1 C. canned unsweetened peach
   slices, drained (reserve
   liquid)
¼ C. raisins
1 T. prepared mustard (or 2 t.
   dry)
4 T. honey
1 T. cornstarch
¼ t. salt
¼ C. plus 2 T. cider vinegar
1 t. Worcestershire sauce
1 T. soy sauce
1 C. brown rice

then stir in the fruit juice mixture and the vinegar. Cook over medium heat, stirring until the mixture comes to boil and becomes clear. Then blend in well the Worcestershire and soy sauces. Pour this over the ham and vegetables. Bake uncovered 45–60 minutes.

Meanwhile, drop 1 C. rice into 2 C. boiling salted (1 t.) water and simmer covered 45–60 minutes. Serve each portion of ham over ½ C. cooked rice.

Yields: 4 servings

--- Tossed Salad ---

4 C. lettuce torn into bite-size
   pieces
⅔ C. thinly sliced red onion
croutons

Gently toss the lettuce with the onion. Add 1 T. Sauce Vinaigrette (see page 14) and 2 T. croutons (see page 46) to each serving.

■ Serve each person 1 C. tomato juice with a slice of lime, and 1 C. skim milk.

	CALORIES	PROTEIN GMS	CARBOHYDRATES GMS	FAT GMS	CALCIUM MGS	IRON MGS	MAGNESIUM MGS	PHOSPHORUS MGS	POTASSIUM MGS	SODIUM MGS	VITAMIN A I.U.	VITAMIN B₁ MGS	VITAMIN B₂ MGS	NIACIN MGS	VITAMIN C MGS
Tomato Juice with Lime, 1 C.	46	2	10	.2	17	2.2	20	44	552	486	1940	.12	.07	1.9	39
Hawaiian Ham	399	12	41	17	43	3	38	185	618	219	3171	.58	.28	4	43
Brown Rice, ½ C.	89	2	19	.6	9	.4	23	55	52	211	0	.07	.02	1	0
Tossed Salad	26	1	6	.25	49	1	10	29	212	9	1090	.4	.06	.26	14
Vinaigrette Dressing, 1 T.	86		5	9.6	t	t	t	t	4.7	36					
Skim Milk, 1 C.	86	8	12	.4	302	.1	28	247	406	126	500	.09	.34	.22	2
TOTAL	732	25	93	28	420	6.7	119	560	1845	1087	6701	1.3	.77	7.4	98

Substitutions
Tomato Juice: 1 C. vegetable juice or Vegetable Juice Cocktail
   (page 20)
Tossed Salad: salad or vegetable of choice
Skim Milk: ½ C. yogurt

Italian Spaghetti
French Bread
Tossed Salad with Italian Dressing
Skim Milk
Fruit Paradise

Calories: 820 per serving   Protein: 40 grams per serving

Italian Spaghetti

12 oz. lean ground beef
½ C. chopped onion
½ C. sliced mushrooms
1 clove garlic, crushed
½ green pepper, sliced
2 C. canned tomatoes
6 oz. tomato paste
1 bay leaf
¼ t. chili powder
¼ t. crushed thyme
¼ C. chopped parsley
1 t. crushed oregano
1½ t. brown sugar
¾ C. water or as needed
8 oz. raw spaghetti
¼ C. grated Parmesan cheese

In a heavy pan or Dutch oven, combine the meat, onion, mushrooms, and garlic. Cook until meat is browned and onion is tender. Skim off excess fat. Add the remaining ingredients except the spaghetti and cheese. Simmer uncovered for 3 hours, stirring occasionally.

Prepare spaghetti noodles according to package instructions.

Serve the sauce over the hot spaghetti and sprinkle each serving with 1 T. Parmesan cheese.

Yields: 4 servings

French Bread

1 T. dry yeast
½ C. warm water
1½ C. hot water
1 T. salt
1 C. yogurt
6 C. whole wheat flour
cornmeal

Dissolve the yeast in the warm water and set aside for 5 minutes.

Combine the hot water, salt, and yogurt. Add the yeast and 4 C. flour. Beat 100 strokes, or 7 minutes on an electric mixer on low speed. Add the remaining flour and knead 10 minutes. Add more flour if the dough is sticky. Put dough into an oiled bowl, turn the dough to coat it with oil, and let it rise in a warm place until double in size. Punch down and divide in two. Shape into 2 long loaves and place on a greased baking sheet sprinkled with cornmeal. Let rise in a warm place for 30 minutes. Meanwhile preheat oven to 400° F.

Slash the tops of the loaves with a sharp knife. Spray with water and bake for 40 minutes or until golden brown.

For a crisp crust, put a pan of water in the oven (for steam), and occasionally spray loaves with water during baking.

Yields: 2 loaves (40 slices)

Tossed Salad

4 C. lettuce torn into bite-size pieces
1 C. sliced mushrooms
2 chopped scallions
4 large pitted black olives

Toss all the ingredients together gently. Serve with 1 T. Italian dressing (see page 71) on each portion.

Yields: 4 servings

Fruit Paradise

1 peach
½ C. mandarin orange or tangerine sections
½ C. grapefruit sections
½ C. blueberries
½ C. grapefruit juice
½ C. orange juice

Divide the peach equally among 4 glasses. Divide the additional fruits and juice among the 4 glasses; mix, and chill.

Yields: 4 servings

■ Serve each person 1 C. skim milk, and 1 slice French bread with 1 t. garlic butter.

	CALORIES	PROTEIN GMS	CARBOHYDRATES GMS	FAT GMS	CALCIUM MGS	IRON MGS	MAGNESIUM MGS	PHOSPHORUS MGS	POTASSIUM MGS	SODIUM MGS	VITAMIN A I.U.	VITAMIN B₁ MGS	VITAMIN B₂ MGS	NIACIN MGS	VITAMIN C MGS
Italian Spaghetti	475	28	60	12	132	6.5	44	352	1063	649	2893	.75	.5	10	62
French Bread, 1 slice	64	1.6	13	.5	15	.6	21	72	75	163	7	.01	.03	.8	t
Tossed Salad	34	1	3	2.2	46	1.2	8	23	197	75	1198	.04	.05	.4	14
Italian Dressing, 1 T.	84	.03	.4	9	1	.02	.3	.8	4	94					1
Skim Milk, 1 C.	86	8	12	.4	302	.1	28	247	406	126	500	.09	.34	.22	2
Fruit Paradise	77	1	19	.4	33	.7	23	29	265	2	621	.08	.06	.7	55
TOTAL	820	40	107	25	529	9	124	724	2010	1109	5219	.97	.98	12	134

Substitutions
French Bread: any whole grain bread
Skim Milk: ½ C. yogurt
Fruit Paradise: 1 C. raspberries or blackberries, or ½ mango;
  ¼ cantaloupe

Lasagna
Fresh Mushroom Sauté
Tossed Salad with Sauce Vinaigrette
French Bread
Fruit Platter with Sauce

Calories: 791 per serving   Protein: 40 grams per serving

Lasagna

8 oz. lean ground beef
2 cloves garlic, minced or crushed
⅓ C. tomato paste
1½ C. canned tomatoes
½ t. salt
¼ t. pepper
½ t. crushed oregano
4 oz. lasagna noodles, uncooked
4 oz. Swiss cheese, sliced
¾ C. cottage cheese
¼ C. grated Parmesan cheese

Brown the ground beef and garlic in a medium saucepan. Add the tomato paste, tomatoes, and seasonings. Stir, cover, and simmer for approximately 20 minutes.

Cook lasagna noodles according to package instructions.

Preheat oven to 350° F.

In a casserole, alternate layers of meat, sauce, noodles, Swiss cheese and cottage cheese, beginning and ending with the meat sauce. Bake 20–30 minutes, and just before serving, sprinkle with grated Parmesan cheese.

Yields: 4 servings

Fresh Mushroom Sauté

1½ lb. mushrooms (3 C. sliced)
2 T. butter

Wash the mushrooms while the butter is melting in a skillet. Slice them if desired. Add the mushrooms to the butter and cook over low heat until tender (8–10 minutes), stirring occasionally. Season to taste.

Yields: 4 servings

Tossed Salad

4 C. lettuce torn into bite-size pieces
1 large carrot, grated
½ green pepper, cut in rings

Gently toss all the ingredients together. Add 1 T. Sauce Vinaigrette (see page 14) to each serving.

Yields: 4 servings

Fruit Platter with Sauce

¼ C. honey
1 T. cornstarch

For the sauce: Stir together in a saucepan the honey, cornstarch, and salt. Add the water, fruit juices, and rinds.

⅛ t. salt
⅜ C. water
½ C. orange juice
2 T. lemon juice
¼ t. grated orange rind
¼ t. grated lemon rind
1 C. green grapes
1 orange, in segments
1 sliced banana
2 sliced peaches
1 C. strawberries

Cook over medium heat, stirring constantly, until the mixture thickens and boils. Continue to boil for 1 minute, stirring constantly. Remove from heat.

Divide the fruits equally among 4 fruit dishes and serve the sauce, warm or chilled, over the fruit.

Yields: 4 servings

■ Serve each person 1 slice French bread with 1 t. butter (see page 31).

	CALORIES	PROTEIN GMS	CARBOHYDRATES GMS	FAT GMS	CALCIUM MGS	IRON MGS	MAGNESIUM MGS	PHOSPHORUS MGS	POTASSIUM MGS	SODIUM MGS	VITAMIN A I.U.	VITAMIN B₁ MGS	VITAMIN B₂ MGS	NIACIN MGS	VITAMIN C MGS
Lasagna	342	30	17	18	401	3	50	429	558	666	1945	.2	.45	5	26
Fresh Mushroom Sauté	97	5	7	11	11	1.2	1	193	753	260	t	.15	.8	7	5
Tossed Salad	23	1	5	.25	47	1	12	25	252	18	3844	.05	.06	.4	16
Vinaigrette Dressing, 1 T.	86		5	9.6	t	t	t	t	4.7	36					
French Bread, 1 slice	64	1.6	13	.5	15	.6	21	72	75	163	7	.01	.03	.8	t
Butter, 1 t.	34	t	t	3.8	1	0	.09	.66	1	47	157	t	t		0
Fruit Platter	145	2	36	.8	39	1	36	47	505	70	923	.12	.11	1.4	64
TOTAL	791	40	83	44	514	6.8	120	767	2149	1260	6876	.53	1.5	15	111

Substitutions
Fresh Mushroom Sauté: optional
French Bread: any whole grain bread
Fruit Platter: 1 C. pineapple, grapefruit, or orange juice; 1 C. pineapple; 1 orange or mango; one 6″ × 1½″ slice of watermelon

Liver Venetian Style
Green Peas with Lemon-Mint Sauce
Sesame Bread
Skim Milk

Calories: 634 per serving   Protein: 38 grams per serving

Liver Venetian Style

4 onions, sliced
2 T. safflower oil
1 lb. calves' liver
dash of salt and pepper

In a large skillet, sauté the onions in the oil until tender.

Cut the liver into thin slices and add it to the onions. Cook until liver is browned, approximately 3 minutes. Season to taste with salt and pepper.

Yields: 4 servings

Green Peas with Lemon-Mint Sauce

2 C. green peas
2 T. butter
2 t. lemon juice
¼ t. grated lemon rind
1½ T. mint leaves, dried or
    fresh

Steam or boil the peas in ½" water just until tender.

Melt the butter and combine it with the lemon juice, rind, and mint. Pour the sauce over the hot peas, mix well, and serve immediately.

Yields: 4 servings

Sesame Bread

⅓ C. honey
¼ C. sesame or safflower oil
2 eggs
1 t. orange rind
1 t. salt
1 T. baking powder
3 C. whole wheat flour
1¼ C. skim milk
½ C. sesame seeds

Preheat oven to 350° F. Grease a 9½" × 5½" loaf pan.

In a large mixing bowl combine the honey and oil. Beat in the eggs and orange rind.

In a separate bowl, stir together the salt, baking powder, and flour. Slowly add the flour mixture alternately with the milk to the egg mixture. Stir well after each addition. Add the sesame seeds and stir gently.

Pour the batter into the loaf pan and bake for 50 minutes or until done.

Yields: 18 slices

■ Serve each person 1 slice of sesame bread with 1 t. butter, and 1 C. skim milk.

	CALORIES	PROTEIN GMS	CARBOHYDRATES GMS	FAT GMS	CALCIUM MGS	IRON MGS	MAGNESIUM MGS	PHOSPHORUS MGS	POTASSIUM MGS	SODIUM MGS	VITAMIN A I.U.	VITAMIN B₁ MGS	VITAMIN B₂ MGS	NIACIN MGS	VITAMIN C MGS
Liver Venetian Style	254	21	13	8	32	7.8	25	430	452	249	11,010	.32	3.7	15	44
Green Peas, ½ C.	108	4	14	6.3	21	1.5	25	80	159	74	667	.23	.09	1.9	16
Sesame Bread, 1 slice	152	5	21	6	42	.9	33	130	117	136	99	.03	.07	1.2	t
Butter, 1 t.	34	t	t	3.8	1	0	.09	.66	1	47	157	t	t		0
Skim Milk, 1 C.	86	8	12	.4	302	.1	28	247	406	126	500	.09	.34	.22	2
TOTAL	634	38	60	25	398	10	111	888	1135	632	12,433	.67	4.2	18	62

Substitutions

Green Peas: vegetable or salad of choice
Sesame Bread: any whole grain bread
Skim Milk: ½ C. yogurt

MENU

Meat Loaf
Baked Potatoes with Sour Cream
Riviera Green Beans
Skim Milk
Berry Gelatin

Calories: 665 per serving   Protein: 44 grams per serving

Meat Loaf

1 C. soft bread crumbs (3 slices bread)
⅓ C. minced onion
2 T. chopped green pepper
1 egg
1 lb. lean ground beef

Preheat oven to 400° F.

Combine the bread crumbs with the onion and green pepper.

In a large bowl, beat the egg slightly and mix in the ground beef and the bread crumb mixture. Add the horseradish, salt, mustard, and two-thirds of the catsup. Combine well.

1 T. horseradish
1 t. salt
½ t. dry mustard
⅓ C. catsup

Shape the meat into an oval loaf. Transfer it to a shallow baking dish, reshape if necessary, and spread top with the remaining catsup. Bake for 50 minutes.

Yields: 4 servings

Riviera Green Beans

2 C. green beans
½ C. peas
2 scallions, chopped fine
1 large carrot, grated
2 medium tomatoes, cut in
  wedges

Cut the green beans into 1″ lengths. Cook the beans and peas for 1–3 minutes in ½″ boiling water or a steamer. Drain and chill.

Combine chilled vegetables with the scallions and carrot. Add salad dressing if desired. Toss and serve with the tomato wedges.

Yields: 4 servings

Berry Gelatin

1 T. unflavored gelatin
½ C. cold water
1½ C. unsweetened blackberry
  juice
1 C. blackberries
pinch salt (optional)

Soak the gelatin in the cold water to dissolve. Heat the juice to boiling; add the gelatin and salt and stir until dissolved. Chill the gelatin until it begins to congeal. Add the blackberries and pour mixture into a mold or pan lightly brushed with oil. Chill.

Suggestion: Heat some honey with the berry juice if a sweeter taste is desired. Any fruit or fruit juice can be used to make gelatin desserts except pineapple.

■ Serve each person 1 baked potato with 1 T. sour cream, and 1 C. skim milk.

	CALORIES	PROTEIN GMS	CARBOHYDRATES GMS	FAT GMS	CALCIUM MGS	IRON MGS	MAGNESIUM MGS	PHOSPHORUS MGS	POTASSIUM MGS	SODIUM MGS	VITAMIN A I.U.	VITAMIN B₁ MGS	VITAMIN B₂ MGS	NIACIN MGS	VITAMIN C MGS
Meat Loaf	291	28	15	13	49	4.4	42	295	503	934	465	.18	.25	6.5	12
Baked Potato, 1	145	4	33	.2	14	1.1	44	101	782	6	t	.15	.07	2.7	31
Sour Cream, 1 T.	30	.5	.6	3	17	.01	1.6	12	21	8	114	.01	.02	.01	t
Riviera Green Beans	58	3	12	.4	57	1.4	42	74	409	17	3955	.16	.12	1.5	32
Skim Milk, 1 C.	86	8	12	.4	302	.1	28	247	406	126	500	.09	.34	.22	2
Berry Gelatin	55	.7	12	.9	23	1.2	30	18	218	1	72	.03	.04	.4	17
TOTAL	665	44	85	18	462	8.2	188	747	2339	1092	5106	.62	.84	11	94

Substitutions

Baked Potato: french- or pan-fried potatoes; optional

Riviera Green Beans: 1 C. cooked spinach, broccoli, brussels
sprouts, cauliflower, chinese cabbage, kohlrabi, rutabaga,
kale, or okra; 1 C. vegetable juice or Vegetable Juice Cocktail
(see page 20).

Skim Milk: ½ C. yogurt or 1 oz. natural cheese

Berry Gelatin: 1 C. boysenberries or raspberries; ½ C.
blackberries; ½ mango

MENU

Moussaka
French Bread
Greek Salad
Papaya

Calories: 738 per serving   Protein: 23 grams per serving

Moussaka

1 medium eggplant (2½ C.)
2 T. olive oil
⅓ C. chopped onion
⅓ C. sliced mushrooms
1 clove garlic, minced or
   crushed
8 oz. ground lamb
⅓ C. chopped green pepper
¾ C. canned tomatoes
½ C. tomato purée
1 T. chopped parsley
1 bay leaf
½ t. crushed oregano
¼ t. ground cinnamon
¼ t. crushed basil
1 t. salt
dash of pepper
¼ C. grated Parmesan cheese

Preheat oven to 400° F.

Prepare the eggplant: Cut it into ¼″ slices, place slices in a
shallow baking dish, and cover with water and salt. Let stand
for 20 minutes. Drain, rinse, pat dry.

In a large skillet, brown the eggplant slices quickly on both
sides in the heated oil. Remove and drain on paper towels.

In another large skillet, brown the onion, mushrooms, and
garlic. Add the meat; sauté, stirring 10 minutes. Add the green
pepper, tomatoes, purée, and seasonings.

Arrange half of the eggplant slices in the bottom of a casserole.
Add the meat mixture and cover with the remaining eggplant.
Pour the white sauce (see below) over the eggplant, sprinkle
with the Parmesan cheese, and bake for 1 hour. Cool for a
few minutes before serving.

Yields: 4 servings

White Sauce

2 T. butter
¼ C. whole wheat flour
1¼ C. skim milk, warmed
2 eggs
dash of grated nutmeg
salt and pepper to taste

Melt the butter in a heavy saucepan over low heat. Slowly add the flour, blending thoroughly with a whisk. Add the milk. Keep whisking until the mixture begins to thicken. Beat in the eggs. Simmer a few minutes. Stir in the seasonings.

Greek Salad

4 C. spinach torn into bite-size
   pieces
8 black or Greek olives
3 T. olive oil
2 T. lemon juice
dash of salt and pepper
feta cheese (optional)

Combine the oil, lemon juice, and salt and pepper in a salad bowl. Add the olives and spinach, and toss gently. Crumble feta cheese over the top if desired.

Yields: 4 servings

■ Serve each person 1 slice of French bread with 1 t. butter (see page 31), and for dessert one half of a papaya.

	CALORIES	PROTEIN GMS	CARBOHYDRATES GMS	FAT GMS	CALCIUM MGS	IRON MGS	MAGNESIUM MGS	PHOSPHORUS MGS	POTASSIUM MGS	SODIUM MGS	VITAMIN A I.U.	VITAMIN B_1 MGS	VITAMIN B_2 MGS	NIACIN MGS	VITAMIN C MGS
Moussaka	435	19	23	29	223	11	56	305	878	907	1747	.27	.33	4.4	35
Greek Salad and Dressing	147	1	3	15	72	2	44	31	268	189	4474	.06	.11	.3	27
French Bread, 1 slice	64	1.6	13	.5	15	.6	21	72	75	163	7	.01	.03	.8	t
Butter, 1 t.	34	t	t	3.8	1	0	.09	.66	1	47	157	t	t		0
Papaya, ½	58	.9	15	t	30	.45	11	24	351	5	2625	.06	.06	.45	84
TOTAL	738	23	54	48	341	14	132	433	1573	1311	9010	.4	.53	6	146

Substitutions
Greek Salad: ½ C. asparagus, collards, or peas; 1 C. Swiss
   chard, kale, green beans, broccoli, or cauliflower
French Bread: any whole grain bread
Papaya: 1 orange, ½ mango, or 1 C. cherries

Pizza
Vegetables and Guacamole
Vanilla Ice Cream

Calories: 826 per serving   Protein: 27 grams per serving

Pizza

Crust

½ T. dry yeast
2 T. warm water
2 T. butter
½ t. salt
½ C. whole milk, scalded
1 C. whole wheat flour

Soften the yeast in the water.

In a separate bowl combine the butter, salt, and milk. Cool to lukewarm.

Stir in the yeast. Gradually add the flour until the dough is stiff. Knead 5 minutes.

Cover and let rise in a warm place to twice its original size.

Sauce

¼ C. chopped onion
2 cloves garlic, chopped
2 t. olive oil
¾ C. tomato paste
1 C. canned tomatoes
dash of pepper
1½ t. crushed oregano
¼ t. crushed basil
¼ t. crushed thyme
¼ t. crushed marjoram
¼ t. cayenne
2 T. chopped parsley

Prepare the sauce: Sauté the onion and garlic in the oil; add the remaining ingredients; cook approximately 30 minutes. Stir occasionally.

Topping

1 C. sliced mushrooms
3 oz. pork sausage, cooked and chopped
5 oz. shredded mozzarella cheese
¼ C. grated Parmesan cheese

Preheat oven to 425° F.

Grease a 12"–13" pizza pan. Roll out the dough, place it in the pan, brush it with some oil and prick with a fork. Bake 3–5 minutes.

Spread the sauce on the dough, then add the mushrooms and sausage. Return the pizza to the oven and bake 10 minutes. Top with cheeses and bake until they are melted.

Yields: 4 servings

Suggestion: Add other toppings such as green pepper, onion, olives. Salami strips or 2 oz. shrimp can be substituted for sausage. Or make it vegetarian and use 8 oz. mozzarella.

Vegetables and Guacamole

1 large carrot, cut in strips
1 large celery stalk, cut in strips
1 C. broccoli flowerets, packed
1 C. cauliflowerets

Guacamole

2 avocados
½ C. minced onion
4 T. sour cream
¼ t. lemon juice
2 cloves garlic, mashed
1 t. salt
1 t. ground cumin (optional)

Mash avocado meat and mix well with remaining guacamole ingredients. Serve as a dip for the raw vegetables.

Yields: 4 servings

Vanilla Ice Cream

½ C. honey
2 eggs or egg yolks
2 C. cream
2 C. whole milk
⅛ t. salt
1½ t. vanilla

Heat the honey in a small saucepan until it is runny. Beat the eggs.

Combine the cream, milk, salt, and vanilla in a large bowl. Slowly add the eggs, then the honey, whisking continuously until all ingredients are well mixed. Follow instructions for your ice cream machine.

Yields: 2 quarts.

■ Serve each person ½ C. ice cream.

	CALORIES	PROTEIN GMS	CARBOHYDRATES GMS	FAT GMS	CALCIUM MGS	IRON MGS	MAGNESIUM MGS	PHOSPHORUS MGS	POTASSIUM MGS	SODIUM MGS	VITAMIN A I.U.	VITAMIN B₁ MGS	VITAMIN B₂ MGS	NIACIN MGS	VITAMIN C MGS
Pizza	442	20	37	25	342	4	67	429	844	560	2865	.4	.38	5	36
Vegetables and Guacamole	238	5	16	20	94	1.6	76	117	1023	603	4207	.2	.35	2.4	75
Vanilla Ice Cream- ½ C.	146	2	11	11	61	.19	7	59	80	44	453	.02	.1	.09	.5
TOTAL	826	27	64	56	491	5.8	150	605	1947	1207	7525	.62	.83	7.5	112

Substitutions

Vegetables and Guacamole: guacamole may be omitted; vegetable or salad of choice; optional

Vanilla Ice Cream: any ice cream; optional

MENU

Polish Sausages and Sauerkraut
Baked Potatoes and Butter
Zucchini Scramble
Fruit Juice Soda (optional)

Calories: 573 per serving   Protein: 21 grams per serving

Polish Sausages and Sauerkraut

4 Polish sausages
2 C. sauerkraut with juice
brown sugar (optional)

Place the sausages, sauerkraut, and juice in a saucepan. Add brown sugar to taste. Bring to a boil and simmer covered for 20–30 minutes or until heated thoroughly. Add water if sauerkraut liquid is insufficient.

Yields: 4 servings

1⅓ C. sliced zucchini
2 T. chopped onion
½ C. sliced mushrooms
2 T. butter
1 T. whole wheat flour
⅛ t. salt
dash of pepper
½ C. whole milk
⅛ C. grated cheddar cheese
½ C. sliced carrots, cooked
½ t. salt
⅛ t. crushed thyme
2 tomatoes, cut in wedges

Sauté the zucchini, onion, and mushrooms in half the butter in a medium skillet.

Prepare the cheese sauce: Melt the remaining butter in a saucepan over medium heat. Blend in the flour, salt, and pepper. Remove from the heat; gradually add the milk, stirring constantly to blend smoothly. Return to the heat, stirring until the sauce thickens. Add the cheese and blend.

Stir the cheese sauce into the zucchini mixture. Add the remaining ingredients; heat through.

Yields: 4 servings

■ Serve each person 1 baked potato with ½ T. butter, and 1 C. Fruit Juice Soda if desired (½ C. unsweetened fruit juice mixed with ½ C. club soda or sparkling mineral water).

	CALORIES	PROTEIN GMS	CARBOHYDRATES GMS	FAT GMS	CALCIUM MGS	IRON MGS	MAGNESIUM MGS	PHOSPHORUS MGS	POTASSIUM MGS	SODIUM MGS	VITAMIN A I.U.	VITAMIN B₁ MGS	VITAMIN B₂ MGS	NIACIN MGS	VITAMIN C MGS
Polish Sausages	214	11	.75	18	6	1.7		124				.24	.1	2.2	
Sauerkraut, ½ C.	21	1	4	.25	42	.5		21	165	561	60	.03	.04	.25	16
Baked Potato, 1	145	4	33	.2	14	1	75	101	782	6	t	.15	.07	2.7	31
Butter, ½ T.	51	t	t	6	1.5	0	.14	1	1.5	70	235	t	t		0
Zucchini Scramble	142	5	9	9	126	.9	32	128	446	473	3172	.11	.2	1.7	29
TOTAL	573	21	47	34	190	4	107	375	1395	1110	3467	.53	.4	6.9	76

Substitutions
Baked Potato: potato made any style
Zucchini Scramble: 1 C. skim milk or ½ C. yogurt, plus ½
    C. asparagus, carrots, or winter squash, or 1 medium tomato

MENU

Porcupine Meatballs
Vegetable-Dill Salad
Whole Wheat Bread
Skim Milk

Calories: 586 per serving   Protein: 36 grams per serving

Porcupine Meatballs

1 egg
1¼ C. condensed tomato soup
¼ C. brown rice
2 T. chopped onion
1 T. chopped parsley
½ t. salt
dash of pepper
12 oz. lean ground beef
1 t. Worcestershire sauce

Beat the egg in a medium bowl and combine it with ¼ C. of the tomato soup, the rice, onion, parsley, salt, and pepper. Add the beef and mix well. Shape into 20 meatballs and place in a skillet.

In a separate bowl, mix the remaining soup, ½ C. water, and the Worcestershire sauce. Pour this over the meatballs and bring the mixture to a boil. Reduce the heat, cover, and simmer for 50 minutes, stirring frequently.

Yields: 4 servings

Vegetable-Dill Salad

¾ C. sliced carrots, cooked
¾ C. sliced cauliflower, cooked
¾ C. peas, cooked
¾ C. canned Italian green beans or fresh snap beans, cooked
½ C. chopped celery
2 T. chopped onion
2 T. low-calorie French dressing
2 T. mayonnaise
1 T. chili sauce
1 t. lemon juice
½ t. salt
dash of pepper
1 t. dill

Chill the vegetables if desired.

Blend together in a medium bowl the French dressing, mayonnaise, chili sauce, lemon juice, salt, pepper, and dill.

Place the vegetables in a large salad bowl, add the dressing, and toss to coat.

Yields: 4 servings

Whole Wheat Bread

Follow the recipe for Whole Wheat Dinner Rolls (page 16). Put the dough into a greased 9½″ × 5½″ loaf pan. Let it rise until double in bulk. Bake in a 350° F. oven for 30–35 minutes or until nicely browned. Let cool on a wire rack.

Yields: 18 slices

■ Serve each person 1 C. skim milk and 1 slice of bread with 1 t. butter.

	CALORIES	PROTEIN GMS	CARBOHYDRATES GMS	FAT GMS	CALCIUM MGS	IRON MGS	MAGNESIUM MGS	PHOSPHORUS MGS	POTASSIUM MGS	SODIUM MGS	VITAMIN A I.U.	VITAMIN B_1 MGS	VITAMIN B_2 MGS	NIACIN MGS	VITAMIN C MGS
Porcupine Meatballs	247	20	15	11	30	3.5	39	227	399	676	542	.15	.2	5	4
Vegetable-Dill Salad	104	3	11	8	45	1.2	32	67	276	403	3319	.3	.1	1.2	25
Whole Wheat Bread, 1 slice	115	5	24	2	38	1	33	125	137	133	74	.17	.07	1.3	t
Butter, 1 t.	34	t	t	3.8	1	0	.09	.66	1	47	157	t	t		0
Skim Milk, 1 C.	86	8	12	.4	302	.1	28	247	406	126	500	.09	.34	.22	2
TOTAL	586	36	62	25	416	5.8	132	667	1219	1385	4592	.7	.7	7.7	31

Substitutions

Vegetable-Dill Salad: ½ C. broccoli, Swiss chard, kale, spinach, winter squash; 1 medium tomato; 1 C. vegetable juice or Vegetable Juice Cocktail (see page 20)

Whole Wheat Bread: any whole grain bread; optional

Skim Milk: ½ C. yogurt or 1 oz. natural cheese

Pork Chops Italiano over Brown Rice
Caesar Salad
Skim Milk

Calories: 877 per serving   Protein: 42 grams per serving

Pork Chops Italiano

4 pork chops (1½–2 lbs. with bone)
1 C. sliced mushrooms
½ C. chopped onion
½ clove garlic, crushed
2 green peppers, sliced
1 T. safflower oil
2 C. tomato purée
1 t. salt
⅛ t. pepper
½ bay leaf
1 T. lemon juice
⅛ t. crumbled sage
1½ t. brown sugar (optional)
1 C. brown rice

Trim excess fat off the pork chops. In a large skillet, brown the chops and drain off any fat. Place the chops in a large roasting pan or 2½-quart casserole.

Preheat oven to 350° F.

In a separate skillet, sauté the mushrooms, onion, garlic, and green pepper in the oil. Add the tomato purée, salt, pepper, bay leaf, lemon juice, and sage. Cover and simmer until vegetables are almost tender.

Pour the sauce over the chops, coating them well. Cover. Bake 1 hour.

Meanwhile, drop 1 C. brown rice into 2 C. boiling salted (1 t.) water and simmer, covered, 45–60 minutes.

Serve each person 1 pork chop over ½ C. rice.

Yields: 4 servings

Caesar Salad

½ C. croutons (approximately 1½ slices old bread)
1 T. olive oil
garlic salt to taste
4 C. romaine lettuce torn into bite-size pieces
3 T. olive oil
1 clove garlic, crushed
1 egg, beaten
juice of ½ lemon
⅓ t. dry mustard
1 t. Worcestershire sauce
paprika to taste
4 T. grated Parmesan cheese
freshly ground pepper

Prepare the croutons: Preheat oven to 300° F. Cut the bread into cubes. Pan fry, stirring constantly, in 1 T. olive oil and garlic salt for 5 minutes. Spread out in a baking tray and bake 10–15 minutes.

Place the olive oil and garlic in a large bowl. Beating with a fork, gradually add the egg, lemon juice, mustard, Worcestershire sauce, and paprika. Mix well. Blend in the cheese. Add the lettuce, coating each piece well.

Serve in individual bowls. Add a grinding of pepper and 2 T. croutons to each serving.

Yields: 4 servings

■ Serve each person 1 C. skim milk.

	CALORIES	PROTEIN GMS	CARBOHYDRATES GMS	FAT GMS	CALCIUM MGS	IRON MGS	MAGNESIUM MGS	PHOSPHORUS MGS	POTASSIUM MGS	SODIUM MGS	VITAMIN A I.U.	VITAMIN B_1 MGS	VITAMIN B_2 MGS	NIACIN MGS	VITAMIN C MGS
Pork Chops Italiano	507	26	16	38	44	6	64	341	1104	1124	2221	1	.45	8.5	122
Brown Rice, ½ C.	89	2	19	.6	9	.4	23	55	52	211	0	.07	.02	1	0
Caesar Salad	195	6	12	18	124	1.3	13	94	180	198	148	.05	.09	.3	4
Skim Milk, 1 C.	86	8	12	.4	302	.1	28	247	406	126	500	.09	.34	.22	2
TOTAL	877	42	59	57	479	7.8	128	737	1742	1659	2869	1.2	.9	10	128

Substitutions
Caesar Salad: tossed salad or vegetable of choice
Skim Milk: ½ C. yogurt

MENU

Porterhouse Steak with Mushroom Sauce
Stuffed Baked Potatoes
Tossed Salad with Thousand Island Dressing
Skim Milk
Peach Puddingcake

Calories: 937 per serving   Protein: 34 grams per serving

Porterhouse Steak with Mushroom Sauce

2 T. butter
1½ C. sliced mushrooms
2 T. whole wheat flour
1½ C. water
2 beef bouillon cubes
2 T. chopped parsley
½ t. crushed thyme
1 t. Worcestershire sauce

Melt the butter in a saucepan and sauté the mushrooms in it.

In a mixing bowl, stir the flour into the water. Add the remaining ingredients, stir well, and add mixture to the mushrooms. Cook the sauce over low heat until thick and bubbly. Taste for seasoning; add ½ C. dry red wine if desired.

Broil the steak: 4 minutes on each side for medium well. Serve

¼ t. salt
½ C. dry red wine (optional)
1 lb. porterhouse steak

the sauce over equal portions of steak.

Yields: 4 servings

Stuffed Baked Potatoes

4 baked potatoes
4 T. sour cream
2 T. chopped parsley
2 t. caraway seeds
½ t. salt
1 t. Worcestershire sauce
   (optional)
pepper to taste
paprika to taste

Cut the baked potatoes in half lengthwise. Scoop out the pulp, mash it well in a bowl, and mix in the sour cream and seasonings, except the paprika. Pack the mixture into the potato skins, sprinkle with paprika, and bake in 400° F. oven for 10 minutes.

Yields: 4 servings

Tossed Salad

1 head iceberg lettuce
½ carrot, grated
1 tomato, cut in wedges
4 T. Thousand Island Dressing

Wash, dry, and tear lettuce into bite-size pieces. Toss the lettuce and carrot together. Garnish with tomato wedges and Thousand Island dressing.

Yields: 4 servings

Thousand Island Dressing

1 C. mayonnaise
¼ C. finely chopped pickles
¼ C. chili sauce
2 hard-boiled eggs, finely
   chopped
2 T. finely chopped onion
1 T. lemon juice

Combine all the ingredients, blend well, and store in the refrigerator.

Yields: approximately 2 cups

Peach Puddingcake

2 C. whole wheat pastry flour
2 t. baking powder
½ t. salt
1 t. ground cinnamon
½ t. ground allspice
2 eggs
½ C. honey
½ t. vanilla extract
2 T. melted butter
3 C. sliced fresh peaches (or
   frozen, thawed)
cream for whipping (optional)

Preheat oven to 350° F.

Sift together the flour, baking powder, salt, and spices.

In a separate bowl mix together with an electric beater the eggs, honey, vanilla, and butter. Add this to the flour mixture and blend thoroughly. Fold in the peaches.

Put the mixture into a buttered 12″ × 8″ baking pan. Bake 35 minutes. Serve warm, with whipped cream if desired.

Yields: 15 pieces

	CALORIES	PROTEIN GMS	CARBOHYDRATES GMS	FAT GMS	CALCIUM MGS	IRON MGS	MAGNESIUM MGS	PHOSPHORUS MGS	POTASSIUM MGS	SODIUM MGS	VITAMIN A I.U.	VITAMIN B₁ MGS	VITAMIN B₂ MGS	NIACIN MGS	VITAMIN C MGS
Porterhouse Steak with Sauce	472	16	4	43	16	2.5	26	184	380	651	467	.1	.25	5	4
Stuffed Baked Potato, 1	177	5	34	7	35	1.2	78	115	817	281	273	.16	.1	3	35
Tossed Salad	26	1	6	.23	56	1.3	8	32	315	13	2025	.1	.06	.6	22
Thousand Island Dressing, 1 T.	58	.6	.8	6	4	.13	1	10	21	116	87	.01	.02	.03	t
Skim Milk, 1 C.	86	8	12	.4	302	.1	28	247	406	126	500	.09	.34	.22	2
Peach Puddingcake, 1 pc.	118	3	24	3	9	.8	21	76	114	27	371	.1	.05	1	1
TOTAL	937	34	81	60	422	6	162	664	2053	1214	3723	.56	.8	6.9	64

Substitutions
Stuffed Baked Potato: potato made any style
Tossed Salad: substitute spinach or endive for iceberg lettuce
Skim Milk: ½ C. yogurt
Peach Puddingcake: 1 C. grape, grapefruit, or pineapple juice;
    1 mango or orange; or one 6″ × 1½″ slice watermelon

MENU

Sloppy Joes
Potato Chips
Carrot Sticks
Dill Pickles
Skim Milk
Maple Nut Ice Cream

Calories: 734 per serving   Protein: 34 grams per serving

Sloppy Joes

8 oz. lean ground beef
¼ C. chopped onion
¼ C. chopped green pepper

Following the recipe for Whole Wheat Dinner Rolls on page 16, make 12 (double-size) rolls for hamburger buns.

¼ C. sliced mushrooms
½ C. chili sauce
4 hamburger buns

Brown the beef in a heavy skillet; add the onion, green pepper, mushrooms, and chili sauce. Cook covered over low heat until tender; about 15 minutes.

Slightly toast each bun and serve Sloppy Joes proportionately on 4 buns.

Yields: 4 servings

Maple Nut Ice Cream

1 T. maple extract
½ C. chopped walnuts

Follow the recipe for vanilla ice cream on page 41, substituting maple extract for the vanilla. Fold in the nuts after processing but before freezing.

Yields: 2 quarts

■ Serve each person ½ C. potato chips, ½ large carrot, 1 dill pickle, 1 C. skim milk, and for dessert ½ C. ice cream.

	CALORIES	PROTEIN GMS	CARBOHYDRATES GMS	FAT GMS	CALCIUM MGS	IRON MGS	MAGNESIUM MGS	PHOSPHORUS MGS	POTASSIUM MGS	SODIUM MGS	VITAMIN A I.U.	VITAMIN B₁ MGS	VITAMIN B₂ MGS	NIACIN MGS	VITAMIN C MGS
Sloppy Joes	315	21	45	9	73	3.5	64	313	520	641	580	.35	.25	5	11
Potato Chips, ½ C.	113	1	10	8	8	.4	9.6	28	226		t	.04	.01	1	3
Raw Carrot, ½	21	.5	5	.1	19	.4	12	18	171	24	5500	.03	.03	.3	4
Dill Pickle, 1 lge.	11	.7	2	.4	26	1	12	21	200	1428	100	t	.02	t	6
Skim Milk, 1 C.	86	8	12	.4	302	.1	28	247	406	126	500	.09	.34	.22	2
Maple Nut Ice Cream, ½ C.	188	3	11	15	66	.6	15	83	103	43	455	.04	.1	.15	t
TOTAL	734	34	85	33	494	6	141	710	1626	2262	7135	.55	.75	6.7	26

Substitutions
Bun: any whole grain bread
Dill Pickle: celery sticks and/or radishes; optional
Carrot: 1 medium tomato; ½ C. broccoli or spinach; 1 C. vegetable juice or Vegetable Juice Cocktail (see page 20)
Skim Milk: ½ C. yogurt
Ice Cream: any ice cream; optional

Vegetable Juice Cocktail
Spaghetti Carbonara
Tossed Delight Salad
Fruit Cocktail

Calories: 998 per serving   Protein: 30 grams per serving

Spaghetti Carbonara

8 oz. spaghetti
8 oz. bacon
1 C. chopped onion
1 C. chopped green pepper
½ C. chopped parsley
3 eggs, beaten
½ C. grated Parmesan cheese
½ t. salt
dash of pepper

Prepare the spaghetti according to package instructions.

Meanwhile, fry the bacon and drain off the fat.

Sauté the onion and green pepper in a little safflower oil in a small skillet. Add the bacon.

Drain the spaghetti and return it to the pot or place it in a large bowl. Add the bacon mixture and parsley. Mix quickly to blend. Pour in the eggs and continue quickly lifting and mixing spaghetti to coat well. Sprinkle in the cheese, salt, and a dash of pepper. Mix and serve.

Yields: 4 servings

Tossed Delight Salad

1½ T. safflower oil
½ T. lemon juice
½ t. salt
herbs to taste
1 C. sliced mushrooms
4 tomatoes
8 leaves leaf lettuce
¼ C. chopped almonds

Combine the oil, lemon juice, salt, and herbs. Marinate the mushrooms in the mixture, covered, for 1 hour in the refrigerator; stir periodically.

Chop the tomatoes and tear the lettuce into bite-size pieces. Add to the dressing. Add the almonds, toss, and serve.

Yields: 4 servings

Fruit Cocktail

1 orange, peeled and sectioned
1 apple, sliced
1 banana, sliced
1 C. canned crushed pineapple, without juice

Combine all the ingredients and chill.

Yields: 4 servings

■ Serve each person 1 C. Vegetable Juice Cocktail (see page 20).

	CALORIES	PROTEIN GMS	CARBOHYDRATES GMS	FAT GMS	CALCIUM MGS	IRON MGS	MAGNESIUM MGS	PHOSPHORUS MGS	POTASSIUM MGS	SODIUM MGS	VITAMIN A I.U.	VITAMIN B₁ MGS	VITAMIN B₂ MGS	NIACIN MGS	VITAMIN C MGS
Vegetable Juice Cocktail, 1 C.	61	3	13	.45	46	3	31	62	757	544	2546	.15	.1	2	54
Spaghetti Carbonara	71	22	49	16	231	4	29	344	413	807	1303	.89	.6	5.5	43
Tossed Delight Salad	135	4	10	10	52	1.3	47	109	546	275	1613	.13	.28	.45	35
Fruit Cocktail	92	1	24	.5	26	.7	26	24	305	2	198	.1	.06	.5	29
TOTAL	998	30	96	27	355	9	133	539	2021	1628	5660	1.3	1	8.5	161

Substitutions
Vegetable Juice Cocktail: 1 C. vegetable juice
Tossed Delight Salad: 1½ C. spinach, kale, or Swiss chard
Fruit Cocktail: 1 C. raspberries or blackberries, or 3 raw figs

═ MENU ═

Spanish Rice
Orange and Onion Salad
Skim Milk

Calories: 658 per serving   Protein: 32 grams per serving

Spanish Rice

¾ C. brown rice
12 oz. lean ground beef
¼ C. chopped onion
½ C. sliced mushrooms
¼ C. diced celery
1 small green pepper, chopped
½ t. chili powder
2 C. whole canned tomatoes
¼ C. catsup (optional)

Drop the rice in 1½ C. boiling salted (½ t.) water. Cover and simmer for 30 minutes.

Brown the ground beef and place it in a bowl.

Sauté the onion, mushrooms, celery, and green pepper lightly in a small amount of safflower oil.

Add the beef to the vegetables and stir in the chili powder, semi-cooked rice, and tomatoes. Bring to a boil, reduce heat, and simmer for 15–20 minutes.

Suggestion: The green pepper may be added in the last 5 to 8 minutes to provide more texture and color.

Yields: 4 servings

Orange and Onion Salad

1 orange, peeled
¼ C. safflower oil
2 T. cider vinegar
1 t. crushed tarragon
¼ t. salt
pepper
½ C. diced onion
4 C. lettuce torn into bite-size
    pieces
1 avocado

Cut the orange into bite-size pieces. Shake the oil, vinegar, and seasonings together in a jar. Pour the dressing over the oranges and onions and marinate in the refrigerator for 1 hour.

Slice the avocado. Toss the lettuce and avocado gently in the marinated mixture.

Yields: 4 servings

■ Serve each person 1 C. skim milk.

	CALORIES	PROTEIN GMS	CARBOHYDRATES GMS	FAT GMS	CALCIUM MGS	IRON MGS	MAGNESIUM MGS	PHOSPHORUS MGS	POTASSIUM MGS	SODIUM MGS	VITAMIN A I.U.	VITAMIN B_1 MGS	VITAMIN B_2 MGS	NIACIN MGS	VITAMIN C MGS
Spanish Rice	326	22	36	9	37	4	55	284	655	471	1169	.25	.25	7	29
Orange and Onion Salad	246	2	11	22	42	1	36	56	549	146	473	.15	.2	1	32
Skim Milk, 1 C.	86	8	12	.4	302	.1	28	247	406	126	500	.09	.34	.22	2
TOTAL	658	32	59	31	381	5	119	587	1610	743	2142	.49	.79	8	63

Substitutions
Orange and Onion Salad: avocado is optional; ½ C. peas or carrots; 1 C. broccoli, cauliflower, or brussels sprouts; 1 baked potato
Skim Milk: ½ C. yogurt or 1 oz. natural cheese

Stuffed Cabbage Rolls
Green Beans and Onions
Chocolate Velvet Ice Cream
Fruit Juice Soda

Calories: 574 per serving   Protein: 27 grams per serving

Stuffed Cabbage Rolls

8 large cabbage leaves
2 C. boiling water
12 oz. lean ground beef
1 onion, sliced
1 T. butter
2 T. chopped onion
⅓ C. brown rice
½ t. salt
dash of pepper
3 T. warm water
1 T. lemon juice
1 T. brown sugar
1 C. tomato sauce
2 C. cold water

Rinse the cabbage leaves and cut off the heavy stem at the base of each leaf. Blanch the cabbage in 2 C. boiling water just until soft. Remove the leaves, pat them dry, and put aside.

Brown the beef. Sauté the sliced onion in the butter.

In a separate bowl mix together the beef, chopped onion, rice, salt, pepper, and 3 T. water.

Place 2 heaping T. of the beef mixture in the center of each leaf. Tuck in the sides and roll up, enclosing the mixture, and secure with a toothpick.

Put the sautéed sliced onion in a saucepan, add the lemon juice, brown sugar, tomato sauce, and 2 C. water. Stir. Place the cabbage rolls in the sauce, folded side down. Cover and cook over low heat for 1–1½ hours or until the rolls are firm. Baste occasionally and add water if necessary.

Yields: 4 servings.

Green Beans and Onions

½ C. chopped onions
1 T. safflower oil
3 C. green beans, steamed

Sauté the onions in the oil. Add the beans, stir, and serve.

Yields: 4 servings

Chocolate Velvet Ice Cream

1½ t. unflavored gelatin
¼ C. water
2 oz. unsweetened baking chocolate
¾ C. evaporated milk
6 T. honey
1 C. whole milk

In a small bowl, soften the gelatin in the water. Melt the chocolate in a small saucepan over low heat.

In another pan, bring the evaporated milk to boiling. Reduce the heat. Add the chocolate, honey, and gelatin to the milk. Cook this mixture, stirring, until well blended. Remove from the heat and allow to cool.

1 C. cream
1 t. vanilla extract

Add and blend the whole milk, cream, and vanilla into the chocolate mixture. Chill in an ice cream can in the refrigerator 2 hours or overnight. Process according to your machine directions.

Yields: 1 quart

■ Serve each person 1 C. Fruit Juice Soda, if desired (½ C. unsweetened fruit juice mixed with ½ C. club soda or sparkling mineral water.

	CALORIES	PROTEIN GMS	CARBOHYDRATES GMS	FAT GMS	CALCIUM MGS	IRON MGS	MAGNESIUM MGS	PHOSPHORUS MGS	POTASSIUM MGS	SODIUM MGS	VITAMIN A I.U.	VITAMIN B₁ MGS	VITAMIN B₂ MGS	NIACIN MGS	VITAMIN C MGS
Stuffed Cabbage Rolls, 2	301	21	27	12	68	4.5	60	251	776	625	1277	.24	.24	6	65
Green Beans and Onions	65	2	8	4	54	.9	29	42	171	6	505	.08	.08	.5	13
Chocolate Velvet Ice Cream, ½ C.	208	4	20	16	121	.4	23	109	176	51	443	.03	.19	.2	t
TOTAL	574	27	55	32	243	5.8	112	402	1123	682	2225	.35	.5	6.7	78

Substitutions
Green Beans and Onions: 1 C. spinach, kale, asparagus, summer squash, or green peas; ½ C. okra, brussels sprouts, or collards
Chocolate Velvet Ice Cream: any ice cream; 1 C. skim milk, ½ C. yogurt, or 1 oz. natural cheese

Stuffed Green Peppers
Scalloped Potatoes
Carrot and Raisin Salad
Skim Milk
Fresh Fruit (optional)

Calories: 733 per serving   Protein: 38 grams per serving

Stuffed Green Peppers

3 T. brown rice
4 green peppers
12 oz. lean ground beef
½ C. chopped onion
1 t. salt
¼ t. crushed thyme
dash of pepper
2 C. tomato juice
3 T. catsup
¼ C. grated Parmesan cheese

Simmer the rice in ½ C. water until tender.

Preheat oven to 350° F.

Cut a small hole at the stem end of each pepper and clean out the seeds and membranes. Bring 3 C. salted water to the boil, add the peppers, and cook for 5 minutes, covered. Drain.

In a separate pan, brown the beef. Add the onion and cook until tender. Add the seasonings, rice, 1 C. of the tomato juice, and catsup. Heat thoroughly, stirring well.

Fill the peppers equally and stand them upright in an ungreased baking dish. Pour ¼ C. tomato juice over each. Bake covered for 45 minutes, then uncovered for 15 minutes. Sprinkle with cheese before the last 5 minutes of cooking time.

Yields: 4 servings

Scalloped Potatoes

3 potatoes
½ C. sliced mushrooms
½ t. salt
2 C. condensed cream of
   mushroom soup
1½ pimento pods, chopped
1 medium onion, cut in rings
   (1 C.)

Preheat oven to 350° F. and grease a 10″ round baking dish. Scrub the potatoes and slice them thin, including the skins. Add the mushrooms and salt to the soup.

Arrange one-third of the potatoes on the bottom of the dish, then one-third of the pimento and onion, then one-third of the mushroom mixture. Repeat, ending with the mushroom mixture. Bake 1½ hours, covered for the first ½ hour and uncovered for the remainder.

Yields: 4 servings

Carrot and Raisin Salad

4 carrots
½ C. raisins

Grate the carrots into a medium-size bowl, and add the raisins. In another bowl, combine all other ingredients and mix well.

½ t. salt
1 t. grated lemon peel
½ T. lemon juice
½ C. sour cream

Pour the sour cream mixture over the carrots and raisins and toss lightly. Cover and refrigerate until ready to serve.

Yields: 4 servings

■ Serve each person 1 C. skim milk, and some fresh fruit for dessert, if desired.

	CALORIES	PROTEIN GMS	CARBOHYDRATES GMS	FAT GMS	CALCIUM MGS	IRON MGS	MAGNESIUM MGS	PHOSPHORUS MGS	POTASSIUM MGS	SODIUM MGS	VITAMIN A I.U.	VITAMIN B₁ MGS	VITAMIN B₂ MGS	NIACIN MGS	VITAMIN C MGS
Stuffed Green Pepper	277	23	22	11	119	5	57	288	819	747	1578	.25	.3	6.5	131
Scalloped Potatoes	207	5	34	5	48	1.5	55	130	727	753	362	.3	.35	2.8	46
Carrot and Raisin Salad	163	2	27	6	86	1.5	34	81	542	343	11,231	.09	.11	.7	9
Skim Milk, 1 C.	86	8	12	.4	302	.1	28	247	406	126	500	.09	.34	.22	2
TOTAL	733	38	95	22	555	8	174	746	2494	1969	13,671	.73	1.1	10	188

Substitutions
Carrot and Raisin Salad: salad or vegetable of choice
Skim Milk: ½ C. yogurt or ice cream, or 1 oz. natural cheese

MENU

Sukiyaki over Rice
Broccoli Spears
Fruit Juice Soda
Apricot Bar

Calories: 539 per serving   Protein: 29 grams per serving

Sukiyaki

1 C. brown rice
12 oz. round steak

Drop the rice into 2 C. boiling salted (1 t.) water and simmer, covered, 45–60 minutes.

1 T. safflower oil
1 bouillon cube, chicken or beef
1 C. boiling water
½ T. cornstarch
1 C. sliced mushrooms
⅔ C. sliced onion
1 C. sliced celery
1 C. bamboo shoots, drained
1⅓ T. honey
¼ C. soy sauce
4 T. chopped chives

Cut the steak diagonally across the grain in thin slices. Brown the meat quickly in the oil.

Dissolve the bouillon cube in the water and stir in the cornstarch. Add the bouillon and the remaining ingredients, except the chives, to the beef and simmer 10–15 minutes over medium heat.

Serve each portion over ½ C. rice and top each with 1 T. chives.

Yields: 4 servings

Apricot Bars

⅔ C. dried apricots
½ C. butter
½ C. plus 2 T. honey
1⅓ C. plus 2 T. whole wheat
  pastry flour
½ t. baking powder
¼ t. salt
2 eggs
½ t. vanilla extract
½ C. chopped walnuts

Put the apricots in a small saucepan and add water to cover. Bring to a boil, lower heat, and simmer for 10 minutes. Drain, cool, and chop.

Preheat oven to 325° F. and grease a 9″ × 9″ × 2″ pan.

In a mixing bowl combine the butter, 1 C. plus 2 T. flour, and 2 T. honey. Blend thoroughly, form into a ball, and press evenly into the pan. Bake 20–25 minutes.

In a separate mixing bowl, sift together the remaining flour, the baking powder, and the salt.

In a large bowl beat ½ C. honey, the eggs, and the vanilla. Gradually stir in the flour mixture. Stir in the walnuts and apricots. Spread this over the baked crust. Bake 30–35 minutes. Cool. Cut into 30 bars.

Yields: 30 bars

■ Serve each person 1 C. steamed broccoli spears, 1 C. Fruit Juice Soda (½ C. unsweetened apple or other juice mixed with ½ C. club soda or sparkling mineral water).

	CALORIES	PROTEIN GMS	CARBOHYDRATES GMS	FAT GMS	CALCIUM MGS	IRON MGS	MAGNESIUM MGS	PHOSPHORUS MGS	POTASSIUM MGS	SODIUM MGS	VITAMIN A I.U.	VITAMIN B₁ MGS	VITAMIN B₂ MGS	NIACIN MGS	VITAMIN C MGS
Sukiyaki	259	20	14	14	50	4	30	245	732	1602	119	.11	.3	5	7
Brown Rice, ½ C.	89	2	19	.6	9	.4	23	55	52	211	0	.07	.02	1	0
Chopped Chives, 1 T.	3	.2	.6	t	7	.2	3	4	25	t	580	.01	.01	.1	6
Broccoli Spears, 1 C.	40	5	7	.5	136	1.2	36	96	414	16	3800	.14	.3	1.2	140
Fruit Juice Soda, 1 C.	59	.1	15	t	8	.08	5	11	125	1		.01	.03	.1	1
Apricot Bar, 1	89	1.5	12	5	9	.5	11	36	64	62	477	.04	.03	.4	t
TOTAL	539	29	68	20	219	6.4	108	447	1412	1892	4976	.38	.69	7.8	154

Substitutions
Chives: optional
Broccoli Spears: 1 C. cooked Swiss chard, kale, or spinach;
  ½ C. cooked collards
Fruit Juice Soda: optional
Apricot Bar: fruit of choice; optional

MENU

Vegetable Juice Cocktail
Sweet Cherry Ham
Honeyed Yams
Peas and Mushrooms
Skim Milk

Calories: 656 per serving   Protein: 24 grams per serving

Sweet Cherry Ham

8 oz. cooked ham
½ C. canned sweet cherries in
  juice
cornstarch (optional)

Preheat oven to 350° F.

Slice the ham into 4 slices and heat them in a casserole for 15–20 minutes.

In a small saucepan, heat the cherries and all their juice. Thicken with cornstarch if desired.

When the ham is thoroughly heated, serve proportionately among 4 persons with the hot cherry sauce.

Yields: 4 servings

Honeyed Yams

4 small yams or sweet potatoes
⅓ C. honey
3 T. butter
1½ T. orange juice (optional)

Preheat oven to 350° F.

Cut the yams in half and arrange them in a greased casserole.

Heat the honey and butter in a small saucepan and pour the mixture over the potatoes. Bake for 30–40 minutes, basting occasionally.

Yields: 4 servings

1 C. sliced mushrooms
1 T. oil or butter
1 C. fresh or frozen peas
¼ C. chopped onion (optional)

Sauté the mushrooms in the oil or butter. Boil or steam the peas and add them to the mushrooms. Stir. Serve ½ C. to each person.

Yields: 4 servings

■ Serve each person 1 C. Vegetable Juice Cocktail (see page 20).

	CALORIES	PROTEIN GMS	CARBOHYDRATES GMS	FAT GMS	CALCIUM MGS	IRON MGS	MAGNESIUM MGS	PHOSPHORUS MGS	POTASSIUM MGS	SODIUM MGS	VITAMIN A I.U.	VITAMIN B₁ MGS	VITAMIN B₂ MGS	NIACIN MGS	VITAMIN C MGS
Vegetable Juice Cocktail, 1 C.	61	3	13	.45	46	3	31	62	757	544	2546	.15	.1	2	54
Sweet Cherry Ham	202	9	3	17	8	1.6	10	98	161	427	16	.4	.11	2	2
Honeyed Yams	259	3	46	9	17	1	30	55	54	109	353	.09	.4	.7	9
Peas and Mushrooms, ½ C.	48	1	6	4	11	.8	11	60	152	4	258	.12	.52	1.6	8
Skim Milk, 1 C.	86	8	12	.4	302	.1	28	247	406	126	500	.09	.34	.22	2
TOTAL	656	24	80	31	384	6.5	110	522	1530	1210	3673	.85	1.5	6.5	75

Substitutions
Vegetable Juice Cocktail: 1 C. vegetable or tomato juice
Peas and Mushrooms: salad or vegetable of choice; optional
Skim Milk: ½ C. yogurt

Vegetable Juice Cocktail
Swiss Steak
Brussels Sprouts Parisienne
Whole Wheat Bread
Pussycat Delight

Calories: 751 per serving   Protein: 40 grams per serving

Swiss Steak

1 lb. rump, round, or chuck
  steak, 1″ thick
½ t. salt
dash of pepper
¼ C. whole wheat flour
½ C. sliced mushrooms
1 T. butter
1 C. canned tomatoes
1 C. diced onions
½ C. sliced green pepper

Cut the meat into 4 equal portions. Season each piece with salt and pepper and dust with ½ T. flour. (To tenderize, pound flour into meat.) Brown in oil in skillet.

In another large skillet, sauté the mushrooms in butter. Add the other ingredients. Add a little water if necessary to prevent sticking. Add the remaining flour to thicken the sauce. Add enough water to achieve a smooth paste. Stir. Add meat, cover, and cook either on the stove or in the oven at 325° F. for 2 hours or until the meat is tender.

Yields: 4 servings

Brussels Sprouts Parisienne

2 T. butter
2 T. whole wheat flour
¼ t. salt
1 C. chicken broth
2 egg yolks
3 C. brussels sprouts, cooked
¼ C. chopped almonds

Melt the butter in a large saucepan over low heat. Add the flour and salt. Stir until smooth. Add the broth and heat to boiling, stirring constantly for 1 minute. Gradually add and blend in the egg yolks. Boil 1 minute, stirring constantly. Add the brussels sprouts and almonds. Heat thoroughly.

Yields: 4 servings

Pussycat Delight

1 sliced banana
1 C. skim milk
1 T. blackstrap molasses
1 C. apricot nectar
1 T. honey

Blend all the ingredients in a blender until smooth. Pour into four glasses.

Yields: 4 servings

■ Serve each person 1 C. Vegetable Juice Cocktail (see page 20) and 1 slice of whole wheat bread with 1 t. butter (see page 44).

	Calories	Protein GMS	Carbohydrates GMS	Fat GMS	Calcium MGS	Iron MGS	Magnesium MGS	Phosphorus MGS	Potassium MGS	Sodium MGS	Vitamin A I.U.	Vitamin B₁ MGS	Vitamin B₂ MGS	Niacin MGS	Vitamin C MGS
Vegetable Juice Cocktail, 1 C.	61	3	13	.45	46	3	31	62	757	544	2546	.15	.1	2	54
Swiss Steak	275	25	12	14	35	4.8	47	290	636	352	630	.2	.3	6.5	28
Brussels Sprouts Parisienne	179	5	8	14	78	2	47	187	416	463	1235	.14	.3	1	116
Whole Wheat Bread, 1 slice	86	4	18	1.7	29	.75	25	94	103	100	56	.13	.05	1	t
Butter, 1 t.	34	t	t	3.8	1	0	.09	.66	1	47	157	t	t		0
Pussycat Delight	116	3	27	.2	117	1.2	34	84	481	36	788	.05	.14	.5	6
TOTAL	751	40	78	34	306	12	184	718	2394	1542	5412	.67	.89	11	204

Substitutions

Vegetable Juice Cocktail: 1 C. vegetable or tomato juice

Brussels Sprouts Parisienne: 1 C. cooked winter squash, spinach, okra, parsnips, broccoli, or cabbage; 1 large raw carrot

Whole Wheat Bread: any whole grain bread

Pussycat Delight: 1 C. skim milk or ½ C. yogurt or ½ C. ice cream, and fruit of choice if desired

MENU

Tacos
Fruity Milk

Calories: 507 per serving   Protein: 31 grams per serving

Tacos

12 oz. lean ground beef
½ C. chopped onion
8 prepared taco shells
½ t. chili powder
1 clove garlic, crushed
¼ t. salt
½ t. ground cumin

Brown the ground beef in a skillet; add the onion and cook until tender.

In a separate pan, combine the chili powder, garlic, salt, cumin, oregano, water, and tomato paste. Stir well, bring to a boil, and simmer for 10 minutes.

Add the sauce to the beef and simmer for 10 minutes.

¼ t. crushed oregano
½ C. water
¼ C. tomato paste
1 small onion, chopped
½ C. grated cheddar cheese
1 C. shredded endive
½ head iceberg lettuce,
  shredded
2 medium tomatoes, chopped

Divide the mixture into equal portions and fill 8 tacos. Top each taco with equal amounts of onion, cheese, endive, lettuce, and tomato. Serve 2 tacos per person.

Yields: 4 servings

Fruity Milk

2 C. skim milk
1½ C. cut-up fresh fruit (or
  frozen)
2 T. honey
12 ice cubes

Select any fresh fruit or combination of fruits. Chop ice cubes in a blender. Combine all the ingredients in a blender and process until smooth. Divide proportionately among 4 persons.

Yields: 4 servings

	CALORIES	PROTEIN GMS	CARBOHYDRATES GMS	FAT GMS	CALCIUM MGS	IRON MGS	MAGNESIUM MGS	PHOSPHORUS MGS	POTASSIUM MGS	SODIUM MGS	VITAMIN A I.U.	VITAMIN B₁ MGS	VITAMIN B₂ MGS	NIACIN MGS	VITAMIN C MGS
Tacos, 2	401	26	38	15	272	6	153	378	736	292	1893	.25	.3	6	32
Fruity Milk	106	5	24	.75	168	.55	29	134	300	64	350	.06	.2	.4	13
TOTAL	507	31	62	16	440	6.6	182	512	1036	356	2243	.31	.5	6.4	45

Substitutions
Fruity Milk: 1 C. skim milk or ½ C. ice cream or ½ C. yogurt,
  and fruit of choice if desired

Vegetable Juice Cocktail
Veal Roll-Ups over Noodles
Creamed Green Beans and Cauliflower
Whole Wheat Dinner Rolls (optional)
Fruit Cup

Calories: 818 per serving   Protein: 44 grams per serving

Veal Roll-Ups

4 veal cutlets
4 slices thin boiled ham
2 slices Swiss cheese
1 egg, beaten
2 T. plus ⅓ C. skim milk
½ C. fine dry bread crumbs
¾ C. condensed cream of
    mushroom soup
dash of paprika
3 C. noodles

Preheat oven to 350° F.

Pound each cutlet to about ⅛" thickness. Place 1 slice of ham on top of each piece. Cut each cheese slice into 4 strips. Place 2 strips on each ham slice. Roll the meat up around the cheese and secure with a toothpick.

Mix the egg and 2 T. milk.

Dip the rolls in the egg mixture and then roll in the crumbs. Place the rolls seam down in a 7" × 11" × 2" baking dish.

Combine the soup and ⅓ C. milk in a small saucepan. Heat until bubbly. Pour around the rolls. Cover dish with foil and bake approximately 1 hour. Uncover, sprinkle with paprika, and bake 10 minutes more to brown the crumbs.

Prepare the noodles according to package instructions. Place a veal roll on ¾ C. noodles per person and spoon sauce on top.

Yields: 4 servings

Creamed Green Beans and Cauliflower

2 C. sliced or French-cut green
    beans
2 C. cauliflowerets
2 T. butter
1 T. whole wheat flour
½ t. salt
¼ t. poppy seeds (optional)
pepper to taste
1¼ C. skim milk
toasted bread crumbs (optional)

Steam or boil the vegetables just until tender.

Melt the butter in a large saucepan over low heat. Add the flour and seasonings. Blend and cook until smooth. Add the milk. Heat to boiling, stirring constantly. Boil and stir 1 minute. Add the vegetables and heat thoroughly. Serve with toasted bread crumbs if desired.

Yields: 4 servings

2 C. sliced peaches
1 C. diced pineapple
1 sliced banana
½ C. cubed cantaloupe
½ C. apricot nectar

Combine the fruits and add the apricot nectar, stirring lightly to coat all the fruit. Serve well chilled in the individual dishes.

Yields: 4 servings

■ Serve each person 1 C. Vegetable Juice Cocktail (see page 20).

	CALORIES	PROTEIN GMS	CARBOHYDRATES GMS	FAT GMS	CALCIUM MGS	IRON MGS	MAGNESIUM MGS	PHOSPHORUS MGS	POTASSIUM MGS	SODIUM MGS	VITAMIN A I.U.	VITAMIN B₁ MGS	VITAMIN B₂ MGS	NIACIN MGS	VITAMIN C MGS
Vegetable Juice Cocktail, 1 C.	61	3	13	.45	46	3	31	62	757	544	2546	.15	.1	2	54
Veal Roll-Ups	396	30	13	24	215	4	33	384	455	554	326	.35	.48	7.5	t
Noodles, ¾ C.	150	5	28	2	12	1		71	53		84	.17	.1	1.4	0
Creamed Green Beans and Cauliflower	107	5	9	7	141	.9	39	128	352	384	771	.1	.21	.6	42
Fruit Cup	104	1	27	.25	30	1.2	39	37	524	8	2785	.1	.09	1	38
TOTAL	818	44	90	34	444	10	142	682	2141	1490	6512	.87	.98	12.5	134

Substitutions
Vegetable Juice Cocktail: 1 C. vegetable or tomato juice
Creamed Green Beans and Cauliflower: 1 C. asparagus, beets, or eggplant; ½ C. peas or spinach; 1 large raw carrot or 1 medium tomato
Fruit Cup: 1 banana or orange, or 1 C. blackberries or raspberries

MENU

Vegetable-Ham Scallop
Sliced Tomatoes
Skim Milk
Apple Pie

Calories: 874 per serving   Protein: 33 grams per serving

Vegetable-Ham Scallop

12 oz. ham slice
2 T. whole wheat flour
1¼ C. condensed cream of
   mushroom soup
1 C. whole milk
¾ t. salt
¼ t. pepper
3 C. sliced potatoes, with skins
1 C. sliced carrots
¼ C. minced onions
1 C. sliced mushrooms
4 parsley sprigs

Preheat oven to 325° F.

Brown the ham on both sides in a large skillet. Remove it from the skillet and cut into serving pieces. Set aside.

Stir the flour into the ham drippings, add the soup, and slowly stir in the milk. Heat until the mixture boils, stirring constantly. Add the seasonings.

In a 2-quart casserole arrange layers of ham, potatoes, carrots, onions, and mushrooms. Pour the soup mixture over the vegetables and ham. Bake covered 1 hour, then uncovered 15 minutes or until vegetables are tender. Garnish each serving with sprig of parsley.

Yields: 4 servings

Apple Pie

Pie Crust

1 C. whole wheat pastry flour,
   chilled
½ t. salt
¼ C. butter, chilled
¼ C. very cold water

Preheat oven to 375° F.

Crust: Mix the flour and salt thoroughly. Cut the butter into the flour until the butter is in pea-size pieces. Sprinkle in the water, tossing the mixture with fork. Stir firmly with the fork until the dough forms a ball. Press a few times with your hands. Roll out the dough and lift it into, or press it into, a 9″ pie pan.

Filling

4 juicy pie apples, peeled
⅓ C. honey, warmed
1 t. lemon juice
½ C. half and half

Filling: Slice the apples and boil or steam them until just tender, not mushy. In a bowl, mix the honey, lemon juice, half and half, flour, and spices. Chop the nuts and finely chop 2 T. Mix the coarser nuts into the honey mixture. Place the

1 T. whole wheat flour
1 t. ground cinnamon
½ t. ground nutmeg
½ C. nuts (optional)

drained apples in a large mixing bowl. Pour in the honey mixture and toss gently. Pour the apple filling into the unbaked pie shell. Bake 35 minutes. After removing the pie from the oven, sprinkle with the finely chopped nuts and some extra cinnamon.

Yields: 8 pieces

	CALORIES	PROTEIN GMS	CARBOHYDRATES GMS	FAT GMS	CALCIUM MGS	IRON MGS	MAGNESIUM MGS	PHOSPHORUS MGS	POTASSIUM MGS	SODIUM MGS	VITAMIN A I.U.	VITAMIN B₁ MGS	VITAMIN B₂ MGS	NIACIN MGS	VITAMIN C MGS
Vegetable-Ham Scallop	495	19	33	32	132	3.5	75	328	996	1426	4086	.8	.45	6.5	33
Sliced Tomato, 1	33	2	7	.3	20	.8	21	40	366	4	1350	.09	.06	1	34
Skim Milk, 1 C.	86	8	12	.4	302	.1	28	247	406	126	500	.09	.34	.22	2
Apple Pie, 1 slice	260	3.5	38	15	38	1	35	107	204	212	127	.14	.07	1	4
TOTAL	874	33	90	48	492	5.4	159	722	1972	1768	6063	1	.9	8.7	73

Substitutions
Sliced Tomato: 1 C. Vegetable Juice Cocktail (see page 20) or vegetable juice, ½ C. cooked beets, 1 C. cooked cabbage or eggplant
Skim Milk: ½ C. yogurt or 1 oz. natural cheese
Apple Pie: fruit or fruit juice of choice; optional

POULTRY

Chicken Cacciatore with Onion Rings
Tossed Salad with Italian Dressing
Skim Milk

Calories: 789 per serving   Protein: 36 grams per serving

Chicken Cacciatore

1¾ C. boned chicken
½ C. whole wheat flour
¼ C. safflower oil
¼ C. sliced mushrooms
1 medium green pepper
3 cloves garlic, crushed
1 lb. tomatoes, chopped, or 2 C. canned
1 C. tomato purée
1 t. salt
1½ C. brown rice

Cut the chicken into bite-size pieces and coat with the flour. Heat the oil in a large, heavy skillet and sauté the chicken pieces over low heat for 15–20 minutes, until they are lightly browned. Remove the chicken from the skillet, and next sauté the mushrooms, green pepper, and garlic in the same skillet until tender. Blend in the tomatoes, purée, and salt; then add the chicken. Cover the skillet tightly and simmer 30–40 minutes.

Meanwhile prepare the rice (see page 24).

Serve each portion of chicken over ¾ C. cooked rice and top with onion rings (see below).

Yields: 4 servings

Onion Rings

3 onions
½ C. whole wheat flour
¼ t. salt
½ beaten egg
½ C. skim milk
1 T. safflower oil
safflower oil for deep-fat frying

Cut the onions into ¼″-thick slices and separate into rings.

In a large bowl combine the flour, salt, egg, milk, and 1 T. oil, and beat thoroughly until moistened.

Coat the onion rings with the batter and fry a few at a time in deep hot fat (375° F.), stirring only once to separate the rings. When golden brown, remove and drain rings on paper towels.

Yields: 4 servings

Tossed Salad

4 C. lettuce torn into bite-size pieces
1 grated carrot
¼ C. raisins
2 T. nuts or seeds—optional

Toss the lettuce with the carrot. Divide among 4 bowls and sprinkle 1 T. raisins and 1 T. Italian Salad Dressing over each. Add nuts, if desired.

Yields: 4 servings

1 C. safflower oil
¼ C. lemon juice
¼ C. cider vinegar
1 t. salt
¼ t. honey
2 cloves garlic, pressed
½ t. onion salt
½ t. crushed oregano
1 t. prepared mustard
½ t. paprika
⅛ t. crushed thyme

Combine and shake all the ingredients together in a tightly covered jar. Refrigerate at least 2 hours to blend the flavors. Shake again before serving.

Yields: 24 servings, 1 T. each

■ Serve each person 1 C. skim milk.

	CALORIES	PROTEIN GMS	CARBOHYDRATES GMS	FAT GMS	CALCIUM MGS	IRON MGS	MAGNESIUM MGS	PHOSPHORUS MGS	POTASSIUM MGS	SODIUM MGS	VITAMIN A I.U.	VITAMIN B₁ MGS	VITAMIN B₂ MGS	NIACIN MGS	VITAMIN C MGS
Chicken Cacciatore	435	24	42	26	101	4	84	382	1195	1024	2383	.4	.3	8	78
Brown Rice, ¾ C.	134	3	29	.9	14	.6	34	83	79	317	0	.1	.02	1.5	0
Tossed Salad	50	1	12	.3	31	.9	14	37	295	22	3000	.08	.07	2.2	7
Italian Salad Dressing, 1 T.	84	.03	.4	9	1	.02	.3	.8	4	94					1
Skim Milk, 1 C.	86	8	12	.4	302	.1	28	247	406	126	500	.09	.34	.22	2
TOTAL	789	36	95	37	449	5.6	160	750	1979	1583	5883	.67	.73	12	88

Substitutions
Tossed Salad: salad or vegetable of choice
Skim milk: ½ C. yogurt

Chicken Kiev with Sauce
Brussels Sprouts Salad
Skim Milk
Fresh Pineapple Boats

Calories: 855 per serving   Protein: 40 grams per serving

Chicken Kiev

4 whole chicken breasts, boned
10 T. butter
1 egg, beaten
½ C. whole milk
½ t. salt
2 T. whole wheat flour
½ C. sliced mushrooms
1 C. sour cream
5 T. chopped chives
½ C. chopped endive (optional)
1 tomato (optional)

Place 1 T. butter on each breast. Roll tightly and fasten with a skewer.

Mix the egg and milk together in a flat dish. Combine the salt and flour in another flat dish. Roll the chicken in the flour, then dip in the egg mixture, roll in the flour again, and fry in 6 T. butter until brown and tender, about 45 minutes.

Remove the chicken from the pan. Drain off the fat. Add the mushrooms to the skillet and simmer 1 minute. Add the sour cream and chives. Simmer to the point of boiling. Place the chicken breasts in a chafing dish, pour the sauce over, and garnish with endive and tomato if desired.

Suggestion: Chicken Kiev may also be finished by placing the browned chicken and the sauce in a casserole and baking at 350° F. until bubbly.

Yields: 4 servings

Brussels Sprouts Salad

3 C. brussels sprouts
3 T. cider vinegar
3 T. safflower oil
1 t. chervil leaves
½ t. salt

Boil or steam the brussels sprouts until tender. Drain.

Shake the vinegar, oil, chervil, salt, and pepper together in a tightly covered jar. Pour the vinegar mixture over the hot

dash of pepper
1 tomato
2 C. spinach leaves
2 T. chopped parsley

brussels sprouts, turning until cool. Cover and refrigerate at least 3 hours.

Cut the tomato in wedges and toss gently with the brussels sprouts. Line a salad bowl with the spinach, fill with the brussels sprouts mixture, and sprinkle with the parsley.

Yields: 4 servings

Fresh Pineapple Boats

1½ C. fresh cubed pineapple
1 sliced banana
½ C. strawberries
½ C. pitted, sliced dates
¼ C. unsweetened orange juice
¼ C. shredded coconut

Mix the fruits together lightly with the orange juice. Spoon each serving into a hollowed-out pineapple quarter and sprinkle with coconut.

Yields: 4 servings

■ Serve each person 1 C. skim milk.

	CALORIES	PROTEIN GMS	CARBOHYDRATES GMS	FAT GMS	CALCIUM MGS	IRON MGS	MAGNESIUM MGS	PHOSPHORUS MGS	POTASSIUM MGS	SODIUM MGS	VITAMIN A I.U.	VITAMIN B₁ MGS	VITAMIN B₂ MGS	NIACIN MGS	VITAMIN C MGS
Chicken Kiev with Sauce	439	24	9.5	37	144	2	48	636	739	629	2669	.15	.4	8	20
Brussels Sprouts Salad	151	6	10	11	74	2.5	58	109	552	300	3191	.15	.24	1.4	127
Skim Milk, 1 C.	86	8	12	.4	302	.1	28	247	406	126	500	.09	.34	.22	2
Fresh Pineapple Boat	179	2	45	.9	45	2	44	55	562	3	186	.15	.1	1.4	55
TOTAL	855	40	77	49	565	6.6	178	1047	2259	1058	6546	.54	1	11	204

Substitutions
Skim Milk: ½ C. yogurt
Brussels Sprouts Salad: 1 C. cooked broccoli, okra, or peas; 1 baked potato or yam
Pineapple Boat: 1 mango or orange, 1 C. pineapple, 2 plums, or 4 large raw figs

Chicken Livers
Garden Pilaf
Yogurt and Pineapple
Fruit Juice Soda (optional)

Calories: 551 per serving   Protein: 35 grams per serving

Chicken Livers

1 lb. chicken livers
1 T. butter

Prepare the pilaf (see below) and keep it warm.

Fry the livers in the butter for 5–10 minutes. Divide into 4 equal portions.

Yields: 4 servings

Garden Pilaf

¾ C. brown rice
¼ C. almonds, chopped or
   slivered
2 T. butter
¼ C. minced onion
⅛ t. pepper
½ t. crushed rosemary
dash of salt
⅔ C. cooked peas, hot
1 tomato, cut in wedges

Drop the rice into 1½ C. boiling salted (¾ t.) water and simmer, covered, 45 minutes.

Sauté the almonds in the butter in a medium saucepan until golden. Add the cooked rice, the onion, and the seasonings. Toss. Add the hot peas and the tomato and toss gently. Divide the pilaf into 4 equal servings and top each with a 4-oz. serving of chicken livers.

Yields: 4 servings

■ Serve each person ½ C. pineapple with ½ C. lowfat yogurt for dessert, and if desired, 1 C. Fruit Juice Soda (½ C. unsweetened fruit juice mixed with ½ C. club soda or sparkling mineral water).

	CALORIES	PROTEIN GMS	CARBOHYDRATES GMS	FAT GMS	CALCIUM MGS	IRON MGS	MAGNESIUM MGS	PHOSPHORUS MGS	POTASSIUM MGS	SODIUM MGS	VITAMIN A I.U.	VITAMIN B_1 MGS	VITAMIN B_2 MGS	NIACIN MGS	VITAMIN C MGS
Chicken Livers	172	22	3	8	14	9	23	268	196	115	13,840	.22	3	12	20
Garden Pilaf	267	6.5	37	12	53	1.8	73	170	316	609	738	.25	.15	3	16
Pineapple, ½ C.	40	.3	10	.15	13	.4	10	6	113	1	55	.07	.02	.25	13
Yogurt, ½ C.	72	6	8	2	207	.09	20	163	2657	9	75	.05	.24	.13	.9
TOTAL	551	35	58	22	287	11	126	607	3282	734	14,708	.59	3.4	15.4	50

Substitutions
Pineapple: Fruit of choice
Yogurt: 1 C. skim milk or 1 oz. natural cheese

MENU

Chicken Oriental with Brown Rice
Chinese Vegetables
Skim Milk
Raspberries

Calories: 745 per serving   Protein: 31 grams per serving

Chicken Oriental

¾ C. cooked chicken, sliced
¼ C. butter
¼ C. whole wheat flour
1½ T. salt
½ C. cream
1½ C. skim milk
1 C. chicken stock
1½ C. brown rice
¼ C. sliced mushrooms
¼ C. almonds, slivered or chopped
6 sliced water chestnuts
2 pods pimiento, cut in strips
⅛ C. sherry (optional)

In a double boiler, melt the butter; add the flour and salt. Stir constantly until smooth and thick. Add the cream, milk, and chicken stock. Stir until smooth. Cook 30 minutes. Add the chicken.

Meanwhile drop the rice into 3 C. boiling salted (1 t.) water and simmer, covered, 45–60 minutes.

While the rice is cooking, add the remaining ingredients to the chicken. Stir and heat thoroughly. Serve over ¾ C. cooked rice per person.

Yields: 4 servings

Chinese Vegetables

2 T. safflower oil
1 C. thinly sliced onion
1 C. finely chopped green pepper
1 C. finely chopped celery
½ C. sliced mushrooms
1 C. bean sprouts

Heat the oil in a skillet over fairly high heat until sizzling. Add the onions and sauté. Add the green pepper and celery. Stir very frequently. When vegetables are almost tender, add the mushrooms. Just before vegetables are done, add the bean sprouts.

Suggestion: Season vegetables with soy sauce, garlic, and/or ginger if desired.

Yields: 4 servings

■ Serve each person 1 C. skim milk, and 1 C. raspberries for dessert.

	CALORIES	PROTEIN GMS	CARBOHYDRATES GMS	FAT GMS	CALCIUM MGS	IRON MGS	MAGNESIUM MGS	PHOSPHORUS MGS	POTASSIUM MGS	SODIUM MGS	VITAMIN A I.U.	VITAMIN B₁ MGS	VITAMIN B₂ MGS	NIACIN MGS	VITAMIN C MGS
Chicken Oriental	354	16	13	30	168	1.4	58	292	543	1078	1129	.14	.35	2.9	4
Brown Rice, ¾ C.	134	3	29	.9	14	.6	34	83	79	317	0	.1	.02	1.5	0
Chinese Vegetables	101	2	8	8	31	.9	16	55	306	47	188	.08	.1	.5	38
Skim Milk, 1 C.	86	8	12	.4	302	.1	28	247	406	126	500	.09	.34	.22	2
Raspberries, 1 C.	70	2	17	.6	27	1.1	24	27	207	1	100	.04	.11	1.1	31
TOTAL	745	31	79	40	542	4.1	160	704	1541	1559	1917	.45	.92	6.2	75

Substitutions
Chinese Vegetables: 1 baked sweet potato; 1 C. spinach; 1 C.
   vegetable juice or Vegetable Juice Cocktail (see page 20); 1
   medium tomato
Skim Milk: ½ C. ice cream or 1 oz. natural cheese
Raspberries: 1 C. strawberries, blueberries, or boysenberries

═══ MENU ═══

Chicken Pie
Georgia Shake

Calories: 543 per serving   Protein: 29 grams per serving

Chicken Pie Pastry

1 C. whole wheat pastry flour,
   chilled
½ t. salt
¼ C. butter, chilled
¼ C. very cold water

Prepare pastry dough, following the instructions on page 66.
Roll out and cut the dough to fit over 4 individual casseroles
or 1 large one.

⅓ C. chopped onion
¼ C. butter
⅓ C. whole wheat flour
1 t. salt
1½ C. chicken stock
1 pimiento pod, chopped
1 C. peas and carrots
1¼ C. cooked chicken, cubed
2 oz. cooked chicken liver, sliced

Preheat over to 450° F.

Sauté the onion in the butter in a large skillet until clear and tender, but not brown. Blend in the flour, salt, and stock. Cook, stirring, until smooth and bubbly. Add the remaining ingredients and heat until bubbly again. Pour into casserole dish(es) and top with the pastry. Bake for 10–12 minutes.

Yields: 4 servings

Georgia Shake

2 C. skim milk
1 T. honey or to taste
1 C. sliced strawberries
1 C. sliced peaches
1 T. malt (optional)

Place all the ingredients in a blender and purée until smooth.

Yields: 4 servings

	CALORIES	PROTEIN GMS	CARBOHYDRATES GMS	FAT GMS	CALCIUM MGS	IRON MGS	MAGNESIUM MGS	PHOSPHORUS MGS	POTASSIUM MGS	SODIUM MGS	VITAMIN A I.U.	VITAMIN B₁ MGS	VITAMIN B₂ MGS	NIACIN MGS	VITAMIN C MGS
Chicken Pie	451	24	33	28	49	4	67	357	585	1170	4787	.35	.5	9	11
Georgia Shake	92	5	18	.5	164	.7	25	141	368	64	938	.07	.2	.9	27
TOTAL	543	29	51	29	213	4.7	92	498	953	1234	5725	.42	.7	9.9	38

Substitutions
Georgia Shake: ½ C. yogurt and a fruit of choice containing
   at least 5 mg. vitamin C.

MENU

Chicken Tetrazzini Casserole
Tossed Salad with Italian Dressing
Whole Wheat Dinner Rolls
Skim Milk
Frozen Green Grapes

Calories: 705 per serving   Protein: 43 grams per serving

Chicken Tetrazzini Casserole

1½ C. cooked chicken
4 oz. spaghetti
¾ C. sliced mushrooms
3 scallions, chopped
¾ C. chopped green pepper
1 T. butter
2 C. canned tomatoes, drained
¼ t. paprika
¼ t. garlic salt
¾ C. tomato sauce
¼ C. grated Parmesan cheese

Preheat oven to 350° F.

Dice the chicken.

Break the noodles into 2″ lengths and cook according to the package instructions. Drain and set aside.

Sauté the mushrooms, scallions, and green pepper in the butter. Add the tomatoes, chicken, and seasonings.

Grease a casserole dish, and put one-third of the cooked spaghetti on the bottom, then one-third of the chicken mixture. Repeat alternating for three layers. Stir the tomato sauce and pour it over the layered casserole. Bake 15 minutes. Then sprinkle evenly with Parmesan cheese and cook another 10 or 15 minutes.

Yields: 4 servings

Tossed Salad

4 C. Romaine lettuce torn into
  bite-size pieces
¼ C. grated cheddar cheese
2 T. sunflower seed kernels
apple chunks (optional)

Toss the lettuce with the other ingredients and serve with 1 T. Italian Dressing per person (see page 71).

Yields: 4 servings

■ Serve each person 1 C. skim milk, 1 dinner roll with 1 t. butter (see page 16), and for dessert ½ C. frozen green grapes (bought fresh, then washed and put in freezer until frozen).

	CALORIES	PROTEIN GMS	CARBOHYDRATES GMS	FAT GMS	CALCIUM MGS	IRON MGS	MAGNESIUM MGS	PHOSPHORUS MGS	POTASSIUM MGS	SODIUM MGS	VITAMIN A I.U.	VITAMIN B₁ MGS	VITAMIN B₂ MGS	NIACIN MGS	VITAMIN C MGS
Chicken Tetrazzini Casserole	299	26	33	8	113	3	45	296	855	459	2268	.4	.3	10	64
Tossed Salad	63	4	3	7	91	1	4	87	138	48	1027	.2	.15	.6	9
Italian Dressing, 1 T.	84	.03	.4	9	1	.02	.3	.8	4	94					1
Whole Wheat Dinner Roll, 1	86	4	18	1.7	29	.75	25	94	103	100	56	.13	.05	1	t
Butter, 1 t.	34	t	t	3.8	1	0	.09	.66	1	47	157	t	t		0
Skim Milk, 1 C.	86	8	12	.4	302	.1	28	247	406	126	500	.09	.34	.22	2
Green Grapes, ½ C.	53	.5	14	.1	10	.3	5	16	139	3	75	.04	.03	.3	3
TOTAL	705	43	80	30	547	5.2	107	742	1646	877	4088	.86	.87	12	79

Substitutions

Whole Wheat Dinner Roll: any whole wheat bread

Skim Milk: ½ C. yogurt

Frozen Green Grapes: 1 medium apple, ½ C. applesauce, 2 apricots, ¼ avocado, ½ C. blueberries or cherries, or 1 orange or peach

MENU

Vegetable Juice Cocktail
Club Chicken Casserole
Tossed Salad with Italian Dressing
Skim Milk

Calories: 494 per serving   Protein: 31 grams per serving

Club Chicken Casserole

½ C. brown rice
1¼ C. diced cooked chicken
1½ pods pimiento, sliced
½ C. diced green pepper
½ C. sliced mushrooms
1⅓ C. condensed cream of mushroom soup
¼ C. almonds, sliced

Drop the rice into 2 C. boiling salted (1 t.) water and simmer, covered, 45–60 minutes.

Preheat oven to 350° F.

Alternate layers of the cooked rice, chicken, vegetables, and soup in a greased baking dish, finishing with the soup. Sprinkle with the almonds and bake for 30 minutes.

Yields: 4 servings

Tossed Salad

4 C. lettuce in bite-size pieces
1 carrot, grated
1 C. diced beets, raw or cooked

Toss all the ingredients together and serve with 1 T. Italian Dressing for each portion (see page 71).

Yields: 4 servings

■ Serve each person 1 C. Vegetable Juice Cocktail (see page 20), and 1 C. skim milk.

	CALORIES	PROTEIN GMS	CARBOHYDRATES GMS	FAT GMS	CALCIUM MGS	IRON MGS	MAGNESIUM MGS	PHOSPHORUS MGS	POTASSIUM MGS	SODIUM MGS	VITAMIN A I.U.	VITAMIN B₁ MGS	VITAMIN B₂ MGS	NIACIN MGS	VITAMIN C MGS
Vegetable Juice Cocktail	61	3	13	.45	46	3	31	62	757	544	2546	.15	.1	2	54
Club Chicken Casserole	228	19	16	10	46	1.6	51	232	388	475	382	.1	.2	6.8	23
Tossed Salad	35	.5	8	.25	52	1.2	19	34	343	37	3808	.06	.07	.5	16
Italian Dressing, 1 T.	84	.03	.4	9	1	.02	.3	.8	4	94					1
Skim Milk, 1 C.	86	8	12	.4	302	.1	28	247	406	126	500	.09	.34	.22	2
TOTAL	494	31	49	21	447	5.9	129	576	1898	1276	7236	.4	.7	9.5	96

Substitutions
Vegetable Juice Cocktail: 1 C. vegetable juice
Tossed Salad: substitute 1 C. broccoli or cauliflower for the beets
Skim Milk: ½ C. ice cream or yogurt

Fried Chicken
Creamy Mashed Potatoes with Gravy
Corn on the Cob
Skim Milk
Cantaloupe

Calories: 733 per serving   Protein: 34 grams per serving

Fried Chicken

3 T. safflower oil
3 T. orange juice
1 egg, beaten
½ C. whole wheat flour
½ t. paprika
½ t. grated orange peel
½ t. salt
1 T. sesame seeds
4 chicken legs

Heat the oil in a baking pan in a 400° F. oven.

Add the orange juice to the beaten egg and mix well. Mix together the flour, paprika, orange peel, salt, and sesame seeds. Dip the chicken first into the liquid, coating it well, then into the dry mixture. Place the chicken in the baking pan, turning to coat it well with the hot oil. Cover and bake for 40 minutes. Turn the chicken occasionally. Uncover and bake 20 minutes more.

Yields: 4 servings

Creamy Mashed Potatoes

3 medium potatoes
¼ C. half and half
¼ C. butter
1 t. salt

Wash the potatoes, leaving the skins on. Boil in water to cover for 30 minutes or until done. Remove from the heat, drain, and add the half and half, butter, and salt. Beat until well blended and smooth.

Yields: 4 servings

Gravy

1½ C. chicken bouillon
3 T. whole wheat flour
3 T. pan drippings

In a small saucepan, combine ¾ C. bouillon with the flour and blend well. Stir in the pan drippings and the rest of the bouillon. Cook, stirring constantly, until thick and bubbly. Serve equal amounts over mashed potatoes.

Yields: 4 servings

■ Serve each person 1 ear of boiled corn on the cob with ½ T. butter, and 1 C. skim milk, and for dessert, a quarter of a cantaloupe.

	Calories	Protein GMS	Carbohydrates GMS	Fat GMS	Calcium MGS	Iron MGS	Magnesium MGS	Phosphorus MGS	Potassium MGS	Sodium MGS	Vitamin A I.U.	Vitamin B₁ MGS	Vitamin B₂ MGS	Niacin MGS	Vitamin C MGS
Fried Chicken	259	17	12	21	27	1.9	67	221	502	375	240	.15	.25	4	9
Creamy Mashed Potatoes	230	4	34	13	33	.85	59	91	608	684	505	.16	.08	2	23
Chicken Gravy	32	1	5	3	7	.45	6	44	20	270		.02	.01	.2	
Corn on the Cob, 1 ear	96	3.5	22	1	3	.7	48	111	280	t	400	.15	.12	1.7	12
Skim Milk, 1 C.	86	8	12	.4	302	.1	28	247	406	126	500	.09	.34	.22	2
Cantaloupe, ¼	30	.7	8	.1	14	.4	17	16	251	12	3400	.04	.03	.6	33
TOTAL	733	34	93	39	386	4.4	225	730	2067	1467	5045	.6	.8	8.7	79

Substitutions

Corn on the Cob: 1 C. cooked winter squash, spinach, or
  rutabaga; ½ C. green peas; 1 C. vegetable juice or Vegetable
  Juice Cocktail (see page 20)

Skim Milk: ½ C. yogurt or 1 oz. natural cheese

Cantaloupe: 2 apricots; ½ mango or papaya; 1 nectarine, peach,
  or persimmon

MENU

Sweet and Sour Chicken
Cashew Rice
Mandarin Spinach Salad
Skim Milk

Calories: 725 per serving   Protein: 39 grams per serving

_____ **Sweet and Sour Chicken** _____

1¼ C. cooked chicken, without
  skin
1½ C. canned pineapple
  chunks, in juice
¾ C. green pepper strips
2 T. honey

First prepare the rice (see next page). While it is cooking,
dice the cooked chicken, and drain the pineapple, reserving
the juice.

Combine the green pepper, pineapple chunks, honey, vinegar,
molasses, and pepper in a saucepan. Add water to the pineapple
juice to make 1½ C. liquid. Add the liquid to the pineapple

½ C. cider vinegar
2 T. blackstrap molasses
dash of pepper
1½ C. brown rice
1½ T. cornstarch
3 T. cold water
¼ C. raisins

mixture and bring it to a boil, stirring constantly. Simmer 5 minutes.

In a separate bowl, combine the cornstarch and cold water. Stir this into the pineapple mixture. Cook over medium heat until thickened, stirring constantly. Add the raisins and the chicken, and simmer 15 minutes.

Yields: 4 servings

Cashew Rice

1 T. butter
½ C. chopped onion
1 C. brown rice
1 t. turmeric
1 t. salt
2 C. water
½ C. cashews

Sauté onions in butter. Add rice and turmeric. Fry a few minutes. Place water and salt in a kettle and bring to boil. Add to rice mixture. Simmer 45–60 minutes. Remove from heat and mix in cashews.

Yields: 4 servings

Mandarin Spinach Salad

4 C. spinach in bite-size pieces
½ C. chopped cucumber
½ C. mandarin oranges, drained
8 ripe olives

Chop the olives and then toss all the ingredients together. Serve with 1 T. Sauce Vinaigrette on each portion (see page 14).

Yields: 4 servings

	CALORIES	PROTEIN GMS	CARBOHYDRATES GMS	FAT GMS	CALCIUM MGS	IRON MGS	MAGNESIUM MGS	PHOSPHORUS MGS	POTASSIUM MGS	SODIUM MGS	VITAMIN A I.U.	VITAMIN B₁ MGS	VITAMIN B₂ MGS	NIACIN MGS	VITAMIN C MGS
Sweet and Sour Chicken	268	24	33	4	105	5	61	273	1097	75	178	.13	.2	11	38
Cashew Rice	222	5	26	12	22	1.2	72	128	167	783	144	.15	.07	1.4	t
Mandarin Spinach Salad	63	2	6	4	84	2	48	48	312	190	5147	.08	.12	.35	36
Sauce Vinaigrette, 1 T.	86		5	9.6	t	t	t	t	4.7	36					
Skim Milk, 1 C.	86	8	12	.4	302	.1	28	247	406	126	500	.09	.34	.22	2
TOTAL	725	39	82	30	513	8.3	209	696	1987	1210	5969	.45	.73	13	76

Substitutions
Cashew Rice: ¾ C. cooked brown rice
Mandarin Spinach Salad: 1 C. broccoli, carrots and peas, kale, or cauliflower
Skim Milk: ½ C. yogurt

Turkey à la King
Corn Pudding
Papaya

Calories: 808 per serving   Protein: 34 grams per serving

Turkey à la King

¼ C. sliced mushrooms
¼ C. diced green pepper
¼ C. butter
¼ C. whole wheat flour
½ t. salt
⅛ t. pepper
1 C. cream
1 C. chicken bouillon
1 C. cooked turkey, diced
1 pimiento pod, chopped
4 slices whole wheat bread, toasted
½ C. slivered almonds

Sauté the mushrooms and green pepper in the butter for 5 minutes. Blend in the flour and seasonings, and cook over low heat, stirring, until bubbly. Remove from the heat, and add the cream and bouillon. Return to the heat and bring to a boil, stirring constantly. Add the turkey and pimiento. Heat thoroughly. Serve over toast, topped with almond slivers.

Suggestion: Chicken may be substituted for the turkey.

Yields: 4 servings

Corn Pudding

2½ C. skim milk
3 T. cornmeal
2 T. whole wheat flour
1 t. salt
1 T. butter
2 eggs, beaten
2 T. minced green pepper
¼ t. crushed marjoram
¼ t. crushed thyme
¼ t. crushed basil
2 C. cooked corn

Preheat oven to 350° F.

Over low heat, heat the milk and gradually add the cornmeal and flour. Stir until blended. Add the salt and butter. Continue cooking until the mixture thickens, stirring frequently. Remove from the heat and blend in the remaining ingredients.

Pour the corn mixture into a greased casserole and place it in a pan of hot water. Bake for 30 minutes or until the center is firm.

Yields: 4 servings

■ Serve each person half a papaya for dessert.

	CALORIES	PROTEIN GMS	CARBOHYDRATES GMS	FAT GMS	CALCIUM MGS	IRON MGS	MAGNESIUM MGS	PHOSPHORUS MGS	POTASSIUM MGS	SODIUM MGS	VITAMIN A I.U.	VITAMIN B₁ MGS	VITAMIN B₂ MGS	NIACIN MGS	VITAMIN C MGS
Turkey à la King	540	22	23	32	121	2.4	81	314	462	760	1339	.19	.39	5.8	15
Corn Pudding	210	11	28	7	205	1	37	291	444	674	1055	.2	.4	1	8
Papaya, ½	58	.9	15	.2	30	.45	11	24	351	5	2625	.06	.06	.45	84
TOTAL	808	34	66	39	356	3.9	129	629	1257	1439	5019	.45	.85	7.3	107

Substitutions

Corn Pudding: 1 C. skim milk or ½ C. yogurt plus: 1 C. broccoli, eggplant, or kale; ½ C. corn, peas, or collards; 1 baked or sweet potato; 1 C. vegetable juice

Papaya: 2″ slice honeydew; ½ C. pineapple or orange juice; 1 orange; 2 plums

MENU

Turkey Divan
Baked Potatoes with Butter
Wassail

Calories: 730 per serving   Protein: 35 grams per serving

Turkey Divan

2 C. cooked broccoli
1⅔ C. cooked turkey breast, diced
1 C. sliced mushrooms
1 oz. grated Parmesan cheese
1 C. condensed cream of mushroom soup
8 oz. evaporated milk
½ C. crushed potato chips

Preheat oven to 350° F.

Place the broccoli in a greased baking dish. Cover it with the turkey and mushrooms. Top with the cheese.

Combine the soup and milk and pour this mixture over the turkey. Bake for 25 minutes. Top with the crushed potato chips and bake 5 minutes more.

Yields: 4 servings

3 oranges
whole cloves
3 C. apple cider or unsweetened
  juice
1 cinnamon stick
1 C. unsweetened pineapple
  juice
¼ C. honey
¼ t. grated nutmeg
3 T. lemon juice
1 t. grated lemon rind

Preheat oven to 350° F.

Stud the oranges with the cloves, about ½″ apart. Place the oranges in a baking pan with enough water to cover bottom of pan. Bake for 30 minutes.

Heat the apple juice and cinnamon stick in large saucepan. Bring to a boil and simmer, covered, for 5 minutes. Add the remaining ingredients and simmer uncovered for 5 minutes. Pour the hot mixture into a punch bowl and float the baked oranges on top.

Yields: 4 servings

■ Serve each person 1 baked potato with ½ T. butter

	CALORIES	PROTEIN GMS	CARBOHYDRATES GMS	FAT GMS	CALCIUM MGS	IRON MGS	MAGNESIUM MGS	PHOSPHORUS MGS	POTASSIUM MGS	SODIUM MGS	VITAMIN A I.U.	VITAMIN B₁ MGS	VITAMIN B₂ MGS	NIACIN MGS	VITAMIN C MGS
Turkey Divan	300	29	16	13	329	1.8	41	385	795	401	2146	.17	.58	8	73
Baked Potato	145	4	33	.2	14	1	75	101	782	6	t	.15	.1	.75	62
Butter, ½ T.	51	t	t	6	1.5	0	.14	1	1.5	70	235	t	t		0
Wassail, 1 C.	234	2	60	.3	62	1.8	31	43	429	4	228	.15	.1	.75	62
TOTAL	730	35	109	20	407	4.6	147	530	2008	481	2609	.47	.78	9.5	197

Substitutions
Baked Potato: serve potato french fried, steamed, or pan fried
Wassail: 1 C. grapefuit, grape, orange, or pineapple juice; or
  a combination of them

FISH AND SEAFOOD

MENU

Baked Haddock in Tomato Sauce
Cauliflower Curry
Green Rice
Apple Juice Soda

Calories: 458 per serving   Protein: 34 grams per serving

Baked Haddock in Tomato Sauce

½ C. sliced onions
2 medium tomatoes, sliced
1 lb. haddock filets
2 T. lemon juice
¼ t. salt
dash of pepper and paprika
½ C. tomato juice
¾ C. diced green pepper,
   sautéed
1 C. sliced mushrooms, sautéed
1 T. chopped parsley

Preheat oven to 350° F.

Arrange the onions and tomatoes in the bottom of 2-quart greased baking dish. Arrange the filets over the vegetables. Season with lemon juice, salt, pepper, and paprika.

Combine the tomato juice, green pepper, and mushrooms, and pour over the fish. Bake for 30–35 minutes, until fish is flaky. Sprinkle with parsley before serving.

Yields: 4 servings

Cauliflower Curry

1 small head cauliflower
1 C. chopped onion
1 clove garlic, crushed
½ t. salt
2 t. curry powder
dash of cayenne pepper
1 T. ground coriander
2 T. safflower oil
1½ C. water

Break the cauliflower into flowerets and steam until crisp-tender.

Sauté the onion, garlic, and seasonings in the oil until the onion is wilted. Add the water and cauliflower and heat just to boiling. Cook over low heat for 20 minutes.

Let stand for 2 hours if possible, then reheat and serve.

Suggestion: Sprinkle chopped peanuts and shredded coconut over the curry.

Yields: 4 servings

Green Rice

1 C. skim milk
1 egg, beaten
½ C. chopped parsley
¼ C. chopped onion
2 C. cooked brown rice
½ C. grated cheddar cheese
¼ t. salt

Preheat oven to 325° F.

Blend the milk and egg in a large bowl. Add the remaining ingredients and mix well. Put into a greased casserole and bake for 30 minutes or until set.

Yields: 4 servings

■ Serve each person 1 C. Apple Juice Soda (½ C. unsweetened apple juice, or fruit juice of choice, mixed with ½ C. club soda or sparkling mineral water).

	CALORIES	PROTEIN GMS	CARBOHYDRATES GMS	FAT GMS	CALCIUM MGS	IRON MGS	MAGNESIUM MGS	PHOSPHORUS MGS	POTASSIUM MGS	SODIUM MGS	VITAMIN A I.U.	VITAMIN B₁ MGS	VITAMIN B₂ MGS	NIACIN MGS	VITAMIN C MGS
Baked Haddock in Tomato Sauce	132	23	9	1	50	1.9	49	282	762	273	1019	.15	.21	5	56
Cauliflower Curry	74	3	8	7	35	.9	23	55	260	279	78	.09	.09	.7	56
Green Rice	193	8	26	7	210	1	39	220	254	803	1047	.1	.2	1	15
Apple Juice Soda, 1 C.	59	.1	15	t	8	.08	5	11	125	1		.01	.03	.1	1
TOTAL	458	34	58	15	303	3.9	116	568	1401	1356	2144	.35	.53	6.8	128

Substitutions
Haddock: white perch
Cauliflower Curry: 1 C. cauliflower, broccoli, or kale; ½ C. peas
    or corn; 1 medium tomato; 1 C. vegetable juice or Vegetable
    Juice Cocktail (see page 20)
Green Rice: ½ C. cooked brown rice plus 1 C. skim milk, ½
    C. yogurt, or 1 oz. natural cheese

MENU

Vegetable Juice Cocktail
Fried Haddock with Tartar Sauce
Eggplant Sauté
Skim Milk
Peanut Puff Cookies

Calories: 838 per serving   Protein: 42 grams per serving

Fried Haddock

2 T. safflower oil   Heat the oil in a large skillet.
¼ C. whole wheat flour
                           Stir together the flour, salt, and pepper. Coat the fish filets

½ t. salt
dash of pepper
1 lb. haddock filets
1 egg, beaten
1 C. dry bread crumbs

in the flour mixture, then dip in the egg, then coat with bread crumbs. Fry 4 minutes or until done. Serve with tartar sauce and a small lemon wedge.

Yields: 4 servings

Tartar Sauce

½ C. mayonnaise
1 T. finely chopped dill pickle
½ T. finely chopped parsley
1 t. finely chopped pimiento
½ t. finely chopped onion

Blend all the ingredients and divide equally among 4 portions of fish.

Yields: 4 servings

Eggplant Sauté

1 small eggplant (1 lb.)
2 T. olive or safflower oil
½ t. salt
pepper to taste
½ t. crushed basil
¼ C. water

Cut the eggplant lengthwise into 8 sections.

Heat the oil in a frying pan over medium heat. Sauté the cut sides of the eggplant a few minutes until browned. Turn eggplant skin side down. Sprinkle with the salt, pepper, and basil, and add the water. Cover, and cook 10–12 minutes or until tender. Stir eggplant frequently while cooking, and add more water if necessary. Serve immediately.

Yields: 4 servings

Peanut Puff Cookies

5 T. butter
2 T. peanut butter
¼ t. salt
3 T. honey
1 t. vanilla extract
1⅛ C. whole wheat pastry flour
⅓ C. chopped roasted peanuts

Preheat oven to 375° F.

Cream the butter with the peanut butter and salt, and gradually add the honey. Blend in the vanilla and flour. Stir in the peanuts and mix well.

Shape the dough into 24 small balls and place them on an ungreased cookie sheet. Bake for 12 minutes or until brown. Cool.

Yields: 24 cookies

■ Serve each person 1 C. Vegetable Juice Cocktail (see page 20), 1 C. skim milk, and 2 Peanut Puff Cookies.

	CALORIES	PROTEIN GMS	CARBOHYDRATES GMS	FAT GMS	CALCIUM MGS	IRON MGS	MAGNESIUM MGS	PHOSPHORUS MGS	POTASSIUM MGS	SODIUM MGS	VITAMIN A I.U.	VITAMIN B₁ MGS	VITAMIN B₂ MGS	NIACIN MGS	VITAMIN C MGS
Vegetable Juice Cocktail	61	3	13	.45	46	3	31	62	757	544	2546	.15	.1	2	54
Fried Haddock	268	27	24	11	67	2.2	61	309	425	534	130	.15	.2	5	t
Tartar Sauce	206	.4	.6	22	8	.5	.6	8	23	142	205	t	t	t	4
Eggplant Sauté	87	1	6	6	12	.7	16	26	214	269	10	.05	.05	.6	5
Skim Milk, 1 C.	86	8	12	.4	302	.1	28	247	406	126	500	.09	.34	.22	2
Peanut Puff Cookies, 2	130	3	12	8	10	.6	22	64	90	110	208	.08	.02	1.3	t
TOTAL	838	42	68	48	445	7	159	716	1915	1725	3599	.52	.7	9	65

Substitutions

Vegetable Juice Cocktail: 1 C. vegetable or tomato juice
Haddock: perch
Eggplant Sauté: 4 spears asparagus; ½ C. broccoli, brussels sprouts, cauliflower, corn, or peas; 1 C. Swiss chard or spinach; 1 medium tomato
Peanut Puff Cookies: optional

MENU

Oven-Crisp Pike
Mushroom, Onion, and Tomato Savory
Skim Milk
Carrot Cake with Cream Cheese Frosting

Calories: 744 per serving   Protein: 47 grams per serving

Oven-Crisp Pike

1 egg
3 T. skim milk
¼ t. salt
½ C. dry bread crumbs
¾ C. grated Swiss cheese
¼ C. chopped parsley

Preheat oven to 475° F. and grease a shallow baking dish.

In a small bowl beat the egg, milk, and salt together. In a separate bowl combine the bread crumbs, cheese, and parsley. Submerge the fish in the egg mixture, then roll in the bread crumb mixture. Coat well.

1 lb. pike or walleye
2 T. butter

Arrange the fish in the baking dish, and sprinkle any remaining crumbs on top. Dot with the butter. Bake 15–20 minutes or until fish is tender and brown.

Yields: 4 servings

Mushroom, Onion, and Tomato Savory

3 small Spanish onions, sliced
in thin rings
¼ C. water
1 T. butter
2 C. sliced mushrooms
4 medium tomatoes, peeled and
sliced
¼ C. dry bread crumbs

Preheat oven to 350° F.

Place the onion rings in the bottom of a greased casserole dish, add the water and dot with ½ T. butter, and bake until fairly tender, 20–30 minutes.

Arrange the mushrooms on top of the cooked onions, and add the tomatoes on top of the mushrooms. Add the bread crumbs, and dot with ½ T. butter. Bake at 350° F. for 20 minutes or until brown.

Yields: 4 servings

Carrot Cake

½ C. honey
2 eggs
½ C. safflower oil
1 t. vanilla extract
1 C. whole wheat pastry flour
1 t. baking powder
1 t. baking soda
1 t. ground cinnamon
½ t. ground nutmeg
¼ t. ground cloves
½ t. ground allspice
½ t. salt
1½ C. packed grated carrots
¾ C. chopped walnuts or
pecans and/or raisins
(optional)

Preheat oven to 325° F. Grease and flour an 8 × 8″ square cake pan.

In a large bowl beat together the honey, eggs, oil, and vanilla. Mix together the dry ingredients and blend them into the liquid mixture. Fold in the carrots, and nuts and raisins if desired. Bake 45–50 minutes. Cool in the pan on a wire rack.

This cake becomes more moist with age and also freezes very well.

Yields: 1 cake, 12 pieces

Cream Cheese Frosting

4 oz. cream cheese
2 T. honey
1 t. skim milk
¼ t. vanilla extract
¼ C. butter (optional)

Beat together all the ingredients and frost the cake when it is completely cooled.

■ Serve each person 1 C. skim milk.

	CALORIES	PROTEIN GMS	CARBOHYDRATES GMS	FAT GMS	CALCIUM MGS	IRON MGS	MAGNESIUM MGS	PHOSPHORUS MGS	POTASSIUM MGS	SODIUM MGS	VITAMIN A I.U.	VITAMIN B_1 MGS	VITAMIN B_2 MGS	NIACIN MGS	VITAMIN C MGS
Oven-Crisp Pike	310	31	11	15	90	1.6	57	427	467	441	602	.3	.35	3	7
Mushroom, Onion, and Tomato Savory	126	5	20	4	53	1.7	37	120	655	99	1503	.16	.28	3	44
Skim Milk, 1 C.	86	8	12	.4	302	.1	28	247	406	126	500	.09	.34	.22	2
Carrot Cake, 1 pc.	177	2	20	10	16	.67	19	68	106	16	1114	.09	.06	.7	1
Cream Cheese Frosting	45	.8	3	3.5	5.8	.05	.75	8	8	24	143	.002	.03	.02	t
TOTAL	744	47	66	33	467	4	142	870	1642	706	3862	.64	1	6.9	54

Substitutions

Mushroom, Onion, and Tomato Savory: 1 C. corn, kale, or
   asparagus; ½ C. peas; 1 C. tomato or vegetable juice or
   Vegetable Juice Cocktail (see page 20)
Skim Milk: ½ C. yogurt or 1 oz. natural cheese
Carrot Cake and Frosting: optional

MENU

Poached Pike with Cucumber Sauce
Stuffed Butternut Squash
Vanilla Ice Cream and Fruit Sauce

Calories: 792 per serving   Protein: 46 grams per serving

Poached Pike

⅔ C. sliced onion
3 lemon slices
¼ C. chopped parsley
1 small green pepper, cut in
   rings
2 peppercorns
1 bay leaf
1 lb. pike filet
lemon wedges (optional)

Fill a skillet with 1½" water and add the onion, lemon, parsley, green pepper, and seasonings. Bring to a boil. Arrange the fish on top of the vegetables, cover, and simmer 4–6 minutes or until the fish flakes easily. Serve four equal pieces of fish with cucumber sauce. Garnish with lemon wedges.

Yields: 4 servings

93

Cucumber Sauce

2 T. butter
1 T. whole wheat flour
½ C. whole milk
1 egg, beaten
½ C. chopped cucumber
½ C. cooked shrimp, chopped
½ t. salt
dash of pepper and ground
   nutmeg

Melt the butter in a saucepan and blend in the flour. Cook over low heat, stirring, until bubbly. Remove from the heat and add the milk. Return to the heat and bring to a boil, stirring constantly for 1 minute. Remove from the heat. Blend a small amount of the hot sauce into the egg. Then add this to the remaining sauce. Simmer 1 minute, stirring constantly. Add the remaining ingredients, heat, and serve over portions of fish.

Yields: 4 servings

Stuffed Butternut Squash

2 butternut squash
1 C. chopped mushrooms
½ C. chopped onion
½ C. chopped celery
¼ C. sunflower seed kernels
2 T. butter
¼ C. chopped parsley
1 C. dry bread crumbs
½ t. crushed sage
salt and pepper to taste
½ C. grated cheddar cheese

Preheat oven to 350° F.

Split each squash in half, remove the seeds, and bake face down on an oiled baking tray for 30 minutes.

Sauté the mushrooms, onion, celery, and seeds in the butter. Add the parsley, bread crumbs, and seasonings. Blend and cook a few minutes. Put the mixture into a bowl and mix in the cheese. Fill the squash cavities with equal amounts of the stuffing and bake another 25 minutes.

Yields: 4 servings

Fruit Sauce

4 peaches or fruit of choice
¼ C. water
½ C. honey
1 t. lemon juice
1 t. butter

Quarter the fruit and steam until soft. Purée the fruit in a blender. Add the honey, lemon juice, and butter. Blend. Pour into a jar, cover, and chill.

Yields: 1 quart

■ Serve each person ½ C. vanilla ice cream (see page 41) with 2 T. fruit sauce.

	CALORIES	PROTEIN GMS	CARBOHYDRATES GMS	FAT GMS	CALCIUM MGS	IRON MGS	MAGNESIUM MGS	PHOSPHORUS MGS	POTASSIUM MGS	SODIUM MGS	VITAMIN A I.U.	VITAMIN B₁ MGS	VITAMIN B₂ MGS	NIACIN MGS	VITAMIN C MGS
Poached Pike with Cucumber Sauce	262	31	9	12	119	2.2	63	389	623	454	711	.35	.32	3.3	47
Stuffed Butternut Squash	361	13	46	12	226	4	56	264	1056	369	2936	.4	.5	4	30
Vanilla Ice Cream, ½ C.	147	2	11	11	60	.35	7	59	75	43	453	.02	.09	.54	.5
Fruit Sauce, 2 T.	22	t	6	t	1.4	t	1.6	2.6	28	1.8	172	t	t	t	1
TOTAL	792	46	72	35	406	6.6	128	715	1782	868	4272	.77	.9	7.5	79

Stuffed Squash: 1 C. asparagus, broccoli, brussels sprouts, collard, kale, peas, or rutabaga; 1 medium tomato; 1 C. tomato or vegetable juice or Vegetable Juice Cocktail (see page 20)
Ice Cream: any ice cream; 1 C. skim milk; ½ C. yogurt; 1 oz. natural cheese; optional
Fruit Sauce: fresh fruit; optional

MENU

Rolled Halibut on Rice with Mushroom Sauce
Asparagus with Dill Cream
Skim Milk
Blueberry Elixir

Calories: 743 per serving   Protein: 45 grams per serving

Rolled Halibut

1⅓ C. brown rice
1 lb. halibut filets
¼ t. salt
2 T. butter
1 T. lemon juice
dash of Tabasco sauce
dash of paprika
1¼ C. condensed cream of mushroom soup
1 C. sliced mushrooms

Drop the rice into 2⅔ C. boiling salted (1 t.) water. Simmer covered 45–60 minutes. Preheat oven to 400° F.

Season the filets on both sides with the salt. Roll them up and place them seam side down in a greased shallow baking pan.

In a separate saucepan, melt 1 T. butter. Blend in the lemon juice and Tabasco sauce. Brush or drizzle this mixture over the filets and sprinkle them with paprika. Bake for 20 minutes.

Sauté the sliced mushrooms in 1 T. butter and add them to the cream of mushroom soup. Heat.

Serve halibut on a bed of rice, topped with mushroom sauce.

Yields: 4 servings

Asparagus with Dill Cream

16 spears asparagus
½ C. sour cream
2 T. chopped scallions

Steam or boil the asparagus in a small amount of water just until tender. Drain and refrigerate.

2 t. crushed dill weed
salt and pepper to taste

Combine the sour cream, scallions, dill, and seasonings. Chill for a few hours, or overnight if possible.

Serve 4 asparagus spears and 2 T. Dill Cream per person.

Yields: 4 servings

Blueberry Elixir

2 C. orange juice
1 C. blueberries
1 T. sesame seeds
1 T. sunflower seed kernels
1 egg
1 T. honey
1 T. wheat germ (optional)

Place all the ingredients in a blender. Blend at medium speed until smooth. Serve immediately.

Yields: 4 servings

■ Serve each person 1 C. skim milk.

	CALORIES	PROTEIN GMS	CARBOHYDRATES GMS	FAT GMS	CALCIUM MGS	IRON MGS	MAGNESIUM MGS	PHOSPHORUS MGS	POTASSIUM MGS	SODIUM MGS	VITAMIN A I.U.	VITAMIN B_1 MGS	VITAMIN B_2 MGS	NIACIN MGS	VITAMIN C MGS
Rolled Halibut on Rice with Mushroom Sauce	452	30	55	12	54	2.2	60	422	763	607	760	.3	.22	14	2
Asparagus with Dill Cream	64	3	5	6	58	.6	30	77	239	16	1252	.16	.22	1.5	28
Skim Milk, 1 C.	86	8	12	.4	302	.1	28	247	406	126	500	.09	.34	.22	2
Blueberry Elixir	141	4	17	5	27	1	36	93	300	15	400	.18	.09	.9	65
TOTAL	743	45	89	23	441	3.9	154	839	1708	764	2912	.73	.87	16.6	97

Substitutions
Asparagus with Dill Cream: ½ C. broccoli, carrots, collards, or kale; 1 C. cooked Swiss chard, peas, or winter squash; 1 C. raw spinach; 1 baked sweet potato; 1 medium tomato; 1 C. tomato or vegetable juice or Vegetable Juice Cocktail (see page 20)
Skim Milk: ½ C. yogurt
Blueberry Elixir: 3 apricots, ½ avocado, 1 banana, ¼ cantaloupe, 1 medium guava, ½ mango, 1 orange, one 6″ × 1½″ slice watermelon; 1 C. pineapple or strawberries

Vegetable Juice Cocktail
Salmon Loaf
Basil Carrots
Creamy Fruit Parfait

Calories: 703 per serving   Protein: 47 grams per serving

Salmon Loaf

1 lb. canned salmon
1 C. soft bread crumbs
2 eggs, beaten
2 T. minced parsley
1 t. grated lemon rind
½ t. salt
⅛ t. crushed thyme
⅛ t. pepper

Preheat oven to 350° F.

Drain the salmon, reserving the liquid. In a bowl, flake the salmon and remove the skin. Add the reserved liquid and other ingredients. Combine thoroughly. Place in a buttered 8″ × 4″ loaf pan. Set in a pan containing 1″ hot water and bake for 30–40 minutes.

Yields: 4 servings

Basil Carrots

2 C. carrots
1 T. butter
dash of salt
½ t. crushed basil

Thinly slice the carrots on the diagonal: enough for 2 C. Melt the butter in a skillet and add the carrots and seasonings. Cover and cook over low heat for 10 minutes, stirring occasionally.

Yields: 4 servings

Creamy Fruit Parfait

2 C. ricotta cheese
2 T. honey
½ t. vanilla extract
2 C. fruit, sliced if necessary

Beat the cheese with an electric mixer at high speed for 5 minutes. Add the honey and vanilla and blend thoroughly. Fold in the fruit. Divide among 4 parfait glasses and chill for 2 hours.

Yields: 4 servings

■ Serve each person 1 C. Vegetable Juice Cocktail (see page 20).

	CALORIES	PROTEIN GMS	CARBOHYDRATES GMS	FAT GMS	CALCIUM MGS	IRON MGS	MAGNESIUM MGS	PHOSPHORUS MGS	POTASSIUM MGS	SODIUM MGS	VITAMIN A I.U.	VITAMIN B_1 MGS	VITAMIN B_2 MGS	NIACIN MGS	VITAMIN C MGS
Vegetable Juice Cocktail	61	3	13	.45	46	3	31	62	757	544	2,546	.15	.1	2	54
Salmon Loaf	280	28	6	11	326	2.4	53	477	484	990	531	.1	.3	9	3
Basil Carrots	50	.75	5	3	26	.45	14	25	173	61	7,993	.04	.04	.4	5
Creamy Fruit Parfait	312	15	23	16	268	.75	23	206	246	105	668	.05	.25	.4	6
TOTAL	703	47	47	30	666	6.6	121	770	1660	1700	11,738	.34	.69	11.8	68

Substitutions
Vegetable Juice Cocktail: 1 C. tomato or vegetable juice
Basil Carrots: ½ C. asparagus, broccoli, Swiss chard, corn,
   eggplant, or peas; 1 C. raw spinach; 1 medium tomato
Creamy Fruit Parfait: fruit of choice; optional

MENU

Salmon Specialty
Brussels Sprouts and Grapes
Skim Milk
Pineapple Boats (optional)

Calories: 648 per serving   Protein: 34 grams per serving

Salmon Specialty

Dough

2⅔ T. skim milk
2⅔ T. butter
1 T. honey
⅓ t. salt
1¼ T. dry yeast
4 t. warm water
1 egg, beaten
1 C. whole wheat flour

Prepare the dough one day before serving.

Scald the milk and allow it to cool to lukewarm.

Cream the butter. Add the honey gradually. Add the salt and blend well.

In a separate bowl, soften the yeast in the water. Add the yeast and the cooled milk to the butter mixture. Add the egg and flour. Beat with a wooden spoon for 2 minutes. Cover and let dough rise in a warm place until double its original size. Stir down. Cover tightly and refrigerate overnight.

½ C. brown rice
3 T. chopped onion
1⅓ T. butter
½ C. sliced mushrooms
8 oz. boneless, skinless salmon
¼ C. white wine or water
1⅓ T. crushed dill weed
⅓ t. salt

Bring 1 C. water to the boil, add the rice, and simmer, covered, for 45–60 minutes.

Sauté the onion in the butter until clear and tender. Add the mushrooms and cook 3 minutes. Allow to cool.

Poach the salmon in the water or wine. Cool. Reserve the poaching liquid. Break the salmon into bite-size pieces. Mix together the cooked rice, dill, onions and mushrooms, and salmon with half of the poaching liquid. Season with the salt and pepper.

Preheat oven to 425° F.

Remove the dough from the refrigerator, stir it down, and turn it out onto a lightly floured pastry cloth or board. Roll and shape the dough into a rectangle at least 8″ × 6″. Shape the salmon mixture into a meatloaf shape and place it in the center of the dough. Fold over the long edges and seal securely. For the ends, cut a triangle from each corner and fold dough envelope style, covering the ends. Turn the loaf over, *very* gently, seam side down, onto a lightly greased and floured cookie sheet. Make steam holes along the length of the dough. Bake 10 minutes or until browned, then reduce heat to 350° F. and bake 10–15 minutes longer.

Suggestion: Prepare a clarified butter sauce, white sauce, or cheese sauce to pour over the loaf before serving.

Yields: 4 servings

Brussels Sprouts and Grapes

14 oz. brussels sprouts
1⅓ T. butter
1 C. green grapes

Boil or steam the sprouts and drain them. Add the butter and grapes and mix thoroughly.

Yields: 4 servings

■ Serve each person 1 C. skim milk. For Pineapple Boats, see page 73.

	CALORIES	PROTEIN GMS	CARBOHYDRATES GMS	FAT GMS	CALCIUM MGS	IRON MGS	MAGNESIUM MGS	PHOSPHORUS MGS	POTASSIUM MGS	SODIUM MGS	VITAMIN A I.U.	VITAMIN B₁ MGS	VITAMIN B₂ MGS	NIACIN MGS	VITAMIN C MGS
Salmon Specialty	457	21	45	22	93	2.3	77	321	473	370	798	.35	.19	7	6
Brussels Sprouts and Grapes	105	5	14	4	43	1.7	34	85	451	61	740	.12	.16	1	104
Skim Milk, 1 C.	86	8	12	.4	302	.1	28	247	406	126	500	.09	.34	.22	2
TOTAL	648	34	71	26	438	4	139	653	1330	557	2038	.56	.69	8.2	112

Substitutions

Brussels Sprouts and Grapes: grapes are optional; ½ C. asparagus, broccoli, collards, kale, spinach, or winter squash; 1 medium tomato; 1 C. tomato or vegetable juice or Vegetable Juice Cocktail (see page 20)

Skim Milk: ½ C. yogurt

MENU

Seafood Pilaf
Broccoli with Yogurt and Almonds
Lemon-Glazed Date Bars

Calories: 411 per serving   Protein: 20 grams per serving

Seafood Pilaf

1 C. brown rice
⅓ C. chopped onion
2 T. chopped celery
⅔ C. chopped green pepper
1⅓ T. butter
1⅓ C. canned tomatoes
⅓ t. salt
⅙ t. paprika
⅓ C. grated cheddar cheese
5 oz. cooked shrimp

Preheat oven to 325° F.

Drop the rice into 2 C. boiling salted (1 t.) water and simmer, covered, 45 minutes.

Sauté the onion, celery, and green pepper in the butter. Add the cooked rice, tomatoes, seasonings, and half the cheese. Stir over medium-low heat until the cheese has melted. Add the shrimp, stir, and put the mixture in a small buttered casserole. Sprinkle the remaining cheese on top. Bake until bubbly, about 5–10 minutes.

Yields: 4 servings

Broccoli with Yogurt and Almonds

4 C. chopped broccoli
1 T. safflower oil
2 T. lemon juice
salt to taste
½ C. lowfat yogurt
¼ C. slivered almonds

Steam or boil the broccoli in a small amount of water until crisp-tender. Place it in a bowl and toss with the oil, lemon juice, and salt. Divide among 4 dishes and top each with 2 T. yogurt and 1 T. almonds.

Yields: 4 servings

Lemon-Glazed Date Bars

½ C. whole wheat pastry flour
¾ t. baking powder
¼ t. salt
1 egg
¼ C. honey
½ T. melted butter
1 C. finely chopped dates
¼ C. chopped walnuts

Preheat oven to 300° F.

Sift the flour, baking powder, and salt together.

In a separate bowl, beat the egg well, adding the honey gradually. Blend in the butter. Stir in the dates, walnuts, and dry ingredients, mixing thoroughly. Pour into a greased cake pan, approximately 8″ × 8″ × 2″. Bake 30–35 minutes. While date bars are cooling, prepare the glaze.

Yields: 16 bars

Glaze

2 T. butter
2 T. honey
1 T. lemon juice
¼ t. grated lemon rind

Heat the butter and honey in a small saucepan. Remove from the heat, and add the lemon juice and rind. Mix well and pour over the date bars while they are still warm.

	CALORIES	PROTEIN GMS	CARBOHYDRATES GMS	FAT GMS	CALCIUM MGS	IRON MGS	MAGNESIUM MGS	PHOSPHORUS MGS	POTASSIUM MGS	SODIUM MGS	VITAMIN A I.U.	VITAMIN B₁ MGS	VITAMIN B₂ MGS	NIACIN MGS	VITAMIN C MGS
Seafood Pilaf	308	14	45	7.7	135	2	77	249	446	874	1022	.22	.13	2.5	44
Broccoli with Yogurt & Almonds	150	8	11	9	209	1.9	65	183	560	36	3819	.17	.4	1.5	144
Lemon-Glazed Date Bar, 1	95	1.4	18	3	12	.6	13	33	102	55	97	.03	.02	.4	t
TOTAL	543	23	74	20	346	4.5	155	465	1108	965	4938	.42	.53	4.4	188

Substitutions
Broccoli with Yogurt and Almonds: 4 spears asparagus; 1 C. cooked eggplant, spinach, peas, green beans, carrots, or cauliflower; 1 C. vegetable juice or Vegetable Juice Cocktail (see page 20)
Lemon-Glazed Date Bar: fruit of choice; optional

MENU

Swiss Crab Pie
Tomato Cups
Apple Juice Soda

Calories: 605 per serving   Protein: 22 grams per serving

Swiss Crab Pie

Pastry

1 C. whole wheat pastry flour, chilled
½ t. salt
¼ C. butter, chilled
¼ C. very cold water

Prepare pastry dough, following the instructions on page 66, and fit the dough into an 8″ pie pan.

Filling

3 oz. Swiss cheese
⅓ C. sliced mushrooms
6 oz. crab meat or cooked shrimp
2 scallions, chopped
2 eggs
⅔ C. cream
1 t. grated lemon rind
¼ t. dry mustard
¼ C. chopped parsley
½ t. salt
dash of ground mace

Preheat oven to 325° F.

Grate the Swiss cheese and sprinkle it over the pie shell. Arrange the mushrooms on the cheese, then top with the crab or shrimp. Sprinkle with the scallions.

In a bowl, beat the eggs, then add the cream, lemon rind, mustard, parsley, salt, and mace. Mix well. Pour the mixture over the crab. Bake for 45 minutes or until set. Remove from the oven and let pie stand for 10 minutes before serving.

Yields: 4 servings

Tomato Cups

4 tomatoes
½ cucumber, sliced
4 scallions, chopped
1 t. grated lemon peel
¼ t. salt
¼ C. lowfat yogurt
¼ head iceberg lettuce

Cut the tops off the tomatoes. Cut slits in the sides of the tomatoes top to bottom and wedge in the sliced cucumber. Combine the scallions, lemon peel, salt, and yogurt. Mix well and place a portion in each tomato with the cucumber slices. Serve on lettuce leaves.

Yields: 4 servings

■ Serve each person 1 C. Apple Juice Soda (½ C. unsweetened apple juice, or other fruit juice, mixed with ½ C. club soda or sparkling mineral water).

	CALORIES	PROTEIN GMS	CARBOHYDRATES GMS	FAT GMS	CALCIUM MGS	IRON MGS	MAGNESIUM MGS	PHOSPHORUS MGS	POTASSIUM MGS	SODIUM MGS	VITAMIN A I.U.	VITAMIN B₁ MGS	VITAMIN B₂ MGS	NIACIN MGS	VITAMIN C MGS
Swiss Crab Pie	495	19	25	38	283	2.5	57	358	293	1020	2103	.25	.3	3	9
Tomato Cup	51	3	9	1	51	1.1	26	66	470	152	1712	.12	.1	1.2	41
Apple Juice Soda, 1 C.	59	.1	15	t	8	.08	5	11	125	1		.01	.03	.1	1
TOTAL	605	22	49	39	342	3.7	88	435	888	1173	3815	.38	.43	4.3	51

Substitutions

Tomato Cup: 1 C. asparagus, broccoli, brussels sprouts, eggplant, kale, okra, or rutabaga; ½ C. peas; 1 C. vegetable juice or Vegetable Juice Cocktail (see page 20)

Apple Juice Soda: 1 C. skim milk

MENU

Tuna Noodle Casserole
Vegetable Tempura
Skim Milk
Peaches Marinade

Calories: 650 per serving   Protein: 32 grams per serving

Tuna Noodle Casserole

4 oz. noodles
3½ oz. tuna, drained
¼ C. mayonnaise
¼ C. chopped celery
¼ C. chopped onion
¼ C. chopped green pepper
2 T. chopped pimiento
¼ t. salt
¼ C. skim milk

Preheat oven to 350° F. and grease a casserole dish.

Cook the noodles according to the package instructions.

Flake the tuna, and combine tuna, mayonnaise, vegetables, pimiento, and salt in a bowl. Blend well.

In a saucepan, heat the milk and soup; add the cheese, stir well, and heat until the cheese has melted. Remove from the heat. Add the tuna mixture to the cheese mixture, then add

½ C. condensed cream of celery
soup
½ C. grated sharp cheddar
cheese
¼ C. wheat flakes (optional)

the cooked noodles. Stir well. Place in the casserole dish and sprinkle with wheat flakes, if desired. Bake for 20 minutes.

Yields: 4 servings

Vegetable Tempura

½ C. whole wheat flour
½ C. cornmeal
½ t. salt
½ t. onion powder
¾ C. water
1 C. broccoli flowerets
1 C. cauliflower flowerets
½ C. sliced zucchini
½ C. sliced green beans
safflower oil for frying

Combine the flour, cornmeal, and seasonings in a bowl. Add the water, blend, and refrigerate for 1 hour before using.

Coat bite-size vegetable pieces with the batter. If batter is too thick, thin it by adding 1 T. water at a time to the desired consistency. Drop the pieces into a preheated deep-fat fryer. When vegetables are lightly browned, remove and drain on paper towels. Keep pieces warm in the oven if needed as you complete the frying.

Yields: 4 servings

Peaches Marinade

1¼ T. lemon juice
1 t. grated orange rind
1 drop almond extract, or more
to taste (optional)
1 T. honey
½ C. lowfat yogurt
mint leaves (optional)
4 C. sliced peaches

Mix the lemon juice, orange rind, almond extract, honey, and yogurt together. Add the mint. Pour over the peaches and marinate, covered, for at least 1 hour in the refrigerator before serving.

Yields: 4 servings

■ Serve each person 1 C. skim milk.

	CALORIES	PROTEIN GMS	CARBOHYDRATES GMS	FAT GMS	CALCIUM MGS	IRON MGS	MAGNESIUM MGS	PHOSPHORUS MGS	POTASSIUM MGS	SODIUM MGS	VITAMIN A I.U.	VITAMIN B₁ MGS	VITAMIN B₂ MGS	NIACIN MGS	VITAMIN C MGS
Tuna Noodle Casserole	334	16	26	19	150	1.9	10	231	278	661	934	.3	.2	5	32
Vegetable Tempura	157	6	26	5	61	1.4	53	136	335	275	1168	.2	.16	1.6	62
Skim Milk, 1 C.	86	8	12	.4	302	.1	28	247	406	126	500	.09	.34	.22	2
Peaches Marinade	73	2	15	2	44	.5	15	47	254	14	1115	.08	.09	1	9
TOTAL	650	32	79	26	557	3.9	106	661	1273	1076	3717	.67	.79	7.8	105

Substitutions

Tempura: substitute eggplant for the zucchini, carrots for the broccoli, green or Spanish onions for the cauliflower, or sweet potatoes for the green beans. Stir-fry vegetables in hot oil if batter and deep-fat frying is not desired.

Skim Milk: ½ C. yogurt

Peaches Marinade: fruit or fruit juice of choice; optional

MEATLESS

Boston Baked Beans
Cool Tomato Salad
Apple Juice Soda

Calories: 510 per serving   Protein: 14 grams per serving

Boston Baked Beans

1 C. dry navy beans
4 C. water
2 slices bacon (optional)
⅛ C. chopped onion
2⅔ T. blackstrap molasses
1 t. dry mustard
¼ t. salt
dash of pepper
1½ T. honey

Place the beans in a large saucepan and cover with the water. Heat to boiling and boil for 2 minutes. Remove from the heat and let stand 1 hour, keeping the beans covered with water.

Place the beans back on the burner and simmer 50 minutes covered or until tender. Do not boil, or the beans will split. Drain the beans, reserving the water.

Preheat oven to 325° F.

Layer the beans, bacon, and onion in an ungreased 2-quart bean pot. Stir together the remaining ingredients with 2 C. of the bean liquid. Pour over the beans. Cover and bake 3–3½ hours, removing the cover for the last hour. Stir occasionally and add liquid if necessary.

Yields: 4 servings

Cool Tomato Salad

3 T. safflower oil
3 T. wine or cider vinegar
1 t. crushed oregano
2 cloves garlic, crushed
½ t. salt
dash of pepper
3 tomatoes, cut into wedges
1 carrot, sliced, steamed lightly
½ head iceberg lettuce
1 T. chopped chives or parsley

Shake the oil, vinegar, and seasonings together in a jar until well blended. Place the tomato wedges and carrot slices in a bowl; pour the dressing over, and refrigerate covered, 2–3 hours.

Arrange the tomatoes and carrots on a lettuce bed for each of 4 servings. Sprinkle with chives or parsley. Drizzle the dressing over the top.

Yields: 4 servings

■ Serve each person 1 C. Apple Juice Soda (½ C. unsweetened apple juice, or other fruit juice, mixed with ½ C. club soda or sparkling mineral water).

	CALORIES	PROTEIN GMS	CARBOHYDRATES GMS	FAT GMS	CALCIUM MGS	IRON MGS	MAGNESIUM MGS	PHOSPHORUS MGS	POTASSIUM MGS	SODIUM MGS	VITAMIN A I.U.	VITAMIN B₁ MGS	VITAMIN B₂ MGS	NIACIN MGS	VITAMIN C MGS
Boston Baked Beans	316	12	46	9	179	5.5	40	245	957	247	2	.45	.15	2.3	t
Cool Tomato Salad	135	2	10	11	35	1.1	25	51	432	284	4032	.11	.75	1.2	32
Apple Juice Soda, 1 C.	59	.1	15	t	8	.08	5	11	125	1		.01	.03	.1	1
TOTAL	510	14	71	20	222	6.7	70	307	1514	532	4034	.57	.93	3.6	33

Substitutions
Cool Tomato Salad: 1 C. asparagus, broccoli, collards, or kale;
   1 C. tomato or vegetable juice or Vegetable Juice Cocktail
   (see page 20)

MENU

Vegetable Juice Cocktail
Cheese Soufflé
Mushroom Salad with Sauce Vinaigrette

Calories: 640 per serving   Protein: 30 grams per serving

Cheese Soufflé

3 T. butter
2 t. dry mustard
2 T. whole wheat flour
1¼ C. hot, scalded skim milk
⅛ t. salt
dash of cayenne pepper
⅛ t. pepper
½ t. Worcestershire sauce
   (optional)
¼ t. basil
2 T. chopped parsley

In a medium saucepan over low heat, melt the butter and stir in the mustard and flour, whisking constantly. Add the milk slowly, stirring and keeping the mixture smooth. Simmer 7 minutes, stirring often. Remove from the heat and add the seasonings, including the parsley. Mix in the cheese. Cool the mixture, stirring it occasionally.

Preheat oven to 350° F.

Beat the egg yolks and add them to the cooled mixture. Beat the egg whites in a large bowl until stiff. Fold one-third of the egg whites into the cheese mixture. Then add the mixture

1½ C. grated sharp cheddar
  cheese, packed
6 eggs, separated

to the remaining egg whites. Fold swiftly and gently with a rubber scraper just until blended. Turn into a well-buttered medium soufflé dish and bake for 40 minutes. Do not open the oven while the soufflé is baking.

Yields: 4 servings

Mushroom Salad

6 C. lettuce in bite-size pieces
2 medium tomatoes
2 C. sliced mushrooms

Cut the tomatoes in wedges and toss all the ingredients together gently. Serve with 1 T. Sauce Vinaigrette on each portion (see page 14).

Yields: 4 servings

■ Serve each person 1 C. Vegetable Juice Cocktail (see page 20).

	CALORIES	PROTEIN GMS	CARBOHYDRATES GMS	FAT GMS	CALCIUM MGS	IRON MGS	MAGNESIUM MGS	PHOSPHORUS MGS	POTASSIUM MGS	SODIUM MGS	VITAMIN A I.U.	VITAMIN B_1 MGS	VITAMIN B_2 MGS	NIACIN MGS	VITAMIN C MGS
Vegetable Juice Cocktail	61	3	13	.45	46	3	31	62	757	544	2546	.15	.1	2	54
Cheese Soufflé	451	25	5	36	546	2.3	38	505	287	644	1992	.12	.5	.3	t
Mushroom Salad	42	2	8	.5	41	2.2	22	81	545	15	1825	.1	.25	2.3	24
Sauce Vinaigrette, 1 T.	86		5	9.6	t	t	t	t	4.7	36					
TOTAL	640	30	31	47	633	7.5	91	648	1594	1239	6363	.37	.85	4.6	78

Substitution
Vegetable Juice Cocktail: 1 C. vegetable or tomato juice

Crunchy Greens with Rice
Broiled Tomatoes
Zucchini Bread

Calories: 595 per serving   Protein: 19 grams per serving

Crunchy Greens with Rice

1 C. brown rice
4 C. raw spinach, packed
2 T. safflower oil
⅓ C. chopped parsley
2 cloves garlic, crushed
⅓ C. slivered almonds
⅛ C. chopped walnuts
½ t. salt
3 oz. Monterey Jack cheese, grated
2 T. grated Parmesan cheese

Drop the rice into 2 C. boiling salted (1 t.) water and simmer, covered, 45–60 minutes.

Wash the spinach thoroughly and steam or boil it in a small amount of water. Cook just until wilted.

In a separate pan, heat the oil and add the remaining ingredients, except the Parmesan cheese. Cook over medium heat until the Monterey Jack cheese is melted. Add a little water for desired consistency.

Divide the rice proportionately, top with spinach, and pour the crunchy sauce over it. Sprinkle with the Parmesan cheese.

Yields: 4 servings

Broiled Tomatoes

4 tomatoes
1½ T. butter
⅓ onion, minced
1½ stalks celery, minced
¼ t. garlic salt
2 T. grated Parmesan cheese

Slice the tops off the tomatoes, remove the cores, and place the tomato shells in a shallow greased pan. Salt the inside of the tomatoes lightly. Mix together all the other ingredients except the Parmesan cheese and fill the tomato centers.

Broil the tomatoes until they are soft to the touch; remove. Sprinkle each with some of the Parmesan cheese, return them to the broiler, and brown them lightly.

Yields: 4 servings

Zucchini Bread

½ C. honey
6 T. melted butter
2 eggs
½ t. vanilla extract
1⅞ C. whole wheat flour
2½ t. baking powder

Preheat oven to 350° F.

Cream together the honey and butter in a medium bowl. Add the eggs and vanilla and beat well.

Sift together the dry ingredients; then add them to the honey mixture. Blend. Fold in the zucchini, and nuts or raisins if

½ t. salt
½ t. ground allspice
½ t. ground coriander
½ t. grated nutmeg
½ t. ground cinnamon
2 C. grated zucchini, packed
½ C. nuts or raisins (optional)

desired. Pour into a 5″ × 9″ loaf pan. Bake 45 minutes or until done.

Suggestion: 1 C. canned pumpkin can be substituted for the zucchini.

Yields: 18 slices

	CALORIES	PROTEIN GMS	CARBOHYDRATES GMS	FAT GMS	CALCIUM MGS	IRON MGS	MAGNESIUM MGS	PHOSPHORUS MGS	POTASSIUM MGS	SODIUM MGS	VITAMIN A I.U.	VITAMIN B₁ MGS	VITAMIN B₂ MGS	NIACIN MGS	VITAMIN C MGS
Crunchy Greens	258	11	7	23	271	3	89	218	432	474	5134	.1	.3	.8	37
Rice, ½ C.	89	2	19	.6	9	.4	23	55	52	211	0	.07	.02	1	0
Broiled Tomato, 1	86	3	9	5	51	1	28	62	459	240	1594	.1	.08	1.1	37
Zucchini Bread, 1 sl.	162	2.7	18	5	14	.67	18	65	92	113	273	.09	.05	.78	3
TOTAL	595	19	53	34	345	5	158	400	1035	1038	7001	.36	.45	3.7	77

Substitutions
Broiled Tomato: 1 baked potato; 1 C. summer squash, eggplant, or Chinese cabbage; ½ C. mushrooms; 1 C. tomato or vegetable juice or Vegetable Juice Cocktail (see page 20)
Zucchini Bread: any whole grain bread; optional

MENU

Egg Foo Yung
Vegetable Chow Mein
Pineapple Boats with Yogurt
Green or Jasmine Tea (optional)

Calories: 640 per serving   Protein: 31 grams per serving

Egg Foo Yung

1 T. safflower oil
3 stalks celery, sliced
1 C. chopped onion

Heat the oil in a large skillet. Sauté the celery and onions; then remove them from the skillet.

8 eggs
1 T. honey
dash of crushed thyme, basil, and/or oregano
½ C. diced cooked chicken
1 C. bean sprouts

In a mixing bowl blend the eggs, honey, and herbs. Pour the mixture into the skillet, cover, and cook over low heat for 1 minute. Before the eggs solidify, add the chicken and sautéed vegetables. Cook until the eggs are firm. Turn over and cook the other side for 30 seconds. Garnish with bean sprouts and divide evenly among 4 persons.

Yields: 4 servings

Vegetable Chow Mein

⅔ C. brown rice
½ C. chopped onions
1 C. chopped celery
½ T. safflower oil
½ C. sliced mushrooms
1 C. bean sprouts
8 water chestnuts, sliced
½ C. vegetable stock
1 T. cornstarch
1 t. salt
2 T. soy sauce
½ pimiento pod, chopped (optional)
2 T. chopped almonds
¼ C. cooked green peas
4 green onion tops, chopped (optional)

Drop the rice into 1⅓ C. boiling salted (⅔ t.) water and simmer, covered, 45 minutes.

Sauté the onions and celery in the oil. Then add the mushrooms and stir until they are just heated. Add the bean sprouts and water chestnuts.

In a bowl, combine the vegetable stock, cornstarch, salt, and soy sauce. Add the mixture to the vegetables and simmer until it thickens. Gently ladle the sauce over the hot rice. Garnish with pimiento, almonds, peas, and green onion tops.

Yields: 4 servings

■ Serve Pineapple Boats (see page 73), each one topped with 3 T. yogurt. Serve Jasmine or Green tea if desired.

	CALORIES	PROTEIN GMS	CARBOHYDRATES GMS	FAT GMS	CALCIUM MGS	IRON MGS	MAGNESIUM MGS	PHOSPHORUS MGS	POTASSIUM MGS	SODIUM MGS	VITAMIN A I.U.	VITAMIN B₁ MGS	VITAMIN B₂ MGS	NIACIN MGS	VITAMIN C MGS
Egg Foo Yung	253	19	12	16	80	3	26	268	435	167	1164	.17	.35	2.5	13
Vegetable Chow Mein	181	8	35	3	48	1.9	43	143	424	1240	152	.22	.17	3	13
Pineapple Boat	179	2	45	.9	45	2	44	55	562	3	186	.15	.1	1.4	55
Yogurt, 3 T.	27	2	3	.8	78	.03	8	60	99	30	27	.02	.09	.04	t
TOTAL	640	31	95	21	251	6.9	121	526	1520	1440	1529	.56	.7	6.9	81

Substitutions
Pineapple Boat: ½ C. softened prunes or blackberries; 1 C. boysenberries, slip-skin grapes, cherries, strawberries, or

raspberries; 2 large fresh figs; 1 mango or orange; one
6" × 1½" slice watermelon; 1 C. apricot nectar, grape, or
grapefruit juice
Yogurt: 1 C. skim milk

MENU

Fresh Mushroom Patties with Mornay Sauce
Saffron Rice and Green Peas
Chocolate Cake

Calories: 694 per serving   Protein: 24 grams per serving

Fresh Mushroom Patties

3 eggs
1½ C. chopped fresh
  mushrooms
2 scallions, chopped
½ t. salt
1 C. grated sharp cheddar
  cheese
1½ T. butter

Beat the eggs well; add the mushrooms, scallions, and salt.
Stir in the cheese. Make 8 patties and fry them in the butter
over medium-low heat until golden. Turn and brown the other
side. The patties become firm with cooking and should be crisp
on the outside, moist on the inside. Serve with Mornay Sauce
(see below).

Yields: 4 servings

Mornay Sauce

1 C. skim milk
1 T. butter
2 T. whole wheat flour
1 T. chopped parsley (optional)
1 T. cream
2 T. grated sharp cheddar
  cheese
⅛ t. Worcestershire sauce

Heat the milk.

In a small saucepan melt the butter and blend in the flour
and parsley. Add this to the milk, stirring with a wire whisk
until thickened. Add the cream and cheese; cook for 1 minute.
Stir the Worcestershire sauce in thoroughly.

Yields: 4 servings

Saffron Rice and Green Peas

1½ C. brown rice
¼ t. crushed saffron
1 C. chopped onion
1 clove garlic, minced

Prepare the rice (see page 24), adding the saffron to the water
before simmering.

Sauté the onion and garlic in the oil. Add the peas and basil.

114

2 T. safflower oil
1 C. cooked green peas
½ t. crushed basil
salt and pepper to taste

Stir. Add the cooked rice and salt and pepper. Blend the ingredients together and cook 1 minute over low heat.

Yields: 4 servings

Chocolate Cake

½ C. butter
1 oz. unsweetened chocolate
1 C. honey
2 eggs
½ t. vanilla extract
½ t. salt
¼ C. powdered cocoa
1 t. baking soda
1 t. baking powder
1½ C. whole wheat pastry flour
1 C. buttermilk

Preheat oven to 350° F.

Melt the butter and chocolate in a double boiler. Cool.

Cream the honey. Add the eggs and vanilla and beat well. Add the butter mixture and blend.

Sift together the dry ingredients and add them to the honey mixture. Blend in the buttermilk. Pour into a 9″ × 13″ cake pan and bake 45 minutes or until done.

Yields: 16 pieces

	CALORIES	PROTEIN GMS	CARBOHYDRATES GMS	FAT GMS	CALCIUM MGS	IRON MGS	MAGNESIUM MGS	PHOSPHORUS MGS	POTASSIUM MGS	SODIUM MGS	VITAMIN A I.U.	VITAMIN B₁ MGS	VITAMIN B₂ MGS	NIACIN MGS	VITAMIN C MGS
Mushroom Patties with Sauce	298	15	9	23	340	1.4	27	341	330	630	1347	.1	.4	1.4	6
Saffron Rice and Green Peas	216	6	37	8	35	1.6	52	138	224	322	233	.2	.08	2.5	12
Chocolate Cake, 1 pc.	180	3	27	8	31	1	21	88	124	161	306	.07	.08	.6	t
TOTAL	694	24	73	39	406	4	100	567	678	1113	1886	.37	.56	4.5	18

Substitutions
Saffron Rice and Green Peas: 1 baked potato
Chocolate Cake: optional

Fruit, Nut, and Rice Casserole
Whole Wheat Dinner Rolls
Skim Milk

Calories: 620 per serving   Protein: 20 grams per serving

Fruit, Nut, and Rice Casserole

1 C. brown rice
1 C. chopped onions
1 C. chopped green pepper
1 C. chopped celery
1½ T. butter
⅓ C. chopped toasted almonds
½ C. raisins
¾ C. chopped dried apricots, softened
½ t. curry powder

Drop the rice into 2 C. boiling salted (1 t.) water and simmer, uncovered, 45–60 minutes.

Preheat oven to 375° F. and grease a baking dish.

Sauté the vegetables in the butter until tender; add the almonds. Add the raisins, apricots, cooked rice, and curry powder and combine well. Put the mixture in the baking dish and bake, covered, for 30 minutes.

Yields: 4 servings

■ Serve each person 1 C. skim milk and 1 Whole Wheat Dinner Roll with 1 t. butter (see page 16).

	CALORIES	PROTEIN GMS	CARBOHYDRATES GMS	FAT GMS	CALCIUM MGS	IRON MGS	MAGNESIUM MGS	PHOSPHORUS MGS	POTASSIUM MGS	SODIUM MGS	VITAMIN A I.U.	VITAMIN B₁ MGS	VITAMIN B₂ MGS	NIACIN MGS	VITAMIN C MGS
Fruit, Nut, and Rice Casserole	414	8	77	10	86	3.7	101	224	731	624	2979	.25	.19	4	35
Whole Wheat Dinner Roll, 1	86	4	18	2	29	.75	25	94	103	100	56	.13	.05	.1	t
Butter, 1 t.	34	t	t	3.8	1	0	.09	.66	1	47	157	t	t		0
Skim Milk, 1 C.	86	8	12	.4	302	.1	28	247	406	126	500	.09	.34	.22	2
TOTAL	620	20	107	16	418	4.6	154	566	1241	897	3692	.47	.58	4.3	37

Substitutions
Whole Wheat Dinner Roll: any whole wheat bread
Skim Milk: ¾ C. yogurt

Garbanzo Stuffed Cabbage
Sliced Tomatoes
Banana-Nut Chocolate Sundae

Calories: 603 per serving   Protein: 20 grams per serving

Garbanzo Stuffed Cabbage

¼ C. brown rice
8 cabbage leaves
⅓ C. cooked garbanzo beans
2 T. parsley
1⅓ T. chopped chives
⅔ T. soy sauce
¼ C. chopped celery
½ C. chopped mushrooms
⅔ C. canned tomatoes
½ C. grated cheddar cheese
⅓ C. yogurt

Drop the rice into ½ C. boiling salted (¼ t.) water and simmer, covered, 30 minutes.

Steam the cabbage leaves in salted water for 2–3 minutes. Reserve the cooking water.

Mash the beans in a medium bowl and add all the ingredients including the rice, except the yogurt and 4 T. of the cheese. Mix thoroughly. Spread equal portions of the mixture on the cabbage leaves. Roll the leaves up and secure them with a toothpick if necessary. Sprinkle the rolls with the remaining cheese and place them in a skillet. Add ¼ C. of the cabbage liquid to prevent sticking if necessary. Cook, covered, over medium heat for approximately 15 minutes or until the cabbage is tender. To serve, top with the yogurt.

Yields: 4 servings

Banana-Nut Sundae

4 bananas
1⅓ C. vanilla ice cream
4 T. Chocolate Syrup (see below)
½ C. toasted peanuts

Cut the bananas lengthwise and arrange 2 halves on each dessert dish. Place ⅓ C. ice cream between the bananas and top with 1 T. Chocolate Syrup (hot or cold). Chop the peanuts and sprinkle each serving with 2 T. of the nuts.

Yields: 4 servings

Chocolate Syrup

1 oz. unsweetened chocolate
¼ C. honey
⅛ t. salt
2 T. water
1½ T. butter
¼ t. vanilla extract

Heat the chocolate, honey, salt, and water in a double boiler over low heat. Cook until mixture is smooth and thickened. Remove from the heat and blend in the butter and vanilla.

Yields: ½ C.

■ Serve each person 1 medium sliced tomato. Sprinkle with parsley, chives, or scallions if desired.

	CALORIES	PROTEIN GMS	CARBOHYDRATES GMS	FAT GMS	CALCIUM MGS	IRON MGS	MAGNESIUM MGS	PHOSPHORUS MGS	POTASSIUM MGS	SODIUM MGS	VITAMIN A I.U.	VITAMIN B₁ MGS	VITAMIN B₂ MGS	NIACIN MGS	VITAMIN C MGS
Garbanzo Stuffed Cabbage	205	10	27	7	193	2	36	215	548	346	972	.15	.2	7	41
Sliced Tomato, 1	33	2	7	3	20	.8	21	40	366	4	1350	.09	.06	1	34
Banana-Nut Chocolate Sundae	365	8	59	14	85	2	99	173	813	51	447	.15	.2	4	16
TOTAL	603	20	93	24	298	4.8	156	428	1727	401	2769	.39	.46	12	91

Substitutions

Sliced Tomato: 1 C. vegetable or tomato juice or Vegetable
    Juice Cocktail (see page 20); 1 C. raw spinach or endive;
    ½ C. cooked summer squash, broccoli, or carrots
Banana-Nut Chocolate Sundae: 1 C. skim milk or ½ C. yogurt;
    optional

MENU

Vegetable Juice Cocktail
Macaroni and Cheese
Herbed Green Beans
Apricots

Calories: 534 per serving   Protein: 22 grams per serving

Macaroni and Cheese

2 C. macaroni noodles, cooked
    and drained
2 T. butter
1 T. whole wheat flour
½ t. dry mustard
½ t. salt
dash of pepper
1¼ C. skim milk
¼ C. chopped onion

Preheat oven to 350° F.

Melt the butter in a saucepan; blend in the flour, mustard, salt, and pepper. Add the milk; stir. Cook until thick and bubbly. Remove from the heat. Add the onion and cheese and stir together well.

Mix the cheese sauce with the noodles; place in a 1-quart casserole dish and cover. Bake 35–40 minutes. If desired, fry the bacon, drain and crumble it, and place it on the casserole

1½ C. grated cheddar cheese
2 slices bacon (optional)

5 minutes before removing from the oven.

Yields: 4 servings

Herbed Green Beans

3 C. green beans
⅓ C. chopped onion
2 T. safflower oil
1 garlic clove, crushed
1 T. minced green pepper
1 medium tomato, chopped
1 T. chopped celery
1 T. minced parsley
¼ t. crushed oregano
¼ t. crushed rosemary
dash of salt

Steam or boil the green beans in a small amount of water just until tender.

Sauté the onion in the oil. Add the remaining ingredients and simmer 8 minutes. Add the beans and mix well.

Yields: 4 servings

■ Serve each person 1 C. Vegetable Juice Cocktail (see page 20) and for dessert, 3 apricots.

	CALORIES	PROTEIN GMS	CARBOHYDRATES GMS	FAT GMS	CALCIUM MGS	IRON MGS	MAGNESIUM MGS	PHOSPHORUS MGS	POTASSIUM MGS	SODIUM MGS	VITAMIN A I.U.	VITAMIN B₁ MGS	VITAMIN B₂ MGS	NIACIN MGS	VITAMIN C MGS
Vegetable Juice Cocktail	61	3	13	.45	46	3	31	62	757	544	2546	.15	.1	2	54
Macaroni and Cheese	340	16	22	21	428	.68	32	339	240	648	876	.15	.35	.95	2
Herbed Green Beans	78	2	3	8	56	.9	33	46	238	27	853	.09	.1	.7	21
Apricots, 3	55	1	14	.2	18	.5	14	25	301	1	2890	.03	.04	.6	11
TOTAL	534	22	52	30	548	5	110	472	1536	1220	7165	.42	.59	4.3	88

Substitutions
Vegetable Juice Cocktail: 1 C. vegetable or tomato juice
Herbed Green Beans: 1 C. broccoli, brussels sprouts, eggplant, or kale; ½ C. collards or peas
Apricots: ½ C. blackberries, blueberries, raspberries, or strawberries; ¼ cantaloupe; one 2″-wide slice honeydew melon; 1 prickly pear or orange; ½ papaya; 2 plums

Vegetable Juice Cocktail
Quiche Lorraine
Spinach Salad

Calories: 717 per serving   Protein: 25 grams per serving

Quiche Lorraine
Pastry

1 C. whole wheat pastry flour, chilled
½ t. salt
¼ C. butter, chilled
¼ C. very cold water

Prepare pastry dough, following the instructions on page 66, and fit into an 8" or 9" pie plate.

Filling

½ C. chopped onion
1 C. sliced mushrooms
1 C. chopped green pepper
1 medium tomato, diced
3 eggs
1 C. half and half
½ t. salt
3 oz. grated gruyère or cheddar cheese
¼ lb. bacon, fried and crumbled (optional)

Preheat oven to 350° F.

Sauté the onion, mushrooms, and green pepper in a little oil. Add the tomato just before the vegetables are done.

Beat the eggs, and add the half and half and salt.

Place the grated cheese in the unbaked pastry shell, cover with the vegetables, and pour the egg mixture over the vegetables. Sprinkle with bacon if desired. Bake 45 minutes or until set. Cool 5 minutes before serving.

Yields: 4 servings

Spinach Salad

6 C. spinach
½ C. sliced cucumber
½ C. chopped green onions

Dressing

¼ C. safflower oil
1 T. cider vinegar
¼ t. salt
½ clove garlic, crushed
½ t. soy sauce

Wash and dry the spinach thoroughly and combine it with the vegetables in a large bowl. Shake together the dressing ingredients in a jar until well blended, pour over the salad and mix well.

Yields: 4 servings

■ Serve each person 1 C. Vegetable Juice Cocktail (see page 20).

	CALORIES	PROTEIN GMS	CARBOHYDRATES GMS	FAT GMS	CALCIUM MGS	IRON MGS	MAGNESIUM MGS	PHOSPHORUS MGS	POTASSIUM MGS	SODIUM MGS	VITAMIN A I.U.	VITAMIN B₁ MGS	VITAMIN B₂ MGS	NIACIN MGS	VITAMIN C MGS
Vegetable Juice Cocktail	61	3	13	.45	46	3	31	62	757	544	2546	.15	.1	2	54
Quiche Lorraine	497	18	41	36	330	3	61	411	494	889	2047	.3	.4	2.5	37
Spinach Salad with Dressing	159	4	6	14	112	4	90	65	668	268	8088	.13	.23	.7	52
TOTAL	717	25	60	51	488	10	182	538	1919	1701	12681	.58	.73	5.2	143

Substitutions
Vegetable Juice Cocktail: 1 C. vegetable or tomato juice
Spinach Salad: salad or vegetable of choice; optional

MENU

Soybean Patties
Tossed Salad (optional)
Fine Fruit Salad
Skim Milk

Calories: 595 per serving   Protein: 26 grams per serving

Soybean Patties

2 medium potatoes, quartered
1 C. toasted soybeans
1 egg, beaten
½ C. tomato sauce
1 T. chopped parsley
2 T. chopped onion
¼ t. salt

Steam the potatoes, with skins, in ½" boiling water for 15–20 minutes. In a large bowl, mash the potatoes (and skins), and mix in all the other ingredients except the bread, ¾ C. tomato sauce, and the oil. Form into 12 patties. Fry the patties in ½ T. hot oil or butter. Serve each person 3 patties with a piece of toasted bread, and 1 T. tomato sauce atop each pattie.

½ t. crushed basil
4 slices whole wheat bread
¾ C. tomato sauce, heated
½ T. safflower oil or butter

Suggestion: Add salt only if soybeans are not salted.

Yields: 12 patties

Fine Fruit Salad

½ C. roasted peanuts
½ apple, sliced
1 banana, sliced
½ tangerine, sectioned
1 peach, sliced
½ C. seedless grapes
¼ C. raisins
1½ T. honey
¾ T. lemon or lime juice
2 T. shredded coconut
2 T. sunflower seed kernels
¼ C. sweet wine (optional)
5–7 mint leaves (optional)

Combine all the ingredients and mix thoroughly. Garnish with mint leaves.

Yields: 4 servings

■ Serve each person 1 C. skim milk.

	CALORIES	PROTEIN GMS	CARBOHYDRATES GMS	FAT GMS	CALCIUM MGS	IRON MGS	MAGNESIUM MGS	PHOSPHORUS MGS	POTASSIUM MGS	SODIUM MGS	VITAMIN A I.U.	VITAMIN B₁ MGS	VITAMIN B₂ MGS	NIACIN MGS	VITAMIN C MGS
Soybean Patties	232	11	38	6	74	3.9	60	198	816	670	1590	.22	.1	3	42
Fine Fruit Salad	277	7	34	12	52	2	90	220	648	8	488	.2	.15	4	12
Skim Milk, 1 C.	86	8	12	.4	302	.1	28	247	406	126	500	.09	.34	.22	2
TOTAL	595	26	84	18	428	6	178	665	1870	804	2578	.5	.59	7	56

Substitutions
Fine Fruit Salad: vary fruits according to season and personal
   taste
Skim Milk: ½ C. yogurt

Spanish Omelet
Skim Milk
Florida Orange Ice

Calories: 579 per serving   Protein: 24 grams per serving

Spanish Omelet

Omelet

6 eggs
½ t. salt
¼ C. plus 2 T. water
2 T. butter

Preheat oven to 325° F.

Separate the eggs. In one bowl, beat the egg yolks. In another bowl, add the salt and 6 T. water to the egg whites and beat until the whites form peaks. Fold the yolks into the whites.

Melt the butter in an omelet pan and heat until sizzling. Pour in the omelet mixture, leveling the surface gently. Cook *slowly* on the stove until puffy on top and slightly browned on the bottom, about 5 minutes. Bake in the oven for 12–15 minutes until a knife inserted in the middle comes out clean. Fold in half.

Sauce

¼ C. chopped onion
1 green pepper, chopped
1 C. sliced mushrooms
2 cloves garlic, minced
2 T. butter
1 C. tomato paste
1 C. water
½ T. honey
1 t. Worcestershire sauce
½ t. crushed basil
½ t. crushed oregano
cayenne pepper to taste

Sauté the onion, green pepper, mushrooms, and garlic in the butter until tender, not brown. Stir in the tomato paste, water, honey, and seasonings. Cook over low heat for 10–15 minutes. Divide the omelet into 4 equal portions with a spatula and pour the sauce over.

Yields: 4 servings of omelet and sauce

Florida Orange Ice

2 C. fresh orange juice
3 oz. frozen orange juice, undiluted
1 t. grated orange rind
1½ T. lemon juice

Partially thaw the frozen orange juice. Add all the ingredients to the fresh orange juice, except the bananas. Stir until honey is absorbed into the mixture, then pour into ice cube trays and freeze. When frozen, cover the trays with foil. Remove the fruit ice from the freezer 5–10 minutes before serving, to

2 T. honey
1 t. rum extract (optional)
2 medium bananas

soften slightly. Divide the cubes among four dishes and top with the bananas.

Yields: 4 servings

■ Serve each person 1 C. skim milk.

	CALORIES	PROTEIN GMS	CARBOHYDRATES GMS	FAT GMS	CALCIUM MGS	IRON MGS	MAGNESIUM MGS	PHOSPHORUS MGS	POTASSIUM MGS	SODIUM MGS	VITAMIN A I.U.	VITAMIN B₁ MGS	VITAMIN B₂ MGS	NIACIN MGS	VITAMIN C MGS
Spanish Omelet	293	14	20	20	64	4	27	212	782	519	3500	.22	.38	3	59
Skim Milk, 1 C.	86	8	12	.4	302	.1	28	247	406	126	500	.09	.34	.22	2
Florida Orange Ice	200	2	49	.6	31	1	50	60	734	3	587	.15	.1	1.3	120
TOTAL	579	24	81	21	397	5	105	519	1922	648	4587	.46	.8	4.5	181

Substitutions
Skim Milk: ½ C. yogurt
Florida Orange Ice: ½ C. cooked prunes, 1 mango, 1 banana,
   or 1 C. unsweetened orange juice; optional

MENU

Vegetable Juice Cocktail
Welsh Rarebit
Peaches

Calories: 479 per serving   Protein: 26 grams per serving

Welsh Rarebit

1 T. safflower oil
1 C. grated cheddar cheese
¼ t. salt
¼ t. dry mustard
dash of cayenne pepper
1 t. soy sauce

Place the oil in a double boiler; stir in the cheese and melt it. Add the seasonings. Add the milk slowly, stirring constantly. Remove from the heat.

Beat the eggs; add a little hot cheese mixture and mix well. Gradually pour all of the egg mixture into the hot sauce, blending well. Return to low heat for several minutes, stirring

1½ C. skim milk
2 eggs
4 slices whole wheat bread

constantly. Remove from the heat. Pour over toasted bread slices.

Yields: 4 servings

■ Serve each person 1 C. Vegetable Juice Cocktail (see page 20) and for dessert, 1 peach.

	CALORIES	PROTEIN GMS	CARBOHYDRATES GMS	FAT GMS	CALCIUM MGS	IRON MGS	MAGNESIUM MGS	PHOSPHORUS MGS	POTASSIUM MGS	SODIUM MGS	VITAMIN A I.U.	VITAMIN B₁ MGS	VITAMIN B₂ MGS	NIACIN MGS	VITAMIN C MGS
Vegetable Juice Cocktail	61	3	13	.45	46	3	31	62	757	544	2546	.15	.1	2	54
Welsh Rarebit	380	22	16	26	571	1.5	47	481	304	613	1048	.1	.4	.8	t
Peach, 1	38	.6	10	.1	9	.5	12	19	202	1	1330	.02	.05	1	7
TOTAL	479	26	39	27	626	5	90	562	1263	1158	4924	.27	.55	3.8	61

Substitutions
Vegetable Juice Cocktail: 1 C. vegetable or tomato juice, or
   ½ C. peas
Peach: fruit of choice

SOUPS, SALADS, AND SANDWICHES

MENU

Chef's Salad
Whole Wheat Dinner Rolls
Peach Melba

Calories: 698 per serving   Protein: 33 grams per serving

Chef's Salad

4 oz. Swiss cheese
2 oz. ham
3 medium tomatoes
2 hard-boiled eggs
1 large carrot
4 C. iceberg lettuce torn into
   bite-size pieces
2 C. Romaine lettuce torn into
   bite-size pieces
1 large celery stalk, chopped
6 scallions, chopped
½ C. diced cooked chicken

Cut the cheese and ham into strips. Cut the tomatoes and eggs into 4 or 8 wedges each. Cut the carrot into 8 strips. Arrange the lettuce in 4 salad bowls, and add all the other ingredients. Serve with 1 T. Italian Dressing on each portion (see page 71).

Peach Melba

½ C. skim milk
¾ C. water
½ C. brown rice
1 egg
3 T. honey
½ T. lemon juice
2 peaches
2 T. jam or jelly

Combine the skim milk and water in a saucepan. Bring to a boil, drop in the rice, and simmer, covered, about 45 minutes. Add more water if necessary; don't allow the rice to become too dry or stick to the pan.

Beat the egg and honey together and add to the rice. Stir well and add the lemon juice. Divide the rice mixture among 4 dessert bowls and chill for at least 1 hour.

Before serving, cut the peaches in half and place a half on each dish. Heat the jam or jelly and spoon ½ T. over each dish.

Suggestion: Should the rice need thickening, add ½ T. cornstarch blended with a small amount of water and cook it in the rice for 2 minutes.

Yields: 4 servings

■ Serve each person 1 Whole Wheat Dinner Roll and 1 t. butter (see page 16).

	CALORIES	PROTEIN GMS	CARBOHYDRATES GMS	FAT GMS	CALCIUM MGS	IRON MGS	MAGNESIUM MGS	PHOSPHORUS MGS	POTASSIUM MGS	SODIUM MGS	VITAMIN A I.U.	VITAMIN B₁ MGS	VITAMIN B₂ MGS	NIACIN MGS	VITAMIN C MGS
Chef's Salad	282	24	12	16	346	3	48	346	736	305	4848	.25	.33	4	38
Italian Dressing, 1 T.	84	.03	.4	9	1	.02	.3	.8	4	94					1
Whole Wheat Dinner Roll, 1	86	4	18	1.7	29	.75	25	94	103	100	56	.13	.05	1	t
Butter, 1 t.	34	t	t	3.8	1	0	.09	.66	1	47	157	t	t		0
Peach Melba	212	5	45	2	59	1	35	119	236	34	858	.1	.1	2	4
TOTAL	698	33	75	33	436	4.8	108	561	1080	580	5919	.48	.48	7	43

Substitutions
Whole Wheat Dinner Roll: any whole wheat rolls; optional
Peach Melba: optional

MENU

Chicken Gumbo Soup
Sunflower Whole Wheat Bread
Skim Milk
Ice Cream and Cherries

Calories: 604 per serving   Protein: 28 grams per serving

Chicken Gumbo Soup

⅓ C. boneless chicken meat
⅔ C. chopped onion
1 T. safflower oil
4 C. chicken stock
1 C. canned tomatoes
1 C. okra, cut up
2 T. chopped parsley
⅓ C. brown rice
1 t. salt
¼ t. pepper
1 t. Worcestershire sauce

Boil the chicken in 4 cups water. Cool, and reserve the stock. Cut into bite-size pieces.

Sauté the onion in the oil, and add the stock, vegetables, rice, seasonings, and chicken. Stir well. Simmer 45 minutes over medium heat.

Yields: 4 servings

■ Serve each person 1 slice Sunflower Whole Wheat Bread with 1 t. butter (see page 167), 1 C. skim milk, and for dessert, ½ C. vanilla ice cream (see page 41) and ½ C. pitted cherries.

	CALORIES	PROTEIN GMS	CARBOHYDRATES GMS	FAT GMS	CALCIUM MGS	IRON MGS	MAGNESIUM MGS	PHOSPHORUS MGS	POTASSIUM MGS	SODIUM MGS	VITAMIN A I.U.	VITAMIN B₁ MGS	VITAMIN B₂ MGS	NIACIN MGS	VITAMIN C MGS
Chicken Gumbo Soup	194	14	21	6	51	1.4	41	171	438	562	881	.18	.12	6	22
Sunflower Whole Wheat Bread, 1 sl.	102	3	18	2	9	.7	22	79	83	67	t	.12	.03	.09	t
Butter, 1 t.	34	t	t	3.8	1	0	.09	.66	1	47	157	t	t		0
Skim Milk, 1 C.	86	8	12	.4	302	.1	28	247	406	126	500	.09	.34	.22	2
Vanilla Ice Cream, ½ C.	147	2	11	11	60	.14	7	59	75	43	453	.02	.19	.54	t
Cherries, ½ C.	41	.7	10	.2	13	.25	9	11	112	1	65	.03	.03	.25	6
TOTAL	604	28	72	23	436	2.6	107	568	1115	846	2056	.44	.7	7	30

Substitutions
Sunflower Whole Wheat Bread: any whole grain bread
Ice Cream and Cherries: ½ C. yogurt and/or fruit of choice; optional

MENU

Chicken Salad Sandwiches
Chicken Liver and Barley Soup
Skim Milk
Bananas

Calories: 689 per serving   Protein: 38 grams per serving

Chicken Salad Sandwiches

1 C. diced cooked chicken
½ C. chopped celery
1½ t. lemon juice

Mix together all the ingredients except the bread and lettuce. Divide the salad into equal portions and make 4 sandwiches with a leaf of lettuce in each.

¼ t. salt
⅛ t. pepper
¼ C. mayonnaise
1 hard-boiled egg, diced
4 lettuce leaves
8 slices whole wheat bread

Yields: 4 servings

Chicken Liver and Barley Soup

3½ C. chicken bouillon
¼ C. pearl barley
½ chopped onion
2 scallions, chopped
⅓ C. diced green pepper
1 large carrot, diced
¼ C. diced celery
1 clove garlic, crushed
½ t. crushed basil
1 bay leaf
½ C. sliced mushrooms
4 oz. chicken livers
2 T. safflower oil

Place the bouillon in a large saucepan and add the barley, the vegetables, and the seasonings. Do not add the mushrooms. Cover, bring to a boil, and simmer 25 minutes. Add the mushrooms and simmer 5 minutes more or until the barley is tender. Remove the bay leaf.

Sauté the livers in the oil. Slice them into thirds and add them to the soup. Stir and serve.

Yields: 4 servings

■ Serve each person 1 C. skim milk and for dessert, 1 banana.

	CALORIES	PROTEIN GMS	CARBOHYDRATES GMS	FAT GMS	CALCIUM MGS	IRON MGS	MAGNESIUM MGS	PHOSPHORUS MGS	POTASSIUM MGS	SODIUM MGS	VITAMIN A I.U.	VITAMIN B_1 MGS	VITAMIN B_2 MGS	NIACIN MGS	VITAMIN C MGS
Chicken Salad Sandwich	292	18	23	15	68	2	47	234	359	510	361	.11	.1	5	4
Chicken Liver and Barley Soup	184	10	15	9	35	4	15	190	177	664	7506	.1	.85	4	20
Skim Milk, 1 C.	86	8	12	.4	302	.1	28	247	406	126	500	.09	.34	.22	2
Banana, 1	127	1.6	33	.3	12	1	49	39	550	2	270	.08	.09	1	15
TOTAL	689	38	83	25	417	7	139	710	1492	1302	8937	.38	1.4	10	41

Substitutions
Chicken Liver and Barley Soup: chicken livers may be omitted
Banana: 1 C. grapes; 1 mango or orange; 2 plums; one 6″ ×
   1½″ slice watermelon

Clam Chowder
Endive and Mushroom Salad with Sauce Vinaigrette
Whole Wheat Crackers

Calories: 404 per serving   Protein: 18 grams per serving

Clam Chowder

10 oz. canned clams
2 potatoes, diced
2 onions, minced
1 C. kernel corn
¼ C. minced celery
1⅓ T. butter
1⅓ C. whole milk
salt and pepper to taste
¼ lb. bacon, fried and crumbled
   (optional)

Drain the clams, reserving the liquid. Chop.

Boil the potatoes approximately 20 minutes. Remove the potatoes and add enough water to the potato water to make 2⅔ C. Set aside.

In a large saucepan, cook the onions, corn, and celery in the clam liquid and butter until tender.

Place the potatoes, milk, and seasonings in a blender. Blend until smooth and add to the onion mixture. Add the potato water and clams. Heat and serve.

Yields: 4 servings

Endive and Mushroom Salad

4 C. endive torn into bite-size
   pieces
½ C. watercress torn into bite-
   size pieces (optional)
1 C. sliced mushrooms

Toss the greens and mushrooms together and serve with 1 T. Sauce Vinaigrette (see page 14) on each portion.

Yields: 4 servings

■ Serve each person 2 whole grain crackers.

	CALORIES	PROTEIN GMS	CARBOHYDRATES GMS	FAT GMS	CALCIUM MGS	IRON MGS	MAGNESIUM MGS	PHOSPHORUS MGS	POTASSIUM MGS	SODIUM MGS	VITAMIN A I.U.	VITAMIN B₁ MGS	VITAMIN B₂ MGS	NIACIN MGS	VITAMIN C MGS
Clam Chowder	247	15	35	19	168	5	44	291	708	109	495	.2	.35	3.5	25
Endive and Mushroom Salad	13	1	2.6	.14	38	.9	6.5	43	195	10	1453	.05	.13	1	8
Sauce Vinaigrette, 1 T.	86		5	9.6	t	t	t	t	4.7	36					
Whole Wheat Crackers, 2	58	2	9	2	10	.2	20	t			7	.03	.02	.5	t
TOTAL	404	18	52	31	216	6	71	334	908	155	1955	.28	.5	5	33

Substitutions
Endive and Mushroom Salad: 4 C. spinach for the endive

MENU

Cottage Cheese Salad
Vegetable Jewel Soup
French Bread

Calories: 491 per serving   Protein: 30 grams per serving

Cottage Cheese Salad

2 C. lowfat cottage cheese
1 C. cubed pineapple, drained
4 peaches, cubed
½ C. roasted peanuts, chopped
4 lettuce leaves

Combine the cottage cheese, fruit, and nuts. Serve each portion on a lettuce leaf.

Yields: 4 servings

Vegetable Jewel Soup

¼ C. chopped onion
¼ C. chopped green pepper
1 T. butter
½ large carrot, sliced
1¼ C. tomato juice
1 beef bouillon cube
1 t. salt
dash of pepper
¼ C. diced potatoes
½ C. peas
2 T. chopped parsley
2 T. whole wheat flour
1¼ C. skim milk

Sauté the onion and green pepper in the butter until tender. Add the carrot, tomato juice, bouillon cube, and seasonings. Cover. Simmer approximately 10 minutes. Add the potatoes, peas, and parsley. Cover, and simmer 15 minutes or until vegetables are tender.

Blend the flour with ½ C. milk and stir into the soup. Cook until bubbly. Add the remaining milk; heat. Season to taste and add water to desired consistency.

Yields: 4 servings

■ Serve each person 1 slice French bread (see page 31) with 1 t. butter.

	CALORIES	PROTEIN GMS	CARBOHYDRATES GMS	FAT GMS	CALCIUM MGS	IRON MGS	MAGNESIUM MGS	PHOSPHORUS MGS	POTASSIUM MGS	SODIUM MGS	VITAMIN A I.U.	VITAMIN B₁ MGS	VITAMIN B₂ MGS	NIACIN MGS	VITAMIN C MGS
Cottage Cheese Salad	266	21	23	11	111	1.4	55	267	410	462	1568	.14	.3	4	15
Vegetable Jewel Soup	127	7	17	3	143	1.6	37	163	532	972	3173	.17	.2	1.9	31
French Bread, 1 sl.	64	1.6	13	.5	15	.6	21	72	75	163	7	.01	.03	.8	t
Butter, 1 t.	34	t	t	3.8	1	0	.09	.66	1	47	157	t	t		0
TOTAL	491	30	53	18	270	3.6	113	503	1018	1644	4905	.32	.53	6.7	46

Substitutions
French Bread: any whole grain bread; optional

═══ MENU ═══

Crab Louis with Avocado
French Bread
Skim Milk

Calories: 672 per serving   Protein: 28 grams per serving

─── Crab Louis ───

2 C. shredded iceberg lettuce, chilled
1 C. shredded leaf lettuce, chilled
1 C. shredded Bibb lettuce, chilled
12 oz. canned crab meat, drained
4 tomatoes, quartered
4 hard-boiled eggs, quartered
1 avocado, peeled and quartered

Arrange the salad greens in 4 salad bowls. Add the crab meat, tomatoes, eggs, and avocado, and top with Louis Dressing (see next page).

Yields: 4 servings

¾ C. chili sauce
1 t. minced onion
¼ t. Worcestershire sauce
½ C. mayonnaise
¼ t. honey
dash of salt

Mix all the ingredients together. Refrigerate for 30 minutes. Serve over Crab Louis.

Yields: 1¼ C.

■ Serve each person 1 slice French bread with 1 t. butter (see page 31) and 1 C. skim milk.

	CALORIES	PROTEIN GMS	CARBOHYDRATES GMS	FAT GMS	CALCIUM MGS	IRON MGS	MAGNESIUM MGS	PHOSPHORUS MGS	POTASSIUM MGS	SODIUM MGS	VITAMIN A I.U.	VITAMIN B₁ MGS	VITAMIN B₂ MGS	NIACIN MGS	VITAMIN C MGS
Crab Louis with Dressing	404	17	23	30	96	3	47	235	783	1235	3960	.28	.3	4	46
Avocado, ¼	84	1	3	8	5	.3	22	21	302	2	145	.05	.1	.8	7
French Bread, 1 sl.	64	1.6	13	.5	15	.6	21	72	75	163	7	.01	.03	.8	t
Butter, 1 t.	34	t	t	3.8	1	0	.09	.66	1	47	157	t	t		0
Skim Milk, 1 C.	86	8	12	.4	302	.1	28	247	406	126	500	.09	.34	.22	2
TOTAL	672	28	51	43	419	4	118	576	1567	1573	4769	.43	.77	5.8	55

Substitutions
Avocado: optional
French Bread: any whole grain bread; optional
Skim Milk: ½ C. yogurt

MENU

Vegetable Juice Cocktail
Creamy Salmon Open Facers
Vegetables Marinade
Peach Ice Cream

Calories: 745 per serving   Protein: 33 grams per serving

Creamy Salmon Open Facers

12 oz. canned salmon, drained, skin removed, and flaked

Mix all the ingredients together, except the bread and lettuce. Arrange a lettuce leaf on each bread slice. Spoon the salmon

4 oz. cream cheese, softened
1 hard-boiled egg, chopped
⅛ C. chopped celery
¼ C. chopped cucumber
3 T. chopped onion
2 T. chopped parsley
1 T. lemon juice
1 t. horseradish
¼ t. salt
8 slices French bread (see page 31)
8 lettuce leaves

mixture equally over the lettuce leaves. Serve 2 open-faced sandwiches to each person.

Yields: 4 servings

Vegetables Marinade

⅓ C. safflower or olive oil
¼ C. cider vinegar
½ clove garlic, crushed
salt, pepper, and herbs to taste
1 C. sliced carrots
1½ C. broccoli flowerets
1 C. cauliflowerets
1 C. halved mushrooms
½ C. red onion rings
1 tomato, diced

Prepare the marinade: Blend the oil, vinegar, garlic, and seasonings in a small bowl. Set aside.

Steam the carrots, broccoli, and cauliflower until just tender. Combine them with the remaining ingredients in a large bowl and pour the marinade over. Refrigerate for several hours or overnight. Stir occasionally.

Suggestion: Use herbs such as thyme, marjoram, oregano, tarragon, parsley, and chives.

Yields: 4 servings

Peach Ice Cream

1½ C. peaches, cut up

Use the recipe for vanilla ice cream (see page 41), and just before freezing, fold in the peaches.

■ Serve each person 1 C. Vegetable Juice Cocktail (see page 20) and for dessert, ½ C. ice cream.

	CALORIES	PROTEIN GMS	CARBOHYDRATES GMS	FAT GMS	CALCIUM MGS	IRON MGS	MAGNESIUM MGS	PHOSPHORUS MGS	POTASSIUM MGS	SODIUM MGS	VITAMIN A I.U.	VITAMIN B₁ MGS	VITAMIN B₂ MGS	NIACIN MGS	VITAMIN C MGS
Vegetable Juice Cocktail	61	3	13	.45	46	3	31	62	757	544	2546	.15	.1	2	54
Creamy Salmon Open Facers	394	24	25	21	269	2.7	31	382	450	905	1224	.19	.35	7.4	9
Vegetables Marinade	139	4	12	10	82	1.4	38	100	518	28	5599	.14	.4	1.9	85
Peach Ice Cream, ½ C.	151	2	12	11	61	.2	8	61	105	45	619	.1	.09	.5	t
TOTAL	745	33	62	43	458	7.3	108	605	1830	1522	9988	.58	.94	12	148

Substitutions

Vegetable Juice Cocktail: 1 C. vegetable or tomato juice

Vegetables Marinade: 1 C. spinach, broccoli, green beans, or peas; 1 baked potato or yam

Peach Ice Cream: any ice cream; substitute blueberries or strawberries for the peaches; 1 C. skim milk or ½ C. yogurt; optional

---

MENU

Egg–Cottage Cheese Salad
Avocadoes
Whole Wheat Date Bread
Skim Milk

Calories: 525 per serving   Protein: 31 grams per serving

Egg–Cottage Cheese Salad

4 hard-boiled eggs
1⅓ C. lowfat cottage cheese
¼ t. salt
⅓ T. prepared mustard
¼ t. crushed marjoram
¼ C. chopped green pepper
⅛ C. chopped scallions
¼ C. diced carrots
1 T. chopped chives
2 T. toasted sunflower seeds
4 ripe olives, chopped
1 C. iceberg lettuce torn into bite-size pieces
1 C. Romaine lettuce torn into bite-size pieces
2 medium tomatoes, cut into wedges
¾ C. mushrooms, chopped
2 T. chopped parsley

Set aside 8 egg slices and coarsely chop all the rest of the eggs. Place the chopped egg in a medium bowl and add the remaining ingredients through the olives. Mix well.

Prepare a bed of lettuce for each serving. Divide the cottage cheese mixture into 4 portions and place on the lettuce. Surround with the tomato wedges and mushrooms. Press in the egg slices and sprinkle the tops with parsley.

Yields: 4 servings

Whole Wheat Date Bread

2½ C. whole wheat flour
1½ t. baking powder
1 t. baking soda
1 t. salt
¼ C. safflower oil
1½ C. buttermilk
¼ C. blackstrap molasses
¼ C. honey
¾ C. chopped dates

Preheat oven to 350° F.

Sift the dry ingredients together. Combine the liquid ingredients and add to the flour mixture. Blend. Fold in the dates. Put into a 9″ × 5″ loaf pan and let stand for 20 minutes. Bake 45–50 minutes or until a toothpick inserted in the center comes out clean.

Yields: 16 slices

■ Serve each person ¼ avocado, 1 slice Whole Wheat Date Bread, and 1 C. skim milk.

	CALORIES	PROTEIN GMS	CARBOHYDRATES GMS	FAT GMS	CALCIUM MGS	IRON MGS	MAGNESIUM MGS	PHOSPHORUS MGS	POTASSIUM MGS	SODIUM MGS	VITAMIN A I.U.	VITAMIN B₁ MGS	VITAMIN B₂ MGS	NIACIN MGS	VITAMIN C MGS
Egg–Cottage Cheese Salad	215	19	11	11	117	2.5	29	285	485	578	2692	.24	.35	1.4	31
Avocado, ¼	84	1	3	8	5	.3	22	21	302	2	145	.05	.1	.8	7
Whole Wheat Date Bread, 1 sl.	140	3	23	4	75	2.5	56	104	451	168	12	.13	.08	1.2	t
Skim Milk, 1 C.	86	8	12	.4	302	.1	28	247	406	126	500	.09	.34	.22	2
TOTAL	525	31	49	23	499	5.4	135	657	1644	874	3349	.5	.87	3.6	40

Substitutions
Avocado: optional
Whole Wheat Date Bread: can be made with raisins
Skim Milk: ½ C. yogurt; optional

Vegetable Juice Cocktail
Egg Salad on Lettuce
Whole Wheat Dinner Rolls
Gingerbread with Orange Sauce

Calories: 488 per serving   Protein: 16 grams per serving

Egg Salad on Lettuce

4 hard-boiled eggs
⅔ C. chopped celery
2 T. chopped green pepper
2 T. chopped onion
3 T. mayonnaise
½ t. Worcestershire sauce
⅔ T. cider vinegar
dash of pepper
¼ t. salt
4 lettuce leaves

Chop the eggs into large pieces. Add all the ingredients except the lettuce and mix well. Serve 4 equal portions on top of lettuce leaves.

Yields: 4 servings

Gingerbread

½ C. honey
½ C. molasses
6 T. melted butter
½ C. firm lowfat yogurt
1 egg
1¾ C. whole wheat pastry flour
2 t. baking soda
2 t. ground cinnamon
1–2 t. ground ginger
¼ t. ground cloves
½ t. salt

Preheat oven to 350° F.

Beat the honey and molasses together for a few minutes with an electric mixer. Add the butter.

Beat the yogurt and egg together. Add to the honey mixture and blend.

Sift the dry ingredients. Add to the liquid mixture and stir just enough to blend. Pour into a 9″ cake pan. Bake for 30–35 minutes or until a toothpick inserted in the center comes out clean.

Yields: 16 pieces

Orange Sauce

3 T. honey
2 T. cornstarch
2 C. water
3 T. butter
6 T. fresh orange juice
1 t. grated orange rind
¼ t. salt

Combine the honey, cornstarch, and water in a pan over medium heat. Stir constantly until the sauce thickens. Remove from the heat and stir in the butter, orange juice, rind, and salt. Glaze the gingerbread with approximately 2 T. Orange Sauce per piece.

■ Serve each person 1 C. Vegetable Juice Cocktail (see page 20) and 1 Whole Wheat Dinner Roll with 1 t. butter (see page 16).

	CALORIES	PROTEIN GMS	CARBOHYDRATES GMS	FAT GMS	CALCIUM MGS	IRON MGS	MAGNESIUM MGS	PHOSPHORUS MGS	POTASSIUM MGS	SODIUM MGS	VITAMIN A I.U.	VITAMIN B₁ MGS	VITAMIN B₂ MGS	NIACIN MGS	VITAMIN C MGS
Vegetable Juice Cocktail	61	3	13	.45	46	3	31	62	757	544	2546	.15	.1	2	54
Egg Salad on Lettuce	162	7	4	14	46	1.5	13	110	211	280	742	.09	.17	.2	8
Whole Wheat Dinner Roll, 1	86	4	18	1.7	29	.75	25	94	103	100	56	.13	.05	1	t
Butter, 1 t.	34	t	t	3.8	1	0	.09	.66	1	47	157	t	t		0
Gingerbread with Orange Sauce, 1 pc.	145	2	17	7	88	1.7	35	147	352	197	313	.05	.06	.5	3
TOTAL	488	16	52	27	210	7	104	414	1424	1168	3814	.42	.38	3.7	65

Substitutions
Vegetable Juice Cocktail: 1 C. vegetable or tomato juice
Whole Wheat Dinner Roll: any whole grain bread
Gingerbread with Orange Sauce: ½ C. yogurt or 1 C. skim milk

MENU

French Dip Sandwiches
Mushroom Buffet Casserole
Skim Milk

Calories: 630 per serving   Protein: 27 grams per serving

French Dip Sandwiches

1 C. hot water
3 beef bouillon cubes
3 T. melted butter
¼ C. steak sauce (tomato type)

In a saucepan, combine the water, bouillon cubes, butter, steak sauce, Worcestershire sauce, and salt. Heat thoroughly.

Toast the bread. Dip the pieces in the sauce and place on a

2 t. Worcestershire sauce
dash of salt
8 slices French bread (see page 31)
8 oz. cooked, sliced beef rump roast, heated

serving plate. Top 4 slices of the bread with a hot slice of beef. Add a second slice of bread to make a sandwich. Spoon the remaining sauce over the sandwiches.

Yields: 4 servings

Mushroom Buffet Casserole

⅓ C. brown rice
½ t. salt
⅓ C. boiling water
1 C. sliced fresh mushrooms
1 C. chopped celery
½ C. chopped onion
¼ C. chopped green pepper
2 T. butter
½ C. condensed cream of mushroom soup
¼ C. chopped pimiento
1 T. soy sauce (optional)

Preheat oven to 350° F.

Place the rice and salt in a 2½-quart casserole dish. Add the boiling water and set aside.

Sauté the mushrooms, celery, onion, and green pepper in the butter.

Blend the mushroom soup with the remaining ingredients. Add the soup and sautéed vegetables to the rice in the casserole; mix well. Cover and bake for 1 hour.

Suggestion: Soy sauce may be added to the casserole or may be put on later by each individual.

Yields: 4 servings

■ Serve each person 1 C. skim milk.

	CALORIES	PROTEIN GMS	CARBOHYDRATES GMS	FAT GMS	CALCIUM MGS	IRON MGS	MAGNESIUM MGS	PHOSPHORUS MGS	POTASSIUM MGS	SODIUM MGS	VITAMIN A I.U.	VITAMIN B₁ MGS	VITAMIN B₂ MGS	NIACIN MGS	VITAMIN C MGS
French Dip Sandwich	389	16	27	22	43	2.2	51	253	440	1203	600	.17	.2	4.5	2
Mushroom Buffet Casserole	155	3	20	7	37	.9	26	86	286	752	505	.1	.15	1	26
Skim Milk, 1 C.	86	8	12	.4	302	.1	28	247	406	126	500	.09	.34	.22	2
TOTAL	630	27	59	29	382	3.2	105	586	1132	2081	1605	.36	.69	5.7	30

Substitutions
French Bread: any whole grain bread

Grilled Cheese Sandwiches
Ripe Tomato Rice Soup
Skim Milk
Peaches

Calories: 592 per serving   Protein: 29 grams per serving

_____ **Grilled Cheese Sandwiches** _____

4 T. butter
8 slices whole wheat or
  pumpernickel bread
4 oz. slices Swiss or brick cheese

Spread the butter on the outside of the slices of bread. Place the cheese inside, between 2 slices, and put the sandwiches in a frying pan. Cover and cook on low heat until the cheese has melted and bread is golden brown.

Yields: 4 sandwiches

_____ **Ripe Tomato Rice Soup** _____

1½ C. water
3 T. brown rice
4 tomatoes, peeled and chopped
1 stalk celery, sliced
3 scallions, chopped
2 C. skim milk
1 T. whole wheat flour
1 T. chopped parsley
1 t. butter

Boil the water, add the rice and cook, covered, on medium heat for about 35 minutes. Add the vegetables and milk. Cook for another 10 minutes.

In a bowl, blend the flour with a little extra water. Add to the soup, stirring constantly. Add the parsley and any other seasonings to taste. Cook for 3 minutes. Add the butter and serve.

Yields: 4 servings

■ Serve each person 1 C. skim milk and for dessert, 1 peach.

	CALORIES	PROTEIN GMS	CARBOHYDRATES GMS	FAT GMS	CALCIUM MGS	IRON MGS	MAGNESIUM MGS	PHOSPHORUS MGS	POTASSIUM MGS	SODIUM MGS	VITAMIN A I.U.	VITAMIN B₁ MGS	VITAMIN B₂ MGS	NIACIN MGS	VITAMIN C MGS
Grilled Cheese Sandwich	319	13	23	21	319	1	46	277	158	452	510	.08	.14	1.2	t
Ripe Tomato Rice Soup	149	7	21	4	187	1.2	48	225	659	112	2055	.2	.24	1.9	40
Skim Milk, 1 C.	86	8	12	.4	302	.1	28	247	406	126	500	.09	.34	.22	2
Peach, 1	38	.6	10	.1	9	.5	12	19	202	1	1330	.02	.05	1	7
TOTAL	592	29	66	26	817	2.8	134	768	1425	691	4395	.39	.77	4.3	49

Substitutions
Peach: 1 C. boysenberries or strawberries; 1 guava

MENU

Vegetable Juice Cocktail
Mulligatawny Soup
Limpa Bread
Skim Milk

Calories: 540 per serving   Protein: 20 grams per serving

Mulligatawny Soup

½ C. chopped onion
¾ C. sliced carrots
¾ C. chopped celery
¼ C. butter
2 T. whole wheat flour
2 t. curry powder
4 C. chicken stock
¼ C. brown rice
½ C. diced cooked chicken
¼ C. diced apple
1 t. salt
¼ t. pepper
½ C. half and half

Lightly sauté the onion, carrot, and celery in the butter. Stir in the flour and curry powder, then cook 3 minutes. Pour in the chicken stock, add the rice, and simmer 30 minutes. Add the chicken, apple, salt, and pepper. Simmer for 15 minutes. Heat the half and half in a small pan over low heat and add it to the soup mixture. Stir and serve.

Yields: 4 servings

■ Serve each person 1 C. Vegetable Juice Cocktail (see page 20), 1 slice Limpa Bread with 1 t. butter (see page 150), and 1 C. skim milk.

	CALORIES	PROTEIN GMS	CARBOHYDRATES GMS	FAT GMS	CALCIUM MGS	IRON MGS	MAGNESIUM MGS	PHOSPHORUS MGS	POTASSIUM MGS	SODIUM MGS	VITAMIN A I.U.	VITAMIN B₁ MGS	VITAMIN B₂ MGS	NIACIN MGS	VITAMIN C MGS
Vegetable Juice Cocktail	61	3	13	.45	46	3	31	62	757	544	2546	.15	.1	2	54
Mulligatawny Soup	260	12	17	16	83	2	32	201	351	784	3661	.09	.1	.8	8
Limpa Bread, 1 sl.	99	3	18	2	167	1.2	30	90	178	94	22	.12	.04	.88	t
Butter, 1 t.	34	t	t	3.8	1	0	.09	.66	1	47	157	t	t		0
Skim Milk, 1 C.	86	8	12	.4	302	.1	28	247	406	126	500	.09	.34	.22	2
TOTAL	540	26	60	23	599	6.3	121	601	1693	1595	6886	.45	.58	3.9	64

Substitutions
Vegetable Juice Cocktail: 1 C. vegetable or tomato juice
Limpa Bread: whole wheat bread
Skim Milk: ½ C. yogurt

MENU

Norwegian Sardine Salad
Minestrone Soup
Apple Juice Soda

Calories: 684 per serving   Protein: 25 grams per serving

Norwegian Sardine Salad

4 oz. sardines
3 potatoes, cooked and diced
½ C. chopped celery
½ C. sliced cucumber
1 hard-boiled egg, diced
1 T. minced parsley
½ T. minced chives
3 T. sour cream
1½ T. lemon juice
⅛ T. dry mustard
dash of salt and pepper
8 leaves lettuce

Drain the sardines and reserve the oil. Set aside.

Combine the potatoes, celery, cucumber, egg, parsley, and chives in a large bowl.

In a small bowl, thoroughly mix the sardines, sardine oil, sour cream, lemon juice, mustard, salt, and pepper. Add the sauce to the potato mixture and mix well. Place in a salad bowl lined with lettuce.

Yields: 4 servings

1 clove garlic, crushed
¾ C. chopped onion
3 T. olive oil
¾ C. diced carrots
¾ C. minced celery
1 t. salt
pepper to taste
1 t. crushed oregano
1 t. crushed basil
3½ C. water
2 C. tomato purée
¾ C. chopped green pepper
1 C. cooked garbanzo beans
½ C. dry macaroni noodles
¼ C. chopped parsley
4 T. grated Parmesan cheese

Sauté the garlic and onion in the oil. Add the carrots, celery, and seasonings. Cook over low heat for 7 minutes. Add the water, tomato purée, green pepper, and beans. Simmer covered for 15 minutes. Add the macaroni and boil gently until tender. Serve topped with the parsley and Parmesan.

Yields: 4 servings

■ Serve each person 1 C. Apple Juice Soda (½ C. apple juice, or other fruit juice, mixed with ½ C. club soda or sparkling mineral water).

	CALORIES	PROTEIN GMS	CARBOHYDRATES GMS	FAT GMS	CALCIUM MGS	IRON MGS	MAGNESIUM MGS	PHOSPHORUS MGS	POTASSIUM MGS	SODIUM MGS	VITAMIN A I.U.	VITAMIN B₁ MGS	VITAMIN B₂ MGS	NIACIN MGS	VITAMIN C MGS
Norwegian Sardine Salad	285	12	26	13	167	2	46	262	878	279	498	.15	.16	3.6	31
Minestrone Soup	340	13	43	14	175	5	46	255	989	1136	5233	.3	.28	3.5	75
Apple Juice Soda, 1 C.	59	.1	15	t	8	.08	5	11	125	1		.01	.03	.1	1
TOTAL	684	25	84	27	350	7	97	528	1992	1416	5731	.46	.47	7.2	107

Oriental Tuna Salad
Winter Squash with Brown Sugar
Whole Wheat Dinner Rolls
Skim Milk
Fresh Fruit Salad

Calories: 689 per serving   Protein: 33 grams per serving

Oriental Tuna Salad

7 oz. water-packed tuna
24 water chestnuts, sliced
1 C. sliced mushrooms
2 C. bean sprouts
4 ripe olives, chopped
1 C. green seedless grapes
¼ dill pickle, chopped
½ avocado
4 T. sour cream
2 T. mayonnaise
1 T. pickle juice
½ t. salt
pepper to taste
¼ t. paprika

Drain the tuna and flake it into a large bowl. Add the water chestnuts, mushrooms, bean sprouts, olives, grapes, and pickle.

Peel and slice the avocado and mix it in gently. Chill.

In a separate bowl, combine the sour cream, mayonnaise, and other seasonings. Combine with the tuna mixture, blending well.

Yields: 4 servings

Winter Squash with Brown Sugar

1 winter squash
¼ C. brown sugar

Preheat oven to 350° F.

Quarter and seed the squash. Bake with one cut side down in a shallow pan with ½" water for 35–40 minutes. Turn right side up and sprinkle with the sugar. Bake 20 minutes longer. Serve hot.

Yields: 4 servings

Fresh Fruit Salad

1 C. raspberries, fresh or frozen
2 bananas
1 C. pineapple chunks

Thaw the raspberries if they are frozen.

Slice the bananas and combine them with the pineapple and a little pineapple juice. Divide into 4 portions and top each with ¼ C. raspberries. Chill.

Yields: 4 servings

■ Serve each person 1 Whole Wheat Dinner Roll (see page 16) with 1 t. butter, and 1 C. skim milk.

	CALORIES	PROTEIN GMS	CARBOHYDRATES GMS	FAT GMS	CALCIUM MGS	IRON MGS	MAGNESIUM MGS	PHOSPHORUS MGS	POTASSIUM MGS	SODIUM MGS	VITAMIN A I.U.	VITAMIN B₁ MGS	VITAMIN B₂ MGS	NIACIN MGS	VITAMIN C MGS
Oriental Tuna Salad	289	19	21	16	58	2.5	22	208	775	928	302	.22	.35	8	18
Winter Squash with Brown Sugar	94	1	21	.2	26	.9	23	27	284	5	2153	.03	.07	.4	7
Whole Wheat Dinner Roll, 1	86	4	18	1.7	29	.75	25	94	103	100	56	.13	.05	1	t
Butter, 1 t.	34	t	t	3.8	1	0	.09	.66	1	47	157	t	t		0
Skim Milk, 1 C.	86	8	12	.4	302	.1	28	247	406	126	500	.09	.34	.22	2
Fresh Fruit Salad	100	1	26	.4	19	.95	36	29	383	2	188	.09	.08	.75	22
TOTAL	689	33	98	23	435	5.3	134	606	1952	1208	3356	.56	.88	10	49

Substitutions
Winter Squash: 1 C. asparagus, broccoli, carrots, or spinach; 1 sweet potato
Whole Wheat Dinner Roll: any whole wheat bread
Skim Milk: ½ C. yogurt
Fresh Fruit Salad: 1 banana, ½ mango, or ½ C. raspberries; optional

MENU

Potato Soup Special
Crisp Cucumber Salad
Whole Wheat Dinner Rolls
Peach

Calories: 496 per serving   Protein: 13 grams per serving

Potato Soup Special

⅓ C. finely chopped leeks
⅔ C. diced onion
1 T. butter

Sauté the leeks and onions in the butter. Add to the chicken stock in a large saucepan.

2 C. chicken bouillon or stock
1 potato
1 C. skim milk
1 C. cream
½ t. salt
cayenne pepper to taste
2 T. chopped parsley
2 slices bacon, fried and
    crumbled (optional)

Cut up the potato (with skin) and boil for 20 minutes. Place the cooked potato, milk, cream, salt, and cayenne in a blender. Blend and add to the chicken stock. Heat, but don't boil. Serve in warm bowls; sprinkle with the parsley, and bacon if desired.

Yields: 4 servings

Crisp Cucumber Salad

2 cucumbers
¼ C. cider vinegar
1 T. honey
2 T. lemon juice
8 lettuce leaves
salt, pepper, and dill seed
    (optional) to taste
1 tomato, cut in wedges

Cut the cucumbers into thin slices. Mix the vinegar, honey, and lemon juice. Pour the dressing over the sliced cucumbers. Cover and marinate in the refrigerator for several hours.

Arrange the lettuce leaves in 4 individual salad bowls and top with the cucumbers. Sprinkle with salt and pepper and dill seed if desired. Garnish with the tomato wedges.

Yields: 4 servings

■ Serve each person 1 Whole Wheat Dinner Roll (see page 16) with 1 t. butter, and 1 peach for dessert.

	CALORIES	PROTEIN GMS	CARBOHYDRATES GMS	FAT GMS	CALCIUM MGS	IRON MGS	MAGNESIUM MGS	PHOSPHORUS MGS	POTASSIUM MGS	SODIUM MGS	VITAMIN A I.U.	VITAMIN B₁ MGS	VITAMIN B₂ MGS	NIACIN MGS	VITAMIN C MGS
Potato Soup Special	291	7	19	22	150	1.5	39	181	472	714	1094	.11	.2	1	18
Crisp Cucumber Salad	47	1	10	.2	38	1	12	33	276	7	993	.05	.05	.6	23
Whole Wheat Dinner Roll, 1	86	4	18	1.7	29	.75	25	94	103	100	56	.13	.05	1	t
Butter, 1 t.	34	t	t	3.8	1	0	.09	.66	1	47	157	t	t		0
Peach, 1	38	.6	10	.1	9	.5	12	19	202	1	1330	.02	.05	1	7
TOTAL	496	13	57	28	227	3.8	88	328	1054	869	3630	.31	.35	3.6	48

Substitutions
Crisp Cucumber Salad: tossed salad or vegetable of choice
Whole Wheat Dinner Roll: any whole wheat bread
Peach: 1 C. strawberries or boysenberries

MENU

Vegetable Juice Cocktail
Reuben Sandwiches
Asparagus Spears
Skim Milk

Calories: 740 per serving   Protein: 36 grams per serving

Reuben Sandwich

8 slices pumpernickel bread
4 T. Thousand Island Dressing
  (see page 48)
4 oz. Swiss cheese
1 C. sauerkraut
8 oz. cooked corned beef
2 T. butter

Spread 4 slices of bread with 1 T. dressing each. Arrange 1 oz. cheese, 2 oz. corned beef, and ¼ C. sauerkraut on each of the 4 slices. Top with the remaining slices of bread. Butter the outside of the sandwiches and grill until cheese is melted and bread is toasted.

Yields: 4 sandwiches

■ Serve each person 1 C. Vegetable Juice Cocktail (see page 20), 4 cooked asparagus spears, and 1 C. skim milk.

	CALORIES	PROTEIN GMS	CARBOHYDRATES GMS	FAT GMS	CALCIUM MGS	IRON MGS	MAGNESIUM MGS	PHOSPHORUS MGS	POTASSIUM MGS	SODIUM MGS	VITAMIN A I.U.	VITAMIN B₁ MGS	VITAMIN B₂ MGS	NIACIN MGS	VITAMIN C MGS
Vegetable Juice Cocktail	61	3	13	.45	46	3	31	62	757	544	2546	.15	.1	2	54
Reuben Sandwich	573	23	38	37	356	4	56	402	457	1796	455	.11	.25	1.9	8
Asparagus Spears, 4	20	2	4	.2	21	.6	21	50	183	1	900	.16	.18	1.4	26
Skim Milk, 1 C.	86	8	12	.4	302	.1	28	247	406	126	500	.09	.34	.22	2
TOTAL	740	36	67	38	725	7.7	136	761	1803	2467	4401	.51	.87	5.4	90

Substitutions
Vegetable Juice Cocktail: 1 C. vegetable or tomato juice
Asparagus Spears: 1 C. cooked summer squash, kale, or
  collards; 1 C. mushrooms

Split Pea Soup
Limpa Bread
Orange Sherbert

Calories: 803 per serving   Protein: 34 grams per serving

Split Pea Soup

1⅓ C. dry split peas
5½ C. water
1 lb. spareribs, cut in half
crosswise
⅔ C. chopped celery
⅔ C. diced carrots
⅓ C. chopped scallions
1 bay leaf
½ t. red pepper sauce
1½ t. salt
¼ t. pepper

Heat the peas and water to boiling. Boil gently for 2 minutes. Remove from the heat; cover, and let stand for 1 hour.

Cut the ribs into serving pieces. In a large skillet, brown the ribs, turning occasionally, over medium-high heat. Add the ribs and remaining ingredients to the peas. Heat to boiling. Reduce heat, cover, and simmer until ribs are tender, about 2½–3 hours.

Suggestion: Substitute sliced frankfurters for the ribs, adding them to the soup 10 minutes before serving.

Yields: 4 servings

Limpa Bread

1 T. dry yeast
1¼ C. warm water
3 T. blackstrap molasses
2 T. honey
1 t. salt
½ T. anise seeds
3 T. melted butter
2 C. rye flour
2 C. whole wheat flour
½ egg, slightly beaten

Dissolve the yeast in the warm water; set in a warm place.

In a large bowl mix together the molasses, honey, salt, anise seeds, and butter. Add the yeast mixture. Add the rye flour and beat 5 minutes. Mix in enough whole wheat flour to make the dough easy to handle. Knead 10 minutes. Shape into a round, slightly flattened loaf. Place on a greased baking sheet. Brush the loaf with the egg. Let the loaf rise in a warm place until almost double in size, about 1 hour. Bake in a preheated 350° F. oven until the crust is brown, about 40 minutes.

Yields: 24 slices

Orange Sherbert

1½ C. orange juice
¼ C. honey
2 t. unflavored gelatin
½ C. cold water
1 C. evaporated milk, chilled
1½ T. lemon juice
1 T. grated orange rind

Heat the juice and honey together and simmer for 5 minutes. Soak the gelatin in the water until it is dissolved. Add the gelatin to the juice; stir and cool. Freeze to a soft mush.

Beat the evaporated milk until it is stiff. Add the juice mixture, lemon juice, and orange rind. Beat until velvety. Freeze to a firm texture.

Yields: 4 servings

■ Serve each person 1 slice Limpa Bread with 1 t. butter.

	CALORIES	PROTEIN GMS	CARBOHYDRATES GMS	FAT GMS	CALCIUM MGS	IRON MGS	MAGNESIUM MGS	PHOSPHORUS MGS	POTASSIUM MGS	SODIUM MGS	VITAMIN A I.U.	VITAMIN B₁ MGS	VITAMIN B₂ MGS	NIACIN MGS	VITAMIN C MGS
Split Pea Soup	488	26	45	23	50	5	54	303	893	361	2937	.8	.3	4.5	8
Limpa Bread, 1 sl.	99	3	18	2	167	1.2	30	90	178	94	22	.12	.04	.9	t
Butter, 1 t.	34	t	t	3.8	1	0	.09	.66	1	47	157	t	t		0
Orange Sherbert	182	5	29	5	172	.35	28	140	334	68	278	.09	.25	.5	35
TOTAL	803	34	92	34	390	6.6	112	534	1406	570	3394	1	.6	5.9	43

Substitutions
Limpa Bread: any whole grain bread
Orange Sherbert: 1 C. skim milk or ½ C. yogurt, plus fruit
   of choice

MENU

Squash Soup
Cornbread and Cheddar Cheese
Honeydew Melon

Calories: 586 per serving   Protein: 24 grams per serving

Squash Soup

3 C. cubed summer (or winter)
   squash
3 slices bacon (optional)
¼ C. chopped onion
1 clove garlic, crushed
1 T. safflower oil
2 C. canned tomatoes
1½ C. vegetable stock
1 C. beef stock or bouillon
¼ C. chopped parsley
1 bay leaf
¼ t. crushed basil
⅛ t. crushed thyme

Prepare the squash: wash the skin, remove the seeds, and cut into ½" cubes. Set aside. If winter squash is used, remove peel.

Fry the bacon and drain it.

Sauté the onion and garlic in the oil until tender. Stir in the tomatoes, stocks, herbs, squash, and sufficient water to make a soupy consistency. Simmer 20–25 minutes. Remove the bay leaf and add the crumbled bacon.

Yields: 4 servings

1 egg
¼ C. honey
¼ C. butter
1 C. buttermilk
1 C. cornmeal
1 C. whole wheat flour
½ t. salt
2 t. baking powder
½ t. baking soda

Preheat oven to 425° F.

In one bowl, beat together the egg, honey, butter, and buttermilk. In another bowl, mix together the dry ingredients. Blend all ingredients and mix well. Pour into an 8"-square cake pan and bake 20–25 minutes or until golden brown.

Yields: 12 pieces

■ Serve each person 1 piece of cornbread, natural cheddar cheese, and for dessert, a 2"-wide slice of honeydew melon.

	CALORIES	PROTEIN GMS	CARBOHYDRATES GMS	FAT GMS	CALCIUM MGS	IRON MGS	MAGNESIUM MGS	PHOSPHORUS MGS	POTASSIUM MGS	SODIUM MGS	VITAMIN A I.U.	VITAMIN B₁ MGS	VITAMIN B₂ MGS	NIACIN MGS	VITAMIN C MGS
Squash Soup	175	6	12	12	45	1.5	32	90	622	340	1521	.25	.4	2.5	50
Cornbread, 1 pc.	138	3	21	5	35	.7	35	108	126	162	301	.13	.07	.8	t
Cheddar Cheese, 2 oz.	224	14	.7	19	422	.4	16	290	56	352	600	.02	.04	.05	0
Honeydew Melon	49	1	12	.5	21	.6	7	24	377	18	60	.06	.05	.9	55
TOTAL	586	24	46	37	523	3.2	90	512	1181	872	2482	.46	.56	4.3	85

Substitutions
Cornbread: any whole grain bread
Cheddar Cheese: 1 C. skim milk or ½ C. yogurt
Honeydew Melon: 1 C. raspberries, strawberries, or boysenberries; 1 guava or peach; ½ mango

MENU

Tuna Salad Niçoise
French Bread
Skim Milk
Chocolate Chip Cookies

Calories: 537 per serving   Protein: 29 grams per serving

Tuna Salad Niçoise

1 C. green beans
2 tomatoes, cut into wedges
½ C. diced cucumber
½ C. sliced mushrooms
¼ t. salt
¼ t. pepper
½ T. cider vinegar
1 T. safflower oil
1 T. chopped parsley
1 T. chopped chives
7 oz. water-packed tuna,
    drained
1 C. endive
4 ripe olives
2 anchovy filets

Cook the beans in ½" boiling water, or steam them, until tender. Chill.

In a bowl, place the tomato wedges, cucumber, mushrooms, and beans. In a separate bowl, whisk the salt, pepper, vinegar, oil, and herbs together. Pour the dressing over the vegetables and toss. Break the tuna into chunks and place them on top. Divide into 4 portions and serve each on a bed of endive. Garnish each with ½ anchovy and 1 olive.

Yields: 4 servings

Chocolate Chip Cookies

1 C. butter
1 C. honey
2 eggs
1 t. vanilla extract
2¼ C. whole wheat pastry flour
1¼ t. baking soda
1 t. salt
12 oz. chocolate chips
1 C. chopped walnuts

Preheat oven to 350° F.

Cream the butter and honey together. Add the eggs and vanilla and beat well.

Mix together the dry ingredients. Add them to the liquid mixture and blend. Fold in the chocolate chips and nuts. Drop by the teaspoonful on a baking sheet and bake 10–12 minutes. Allow cookies to sit on the baking sheet a few minutes before removing.

Yields: about 5 dozen

■ Serve each person 1 slice French bread with 1 t. butter (see page 31), 1 C. skim milk, and 2 chocolate chip cookies.

	CALORIES	PROTEIN GMS	CARBOHYDRATES GMS	FAT GMS	CALCIUM MGS	IRON MGS	MAGNESIUM MGS	PHOSPHORUS MGS	POTASSIUM MGS	SODIUM MGS	VITAMIN A I.U.	VITAMIN B_1 MGS	VITAMIN B_2 MGS	NIACIN MGS	VITAMIN C MGS
Tuna Salad Niçoise	155	17	7	7	67	2	25	155	499	650	1524	.14	.2	8	29
French Bread, 1 sl.	64	1.6	13	.5	15	.6	21	72	75	163	7	.01	.03	.8	t
Butter, 1 t.	34	t	t	3.8	1	0	.09	.66	1	47	157	t	t		0
Skim Milk, 1 C.	86	8	12	.4	302	.1	28	247	406	126	500	.09	.34	.22	2
Chocolate Chip Cookies, 2	198	2.8	22	14	16	1	14	82	126	150	390	.06	.06	.6	t
TOTAL	537	29	54	26	401	3.7	88	557	1107	1136	2578	.3	.63	9.6	31

Substitutions
French Bread: any whole grain bread; optional
Chocolate Chip Cookies: optional

MENU

Vegetable-Beef Soup
French Bread
Tangy Tossed Green Salad

Calories: 613 per serving   Protein: 26 grams per serving

Vegetable-Beef Soup

½ C. chopped celery
½ C. chopped green pepper
1 T. butter
4 oz. lean ground beef
1 C. tomato juice
½ C. diced potato, unpeeled
1 large carrot, diced
2 C. skim milk
½ C. instant skim milk powder
¼ C. whole wheat flour
¼ t. salt

Sauté the celery and green pepper in the butter. Then add the ground beef, stirring constantly until brown. Add the tomato juice, potato, and carrot. Simmer, covered, until the vegetables are tender.

In a bowl, combine the skim milk and milk powder; add the flour and salt gradually. Blend well. Add to the soup, stirring constantly, and heat until thickened.

Yields: 4 servings

Tangy Tossed Green Salad

4 C. iceberg lettuce torn into
  bite-size pieces
1 C. endive torn into bite-size
  pieces
1 banana, sliced
1 orange, sectioned
½ C. sliced green pepper
¼ C. sliced red onion
4 oz. diced Monterey Jack
  cheese

Toss all the salad ingredients together, except the cheese.

Dressing

3 T. safflower oil
1 T. cider vinegar
1 T. lemon juice
½ t. honey
½ t. dry mustard

Shake together the dressing ingredients in a jar, blending well. Divide the salad into 4 portions, add the dressing, and top with the cheese.

Yields: 4 servings

■ Serve each person 1 slice of French bread (see page 31) with 1 t. butter.

	CALORIES	PROTEIN GMS	CARBOHYDRATES GMS	FAT GMS	CALCIUM MGS	IRON MGS	MAGNESIUM MGS	PHOSPHORUS MGS	POTASSIUM MGS	SODIUM MGS	VITAMIN A I.U.	VITAMIN B₁ MGS	VITAMIN B₂ MGS	NIACIN MGS	VITAMIN C MGS
Vegetable-Beef Soup	241	15	23	7	236	1.7	59	342	888	466	3645	.17	.25	2.6	31
French Bread, 1 sl.	64	1.6	13	.5	15	.6	21	72	75	163	7	.01	.03	.8	t
Butter, 1 t.	34	t	t	3.8	1	0	.09	.66	1	47	157	t	t		0
Tangy Tossed Green Salad	172	9	17	9	258	1	35	172	432	164	111	.16	.2	.9	40
Tangy Dressing	102	t	2	10	.3	.03	.1	.8	10	.08			.001	.008	2
TOTAL	613	26	55	30	510	3.3	115	588	1406	840	4920	.34	.48	4.3	73

Substitutions
French Bread: any whole grain bread
Tangy Tossed Green Salad: 1 C. corn, asparagus, or okra; ½
  C. peas; 1 baked potato; plus fruit of choice

Vegetable-Flower Soup
Green Peas
Skim Milk
Chocolate Brownies

Calories: 398 per serving   Protein: 23 grams per serving

Vegetable-Flower Soup

4 C. chicken stock
¼ C. bean sprouts
¼ C. sliced mushrooms
¼ C. chopped onions
8 water chestnuts, sliced
¼ C. bamboo shoots
1½ pimiento pods, chopped
3 eggs
2 T. soy sauce

Bring the stock to a boil, then add the vegetables. Lower the heat and simmer 5–10 minutes.

Beat the eggs. Increase the heat and pour the eggs into the stock. The egg mixture will set like a flower. Heat for 5 minutes, stirring constantly, then season with the soy sauce.

Yields: 4 servings

Chocolate Brownies

½ C. whole wheat pastry flour
½ C. butter, softened
2½ oz. unsweetened baking
   chocolate
2 eggs
½ C. honey
1 t. vanilla extract
½ C. chopped walnuts

Preheat oven to 350° F.

Melt the butter and chocolate together. Cool slightly. Beat the eggs; add the honey and vanilla and beat for several minutes. Add the chocolate mixture. Add the flour and blend until well mixed. Fold in the nuts. Spread mixture in a greased 8″-square cake pan and bake 20–25 minutes or until a toothpick inserted in the center comes out clean. Cool.

Yields: 16 squares

■ Serve each person 1 C. skim milk, ½ C. green peas, and 1 chocolate brownie for dessert.

	CALORIES	PROTEIN GMS	CARBOHYDRATES GMS	FAT GMS	CALCIUM MGS	IRON MGS	MAGNESIUM MGS	PHOSPHORUS MGS	POTASSIUM MGS	SODIUM MGS	VITAMIN A I.U.	VITAMIN B_1 MGS	VITAMIN B_2 MGS	NIACIN MGS	VITAMIN C MGS
Vegetable Flower Soup	106	9	8	5.3	45	3	7	177	232	1427	685	.08	.19	.7	15
Green Peas, ½ C.	57	4	9	.3	18	1.4	25	79	157	1	430	.22	.09	1.9	16
Skim Milk, 1 C.	86	8	12	.4	302	.1	28	247	406	126	500	.09	.34	.22	2
Chocolate Brownie, 1	158	2	14	12	15	.5	18	9	114	78	305	.06	.05	.2	t
TOTAL	407	23	43	17	380	5	78	512	909	1632	1920	.45	.67	3	33

Substitutions

Green Peas: 1 C. tomato or vegetable juice or Vegetable Juice
   Cocktail (see page 20)
Skim Milk: ½ C. yogurt or ice cream, or 1 oz. natural cheese

BREAKFASTS

Banana Bread
Georgia Shake

Calories: 282 per serving   Protein: 8 grams per serving

────────────────────────── **Banana Bread** ──────────────────────────

2 C. whole wheat flour
1 t. salt
1 t. baking soda
1 t. baking powder
6 T. butter
½ C. honey
1½ C. mashed bananas
   (approximately 3)
2 eggs
½ C. buttermilk
½ C. chopped walnuts

Preheat oven to 325° F.

Sift together the dry ingredients in a large bowl.

Cream together the butter and honey. Blend in the bananas and eggs. Add to the dry mixture. Add the buttermilk, blending well but only until combined. Fold in the nuts. Pour into a 9″ × 5″ greased loaf pan. Bake 50–55 minutes or until done.

Yields: 18 slices

■ Serve each person 1 t. butter with 1 slice of bread and a Georgia Shake (see page 77).

	CALORIES	PROTEIN GMS	CARBOHYDRATES GMS	FAT GMS	CALCIUM MGS	IRON MGS	MAGNESIUM MGS	PHOSPHORUS MGS	POTASSIUM MGS	SODIUM MGS	VITAMIN A I.U.	VITAMIN B₁ MGS	VITAMIN B₂ MGS	NIACIN MGS	VITAMIN C MGS
Banana Bread, 1 sl.	156	3	25	7	23	.8	29	82	176	180	222	.1	.07	.8	3
Butter, 1 t.	34	t	t	3.8	1	0	.09	.66	1	47	157	t	t		0
Georgia Shake	92	5	18	.5	164	.7	25	141	368	64	938	.07	.2	.9	27
TOTAL	282	8	43	11	188	1.5	54	107	545	291	1317	.17	.27	1.7	30

MENU

Tomato Juice
Blueberry Pancakes with Butter and Syrup
Skim Milk

Calories: 714 per serving   Protein: 21 grams per serving

Blueberry Pancakes

⅓ C. brown rice
⅔ C. whole wheat flour
2 t. baking powder
½ t. salt
2 eggs, separated
1 C. skim milk
2 T. safflower oil
1 t. honey
¼ C. sesame seeds
1 C. blueberries
¾ C. maple syrup
4 T. butter

Drop the rice in 1 C. boiling salted (½ t.) water and simmer, covered, 45 minutes.

In a medium bowl, combine the flour, baking powder, and salt. In a separate bowl, beat the egg yolks and blend in the milk, oil, and honey. In a blender, blend the cooked rice and the sesame seeds with the egg mixture until smooth. Combine the wet and dry ingredients with as few strokes as possible, but be sure to combine thoroughly.

Beat the egg whites until stiff. Fold the egg whites and blueberries carefully into the batter. Cook the pancakes on a hot, oiled griddle. Serve with 3 T. maple syrup and 1 T. butter on each portion.

Yields: 4 servings, 12 cakes

■ Serve each person 1 C. tomato juice and 1 C. skim milk.

	CALORIES	PROTEIN GMS	CARBOHYDRATES GMS	FAT GMS	CALCIUM MGS	IRON MGS	MAGNESIUM MGS	PHOSPHORUS MGS	POTASSIUM MGS	SODIUM MGS	VITAMIN A I.U.	VITAMIN B_1 MGS	VITAMIN B_2 MGS	NIACIN MGS	VITAMIN C MGS
Tomato Juice, 1 C.	46	2	10	.2	17	2.2	20	44	552	486	1940	.12	.07	1.9	39
Blueberry Pancakes, 3	330	11	39	15	120	2	66	276	276	327	423	.3	.15	2.9	6
Maple Syrup, 3 T.	150	0	39	0	99	.6		9	78	9	0				0
Butter, 1 T.	102	t	t	12	3	0	.27	2	3	141	471	t	t		0
Skim Milk, 1 C.	86	8	12	.4	302	.1	28	247	406	126	500	.09	.34	.22	2
TOTAL	714	21	100	28	541	4.9	114	578	1315	1089	3334	.51	.56	5	47

Substitutions
Tomato Juice: 1 C. vegetable juice or Vegetable Juice Cocktail
  (see page 20).

Cantaloupe
Bran Muffins and Butter
Skim Milk

Calories: 394 per serving   Protein: 15 grams per serving

Bran Muffins

¾ C. whole wheat pastry flour
¼ C. cornmeal
1 C. bran
½ t. salt
1 T. baking powder
1 egg
1 C. skim milk
¼ C. honey
2 T. safflower oil

Preheat oven to 375° F.

Combine the dry ingredients. In a large bowl, beat together the egg, milk, honey, and oil. Add the dry ingredients and mix well with as few strokes as possible. Fill greased muffin tins and bake 20–25 minutes or until done.

Yields: 12 muffins

■ Serve each person ¼ cantaloupe, 2 bran muffins with 2 t. butter, and 1 C. skim milk.

	CALORIES	PROTEIN GMS	CARBOHYDRATES GMS	FAT GMS	CALCIUM MGS	IRON MGS	MAGNESIUM MGS	PHOSPHORUS MGS	POTASSIUM MGS	SODIUM MGS	VITAMIN A I.U.	VITAMIN B_1 MGS	VITAMIN B_2 MGS	NIACIN MGS	VITAMIN C MGS
Cantaloupe	30	.7	8	.1	14	.4	17	16	251	12	3400	.04	.03	.6	33
Bran Muffins, 2	210	6	34	8	72	2	76	242	246	208	168	.16	.16	2.8	t
Butter, 2 t.	68	t	t	7.6	2	0	.18	1.3	2	94	314	t	t		0
Skim Milk, 1 C.	86	8	12	.4	302	.1	28	247	406	126	500	.09	.34	.22	2
TOTAL	394	15	54	16	390	2.5	121	506	905	440	4382	.29	.53	3.6	35

Substitutions
Cantaloupe: ¼ mango, 1 peach, or ½ papaya
Skim Milk: ½ C. yogurt

MENU

Tomato Juice
Strawberries
Cornmeal Griddle Cakes with Fruit Sauce

Calories: 612 per serving   Protein: 15 grams per serving

Cornmeal Griddle Cakes

1½ C. cornmeal
¼ C. whole wheat flour
1 t. baking soda
1 t. salt
2 C. buttermilk
2 T. safflower oil
1 egg, separated
1 t. honey

Sift all the dry ingredients together in a medium bowl. Add the buttermilk, oil, egg yolk, and honey to the dry ingredients. Mix well.

Beat the egg white until stiff. Fold the egg white into the cornmeal mixture. Let batter stand 10 minutes while griddle is heating. Cook on a hot greased griddle until golden brown on both sides.

Yields: 16 4″ cakes, 4 servings

■ Serve 1 C. tomato juice, 1 C. strawberries, and 4 griddle cakes with ½ C. Fruit Sauce (see page 94) and 1 T. butter.

	CALORIES	PROTEIN GMS	CARBOHYDRATES GMS	FAT GMS	CALCIUM MGS	IRON MGS	MAGNESIUM MGS	PHOSPHORUS MGS	POTASSIUM MGS	SODIUM MGS	VITAMIN A I.U.	VITAMIN B₁ MGS	VITAMIN B₂ MGS	NIACIN MGS	VITAMIN C MGS
Tomato Juice, 1 C.	46	2	10	.2	17	2.2	20	44	552	486	1940	.12	.07	1.9	39
Cornmeal Griddle Cakes, 4	320	12	44	12	164	1.2	72	260	336	676	384	.24	.24	1.5	1
Butter, 1 T.	102	t	t	12	3	0	.27	2	3	141	471	t	t		0
Fruit Sauce, ½ C.	88	t	24	t	5.6	t	6.4	10	112	7	688	t	t	t	1
Strawberries, 1 C.	56	1	13	.8	32	1.5	18	32	246	2	90	.04	.1	.9	88
TOTAL	612	15	91	25	222	4.9	117	348	1249	1312	3573	.4	.41	4.3	129

Substitutions
Tomato Juice: 1 C. vegetable juice or Vegetable Juice Cocktail
  (see page 20)
Strawberries: 1 C. raspberries or boysenberries

Tomato Juice
French Toast with Butter and Syrup
Boysenberries

Calories: 516 per serving   Protein: 15 grams per serving

_____ **French Toast** _____

4 eggs
½ C. lowfat yogurt
2 T. safflower oil
8 slices whole grain bread
8 t. butter
8 T. maple syrup

Beat the eggs and yogurt together. Heat a griddle and add sufficient oil to fry the bread. Dip the bread into the egg mixture and saturate; place on the hot griddle and cook until golden brown. Turn and cook the other side. Serve each portion with 2 t. butter and 2 T. maple syrup.

Yields: 4 servings

■ Serve each person 1 C. tomato juice, 2 pieces French toast with 2 t. butter and 2 T. maple syrup, and ½ C. boysenberries.

	CALORIES	PROTEIN GMS	CARBOHYDRATES GMS	FAT GMS	CALCIUM MGS	IRON MGS	MAGNESIUM MGS	PHOSPHORUS MGS	POTASSIUM MGS	SODIUM MGS	VITAMIN A I.U.	VITAMIN B₁ MGS	VITAMIN B₂ MGS	NIACIN MGS	VITAMIN C MGS
Tomato Juice, 1 C.	46	2	10	.2	17	2.2	20	44	552	486	1940	.12	.07	1.9	39
French Toast, 2	272	12	24	15	102	2	49	221	225	305	567	.14	.2	1.3	t
Butter, 2 t.	68	t	t	7.6	2	0		.18	1.3	2	94	314	t	t		0
Maple Syrup, 2 T.	100	0	26	0	66	.4		6	52	6	0				0
Boysenberries, ½ C.	30	.7	7	.2	16	1	1	15	96	.5	105	.02	.08	.7	8
TOTAL	516	15	67	23	203	5.6	70	287	927	892	2926	.28	.35	3.9	47

Substitutions
Tomato Juice: 1 C. vegetable juice or Vegetable Juice Cocktail
    (see page 20)
Boysenberries: ¾ C. strawberries

MENU

Orange Juice
Granola
Yogurt

Calories: 472 per serving   Protein: 17 grams per serving

Granola

½ C. safflower oil
½ C. honey
1 T. vanilla extract
1 C. wheat germ
1 C. sesame seeds
1 C. coconut
1 C. bran
7 C. rolled oats
1 C. sunflower seed kernels
1 C. chopped almonds
1 C. peanuts, chopped
1 C. raisins or diced dates
1 C. diced dried apricots

Heat oven to 300° F.

In a large skillet on low heat, heat the oil, honey, and vanilla until the mixture is thin. Stir in the remaining ingredients except the raisins or dates and apricots. Stir well until the dry ingredients are well coated. Put the cereal in a large shallow pan or baking sheet. Bake until brown, about 45 minutes, stirring occasionally. Add the raisins and apricots. Stir well.

Yields: 30 ½-C. servings

■ Serve each person 1 C. orange juice, and ½ C. granola over ½ C. lowfat yogurt.

	CALORIES	PROTEIN GMS	CARBOHYDRATES GMS	FAT GMS	CALCIUM MGS	IRON MGS	MAGNESIUM MGS	PHOSPHORUS MGS	POTASSIUM MGS	SODIUM MGS	VITAMIN A I.U.	VITAMIN B₁ MGS	VITAMIN B₂ MGS	NIACIN MGS	VITAMIN C MGS
Orange Juice, 1 C.	112	2	26	.5	27	.5	49	42	496	2	500	.22	.07	1	124
Granola, ½ C.	288	9	31	16	46	2.6	85	252	313	5	476	.3	.13	2.3	1
Yogurt, ½ C.	72	6	8	2	207	.09	20	163	265	79	75	.05	.24	.1	.5
TOTAL	472	17	65	19	280	3	154	457	1074	86	1051	.57	.44	3.4	126

Substitutions
Orange Juice: 1 banana, guava or peach; 1 C. boysenberries, raspberries or strawberries; ½ mango; 1 2″-wide slice honeydew melon
Yogurt: 1 C. skim milk

Tomato Juice
Oatmeal
Whole Wheat Toast

Calories: 434 per serving   Protein: 16 grams per serving

Oatmeal

2 C. oatmeal (or enough to make 4 C. cooked)
4 T. honey
2 C. skim milk

Cook the oatmeal according to the package instructions. Serve hot with 1 T. honey and ½ C. milk per person.

Yields: 4 servings

■ Serve each person 1 C. tomato juice and 1 piece toasted Whole Wheat Bread with 1 t. butter (see page 44).

	CALORIES	PROTEIN GMS	CARBOHYDRATES GMS	FAT GMS	CALCIUM MGS	IRON MGS	MAGNESIUM MGS	PHOSPHORUS MGS	POTASSIUM MGS	SODIUM MGS	VITAMIN A I.U.	VITAMIN B₁ MGS	VITAMIN B₂ MGS	NIACIN MGS	VITAMIN C MGS
Tomato Juice, 1 C.	46	2	10	.2	17	2.2	20	44	552	486	1940	.12	.07	1.9	39
Oatmeal, 1 C.	132	5	23	2	22	1.4	50	137	146	523	0	.19	.05	.2	0
Honey, 1 T.	64	.1	17	0	1	.1	.6	1	11	1	0	.002	.014	.1	t
Skim Milk, ½ C.	43	4	6	.2	151	.05	14	123	203	63	250	.05	.17	.11	1
Whole Wheat Toast, 1 sl.	115	5	24	2	38	1	33	125	137	133	74	.17	.07	1.3	t
Butter, 1 t.	34	t	t	4	1	0	.09	.66	1	47	157	t	t		0
TOTAL	434	16	80	8	230	4.8	118	431	1050	1253	2421	.53	.37	3.6	40

Substitutions
Tomato Juice: 1 C. vegetable juice or Vegetable Juice Cocktail (see page 20)

MENU

Tomato Juice
Poached Eggs with Cream Sauce
Sunflower Whole Wheat Bread
Peaches

Calories: 483 per serving   Protein: 23 grams per serving

Poached Eggs

8 eggs

Bring 1½" salted water to the boil in a shallow pan. Turn down the heat until the water has stopped boiling. Gently slip in the eggs, cover, and simmer 8 minutes or until the whites are firm. (Meanwhile begin the Cream Sauce.) Remove them from the water with a pancake turner. Serve 2 eggs per person.

Cream Sauce

2 T. butter
¼ C. whole wheat pastry flour
2 C. skim milk
1 t. salt
¼ t. pepper
¼ t. paprika
1 t. Worcestershire sauce
   (optional)

Melt the butter in a medium saucepan. Add the flour and blend it in well. Gradually add the milk, stirring constantly. When the mixture is smooth, add the seasonings and simmer 10 minutes. Pour over the poached eggs.

Yields: 4 servings

Sunflower Whole Wheat Bread

3 C. warm skim milk
2½ T. dry yeast
¾ C. honey
¼ C. safflower oil
7½ C. whole wheat flour
1¾ t. salt
⅓ C. shredded coconut
⅓ C. sunflower seed kernels

All the ingredients must be at room temperature.

Combine the warm milk, yeast, and honey in a large mixing bowl. Let the mixture rest for 5 minutes. Then add the oil, 5 cups of the flour, and the salt. Beat these ingredients for 7 minutes with an electric mixer at low speed or 100 hand strokes. Stir in the remaining 2½ C. flour, or enough flour to stiffen the dough.

Sprinkle the coconut, sunflower seeds, and 2 T. flour on a board. Knead these ingredients into the dough, adding flour if the dough sticks to the board. Knead until the dough is smooth, approximately 10 minutes.

Oil a large bowl and place the dough in it, lightly coating it with oil to prevent crusting. Cover and set in a warm place.

Let the dough rise 1 hour or until twice its original size. Then punch the dough down to its original size, cover, and let it rise as before. Knead the dough again and divide it into 3 equal parts. Shape them into loaves in 3 buttered bread pans. Cover and let the dough rise until it reaches the top of the pans.

Heat oven to 350° F.

Bake for 50 minutes or until the tops are deep brown. Remove from pan. Brush lightly with butter and cool on a wire rack.

Yields: 3 loaves, 48 slices

■ Serve each person 1 C. tomato juice, 1 slice of bread with 1 t. butter, and 1 peach.

	CALORIES	PROTEIN GMS	CARBOHYDRATES GMS	FAT GMS	CALCIUM MGS	IRON MGS	MAGNESIUM MGS	PHOSPHORUS MGS	POTASSIUM MGS	SODIUM MGS	VITAMIN A I.U.	VITAMIN B₁ MGS	VITAMIN B₂ MGS	NIACIN MGS	VITAMIN C MGS
Tomato Juice, 1 C.	46	2	10	.2	17	2.2	20	44	552	486	1940	.12	.07	1.9	39
Poached Eggs with Cream Sauce	263	17	12	18	207	2	33	330	346	774	1525	.19	.43	.5	1
Sunflower Whole Wheat Bread, 1 sl.	102	3	18	2	9	.7	22	79	83	67	t	.12	.03	.09	t
Butter, 1 t.	34	t	t	3.8	1	0	.09	.66	1	47	157	t	t		0
Peach, 1	38	.6	10	.1	9	.5	12	19	202	1	1330	.02	.05	1	7
TOTAL	483	23	50	24	243	5.4	87	473	1184	1375	4952	.45	.58	3.5	47

Substitutions
Tomato Juice: 1 C. vegetable juice or Vegetable Juice Cocktail (see page 20)
Sunflower Bread: any whole grain bread
Peach: 1 C. boysenberries, raspberries, or strawberries; 1 guava; 1 2″-wide slice honeydew melon

Prune Nut Bread and Butter
Skim Milk

Calories: 257 per serving   Protein: 11 grams per serving

Prune Nut Bread

1 C. chopped dried prunes
2 t. grated orange rind
1⅓ C. unsweetened orange
    juice
1⅞ C. whole wheat flour
3 t. baking powder
½ t. salt
½ t. ground cinnamon
6 T. honey
2 T. safflower oil
2 eggs
½ C. chopped walnuts

Preheat oven to 350° F.

In a saucepan combine the chopped prunes, orange rind, and juice. Cook 5–10 minutes. Cool.

Sift the dry ingredients together and set aside.

In a mixing bowl, cream the honey and oil together. Add the eggs, and beat. Add the prune mixture, beating continuously. Add the dry ingredients, mixing well. Fold in the nuts. Turn into a greased loaf pan and bake for 40–55 minutes or until done.

Yields: 18 slices

■ Serve each person 1 slice bread with 1 t. butter, and 1 C. skim milk.

	CALORIES	PROTEIN GMS	CARBOHYDRATES GMS	FAT GMS	CALCIUM MGS	IRON MGS	MAGNESIUM MGS	PHOSPHORUS MGS	POTASSIUM MGS	SODIUM MGS	VITAMIN A I.U.	VITAMIN B₁ MGS	VITAMIN B₂ MGS	NIACIN MGS	VITAMIN C MGS
Prune Nut Bread, 1 sl.	137	3	25	4	18	1	25	81	171	67	239	.1	.06	.08	10
Butter, 1 t.	34	t	t	3.8	1	0	.09	.66	1	47	157	t	t		0
Skim Milk, 1 C.	86	8	12	.4	302	.1	28	247	406	126	500	.09	.34	.22	2
TOTAL	257	11	37	8	321	1.1	53	329	578	240	896	.19	.4	1	12

Tiger's Bread
Hot Cocoa
Strawberries

Calories: 389 per serving   Protein: 14 grams per serving

────────────────────── **Tiger's Bread** ──────────────────────

½ C. honey
½ C. chunky peanut butter
3 T. safflower oil
2 eggs
2 C. grated carrots
2 bananas, mashed
1¾ C. whole wheat flour
½ t. salt
1 t. baking powder
1 t. baking soda
¼ t. ground allspice
¼ t. grated nutmeg
1 t. vanilla extract
¼ C. skim milk

Preheat oven to 325° F.

In a large bowl, cream together the honey, peanut butter, oil, and eggs. Add the carrots and bananas. In a separate bowl combine the dry ingredients. In a small bowl combine the milk and vanilla. Alternately blend the dry mixture and the milk into the creamed mixture. Mix well and turn into a greased 9″ × 5″ × 3″ loaf pan. Bake for 70 minutes or until done. Cool in the pan for 10 minutes. Remove the bread from the pan and continue cooling on a wire rack.

Yields: 18 slices

────────────────────── **Hot Cocoa** ──────────────────────

4 C. skim milk
4 T. powdered cocoa
4 T. honey

Heat the milk. Add the cocoa and blend well. Add the honey and stir again.

Yields: 4 servings

■ Serve each person 1 slice of bread and 1 C. strawberries.

	CALORIES	PROTEIN GMS	CARBOHYDRATES GMS	FAT GMS	CALCIUM MGS	IRON MGS	MAGNESIUM MGS	PHOSPHORUS MGS	POTASSIUM MGS	SODIUM MGS	VITAMIN A I.U.	VITAMIN B₁ MGS	VITAMIN B₂ MGS	NIACIN MGS	VITAMIN C MGS
Tiger's Bread, 1 sl.	162	4	23	5	23	.6	30	89	154	79	1815	.08	.06	1.7	1
Hot Cocoa, 1 C.	171	9	32	2	312	1	29	298	515	127	502	.1	.38	.52	2
Strawberries, 1 C.	56	1	13	.8	32	1.5	18	32	246	2	90	.04	.1	.9	88
TOTAL	389	14	68	8	367	3.1	77	419	915	208	2407	.22	.54	3	91

Hot Cocoa: 1 C. skim milk or ½ C. yogurt
Strawberries: 1 guava, 1 2"-wide slice honeydew melon, ½
    mango, or 1 C. raspberries

MENU

Tomato Juice
Whole Wheat Waffles with Butter and Syrup
Skim Milk
Cantaloupe

Calories: 442 per serving   Protein: 17 grams per serving

Whole Wheat Waffles

¾ C. whole wheat flour
2 t. baking powder
¼ t. salt
1 egg, separated
¾ C. skim milk
2 T. safflower oil

Preheat a waffle iron.

Mix the dry ingredients thoroughly. Beat the egg white until it peaks.

In a separate bowl combine well-beaten egg yolk and milk; add this to the dry ingredients gradually, stirring until well blended and smooth. Stir in the oil and fold in the egg white. Bake at once in the hot waffle iron, filling each compartment two-thirds full. Waffles are done when steam no longer escapes from the waffle iron. Top each waffle with 2 T. maple syrup and 1 t. butter.

Yields: 4 waffles

■ Serve each person 1 C. tomato juice, 1 C. skim milk, and ¼ cantaloupe.

	CALORIES	PROTEIN GMS	CARBOHYDRATES GMS	FAT GMS	CALCIUM MGS	IRON MGS	MAGNESIUM MGS	PHOSPHORUS MGS	POTASSIUM MGS	SODIUM MGS	VITAMIN A I.U.	VITAMIN B₁ MGS	VITAMIN B₂ MGS	NIACIN MGS	VITAMIN C MGS
Tomato Juice, 1 C.	46	2	10	.2	17	2.2	20	44	552	486	1940	.12	.07	1.9	39
Whole Wheat Waffle, 1	146	6	22	9	75	.5	32	157	170	183	241	.12	.1	.95	t
Butter, 1 t.	34	t	t	3.8	1	0	.09	.66	1	47	157	t	t		0
Maple Syrup, 2 T.	100	0	26	0	66	.4		6	52	6	0				0
Skim Milk, 1 C.	86	8	12	.4	302	.1	28	247	406	126	500	.09	.34	.22	2
Cantaloupe, ¼	30	.7	8	.1	14	.4	17	16	251	12	3400	.04	.03	.6	33
TOTAL	442	17	78	14	475	3.6	97	471	1432	860	6238	.37	.54	3.7	74

Substitutions
Tomato Juice: 1 C. vegetable juice or Vegetable Juice Cocktail
   (see page 20)
Skim Milk: ½ C. yogurt
Cantaloupe: ½ C. raspberries; ¾ C. strawberries; 1 peach; 3
   apricots; ¹⁄₁₀ casaba melon; optional

CALORIE AND NUTRIENT ALLOWANCE CHART

The following chart is designed to give you a better understanding of the calories and nutrients your body requires daily. The figures are based on *Recommended Dietary Allowances (RDA)* by the National Research Council.[1] Any variations from this chart are footnoted.

The chart is divided into three categories—children, girls and women, and boys and men. The women's and men's sections are further divided into different ages and weights.

LEVEL OF ACTIVITY

Resting Metabolic Rate—

represents the minimum energy needs for day and night with no exercise or exposure to cold.

Sedentary—

includes occupations that involve sitting most of the day, such as secretarial work and studying.

Light—

includes activities which involve standing most of the day, such as teaching or laboratory work.

Moderate—

may include walking, gardening, and housework.

Active—

may include dancing, skating, and manual labor such as farm or construction work.

The Calorie and Nutrient Allowance Chart includes the requirements for Resting Metabolic Rate and for Light Activity. The chart below is included to allow calculation of calorie requirements for sedentary, moderate, and active levels. Although calorie requirements vary with the level of activity, nutrient requirements remain the same as stated under an individual's desirable weight in the Calorie and Nutrient Allowance Chart.

METABOLIC RATE	Men
Resting	See Nutrient Allowance Chart
Sedentary	16 calories/lb. body weight
Light	See Nutrient Allowance Chart
Moderate	21 calories/lb. body weight
Active	26 calories/lb. body weight

	Women
Resting	See Nutrient Allowance Chart
Sedentary	14 calories/lb. body weight
Light	See Nutrient Allowance Chart
Moderate	18 calories/lb. body weight
Active	22 calories/lb. body weight

It can be seen from the chart above that a moderately active man of 180 pounds requires approximately 3780 calories. This figure is ob-

[1] *Recommended Dietary Allowances,* Food and Nutrition Board, National Academy of Sciences, National Research Council. Revised 1968.

tained by multiplying 180 pounds by 21 calories. These estimates do not take into account body build and height, which also affect calorie requirements.

For the purpose of dieting, the "Desirable Height and Weight Chart" is included on the following page so that you may estimate the weight that you should be, based on your sex, height, and body frame. This information should be used in connection with the "Calorie and Nutrient Allowance Chart" in order to determine what nutrients and calories you require, so that you may cut calories accordingly. If popular fad diets are used, there is great risk of illness occurring, due to any one of the nutrient deficiencies.

The age categories used in the "Calorie and Nutrient Allowance Chart" differ slightly from those used in RDA. Therefore, those nutrients marked with asterisks have minute variations from those listed by the RDA. Average or adequate daily intakes, as stated in the RDA, have been listed for those nutrients which have no established minimum daily requirement. Requirements or adequate intakes are not listed by the RDA, for inositol, PABA, and vitamin K; these figures were obtained from other sources.

Charts 1 and 2 were the generally accepted height and weight charts for many years. Charts 3 and 4 are new tables based on a mortality study of 4 million healthy adults over a 22-year period. These tables set forth the weights at which men and women of various heights and bone structures can expect to live a long life. The new tables allow for higher weight than the old ones, but many people feel that these may not be ideal. Therefore, both sets are included.

DESIRABLE HEIGHT AND WEIGHT CHART

Chart 1
Desirable Weights for Men Aged 25 and Over*

Height with Shoes (1-in. heels) Feet	Inches	Small Frame	Medium Frame	Large Frame
5	2	112-120	118-129	126-141
5	3	115-123	121-133	129-144
5	4	118-126	124-136	132-148
5	5	121-129	127-139	135-152
5	6	124-133	130-143	138-156
5	7	128-137	134-147	142-161
5	8	132-141	138-152	147-166
5	9	136-145	142-156	151-170
5	10	140-150	146-160	155-174
5	11	144-154	150-165	159-179
6	0	148-158	154-170	164-184
6	1	152-162	158-175	168-189
6	2	156-167	162-180	173-194
6	3	160-171	167-185	178-199
6	4	164-175	172-190	182-204

* Weight in pounds according to frame (in indoor clothing). For nude weight, deduct 5 to 7 lb. This chart prepared by Metropolitan Life Insurance Company.

Chart 2
Desirable Weights for Women Aged 25 and Over*

Height with Shoes (2-in. heels) Feet	Inches	Small Frame	Medium Frame	Large Frame
4	10	92-98	96-107	104-119
4	11	94-101	98-110	106-122
5	0	96-104	101-113	109-125
5	1	99-107	104-116	112-128
5	2	102-110	107-119	115-131
5	3	105-113	110-122	118-134
5	4	108-116	113-126	121-138
5	5	111-119	116-130	125-142
5	6	114-123	120-135	129-146
5	7	118-127	124-139	133-150
5	8	122-131	128-143	137-154
5	9	126-135	132-147	141-158
5	10	130-140	136-151	145-163
5	11	134-144	140-155	149-168
6	0	138-148	144-159	153-173

* Weight in pounds according to frame (in indoor clothing). For nude weight, deduct 2 to 4 lb. This chart prepared by Metropolitan Life Insurance Company.

Chart 3

Height Feet	Inches	Small Frame	Medium Frame	Large Frame
5	2	128-134	131-141	138-150
5	3	130-136	133-143	140-153
5	4	132-138	135-145	142-156
5	5	134-140	137-148	144-160
5	6	136-142	139-151	146-164
5	7	138-145	142-154	149-168
5	8	140-148	145-157	152-172
5	9	142-151	148-160	155-176
5	10	144-154	151-163	158-180
5	11	146-157	154-166	161-184
6	0	149-160	157-170	164-188
6	1	152-164	160-174	168-192
6	2	155-168	164-178	172-197
6	3	158-172	167-182	176-202
6	4	162-176	171-187	181-207

Weights at ages 25-59 based on lowest mortality. Weight in pounds according to frame (in indoor clothing weighing 5 lb., shoes with 1-inch heels).

Chart 4

Height Feet	Inches	Small Frame	Medium Frame	Large Frame
4	10	102-111	109-121	118-131
4	11	103-113	111-123	120-134
5	0	104-115	113-126	122-137
5	1	106-118	115-129	125-140
5	2	108-121	118-132	128-143
5	3	111-124	121-135	131-147
5	4	114-127	124-138	134-151
5	5	117-130	127-141	137-155
5	6	120-133	130-144	140-159
5	7	123-136	133-147	143-163
5	8	126-139	136-150	146-167
5	9	129-142	139-153	149-170
5	10	132-145	142-156	152-173
5	11	135-148	145-159	155-176
6	0	138-151	148-162	158-179

Weights at ages 25-59 based on lowest mortality. Weight in pounds according to frame (in indoor clothing weighing 3 lb., shoes with 1-inch heels).

Source 1979 Build Study, Society of Actuaries and Association of Life Insurance Medical Directors of America, 1980

CALORIE AND NUTRIENT ALLOWANCE CHART

	CHILDREN (Boys and Girls)								
Age:	0-1 mo.	1-6 mo.	6-12 mo.	1-2 yr.	2-3	3-4	4-6	6-8	8-10
Weight (in pounds)	9	15	20	26	31	35	42	51	62
Weight (in kilograms)	4	7	9	12	14	16	19	23	28
Calories required for: Resting Metabolic Rate Light Activity	480	770	900	1100	1250	1400	1600	2000	2200
Carbohydrate grams	72	115	135	165	187	210	240	300	330
Fats in grams	17	28	33	38	44	49	58	73	80
Protein in grams	9	14	16	25	25	30	30	35	40
Minerals Calcium — mg.	400	500	600	700	800	800	800	900	1000
Iodine — mcg.	25	40	45	55	60	70	80	100	110
Iron — mg.	6	10	15	15	15	10	10	10	10
Magnesium — mg.	40	60	70	100	150	200	200	250	250
Phosphorus — mg. Potassium — mg. Sodium — mg.	200	400	500	700	800	800	800	900	1000
Vitamins Vitamin A — I.U. Vitamin B complex:	1500	1500	1500	2000	2000	2500	2500	3500	3500
Thiamine (B_1) — mg.	0.2	0.4	0.5	0.6	0.6	0.7	0.8	1.0	1.1
Riboflavin (B_2) — mg.	0.4	0.5	0.6	0.6	0.7	0.8	0.9	1.1	1.2
Pyridoxin (B_6) — mg.	0.2	0.3	0.4	0.5	0.6	0.7	0.9	1.0	1.2
Cyanocobalamin (B_{12}) — mcg.	1.0	1.5	2.0	2.0	2.5	3.0	4.0	4.0	5.0
Biotin — mcg.			Adequate daily intake — 150-300 mcg.						
Choline — mg.			Average daily intake — 500-900 mg.						
Folic Acid — mg.	.05	.05	0.1	0.1	0.2	0.2	0.2	0.2	0.3
Inositol — mg.[1] Niacin —mg.	5.0	7.0	8.0	8.0	8.0	9.0	11	13	15
Para-Aminobenzoic Acid (PABA) — mg. Pantothenic Acid — mg.			No Minimum Daily Requirement						
Vitamin C (Ascorbic Acid) — mg.	35	35	35	40	40	40	40	40	40
Vitamin D — I.U.	400	400	400	400	400	400	400	400	400
Vitamin E — I.U. Vitamin K — mg.[2]	5.0	5.0	5.0	10	10	10	10	15	15

[1]Goodhart, Robert S. and Shils, Maurice E. Modern Nutrition in Health and Disease. 5th ed., (Philadelphia: Lea and Febiger, 1973), p. 263.
[2]Ibid., p. 172.

CALORIE AND NUTRIENT ALLOWANCE CHART

GIRLS					WOMEN							
10-12	12-14	14-16	16-18	18-22	22-45							
77	97	114	119	128	88	99	110	121	128	132	143	154
35	44	52	54	58	40	45	50	55	58	60	65	70
2250	2300	2400	2300	2000	1280	1380	1460	1560	1620	1640	1740	1830
					1550	1700	1800	1950	2000	2050	2200	2300
337	345	360	345	346	232	255	270	292	300	307	330	345
78	80	82	78	79	53	58	60	65	66	67	72	74
50	50	55	55	52	36	40	45	49	52	54	58	63
1200	1300	1300	1300	800	800	800	800	800	800	800	800	800
110	115	120	115	100	100	100	100	100	100	100	100	100
18	18	18	18	18	18	18	18	18	18	18	18	18
300	350	350	350	350	300	300	300	300	300	300	300	300
1200	1300	1300	1300	800	800	800	800	800	800	800	800	800
					Average daily intake — 1950-5850 mg.							
					Average daily intake — 2300-6900 mg.							
4500	5000	5000	5000	5000	5000	5000	5000	5000	5000	5000	5000	5000
1.1	1.2	1.2	1.2	1.0	1.0	1.0	1.0	1.0	1.0	1.0	1.0	1.0
1.3	1.4	1.4	1.5	1.5	1.5	1.5	1.5	1.5	1.5	1.5	1.5	1.5
1.4	1.6	1.8	2.0	2.0	2.0	2.0	2.0	2.0	2.0	2.0	2.0	2.0
5.0	5.0	5.0	5.0	5.0	5.0	5.0	5.0	5.0	5.0	5.0	5.0	5.0
					Adequate daily intake — 150-300 mg.							
					Average daily intake — 500-900 mg.							
0.4	0.4	0.4	0.4	0.4	0.4	0.4	0.4	0.4	0.4	0.4	0.4	0.4
					Average daily intake — 1000 mg.							
15	15	16	15	13	13	13	13	13	13	13	13	13
					No Minimum Daily Requirement							
					Adequate daily intake — 5-10 mg.							
40	45	50	50	55	55	55	55	55	55	55	55	55
400	400	400	400	400	Adequate daily intake — 400 I.U.							
20	20	25	25	25	25	25	25	25	25	25	25	25
					Adequate daily intake — 300-500 mcg.							

CALORIE AND NUTRIENT ALLOWANCE CHART
WOMEN

Age:	Preg-nant	Nurs-ing	45-65							
Weight (in pounds)			88	99	110	121	128	132	143	154
Weight (in kilograms)			40	45	50	55	58	60	65	70
Calories required for: Resting Metabolic Rate Light Activity	+200	+1000	1450	1550	1650	1800	1850	1900	2000	2100
Carbohydrate grams			217	232	247	270	277	285	300	315
Fats in grams			48	51	53	58	59	60	58	63
Protein in grams	65	75	36	40	45	49	52	54	63	65
Minerals										
Calcium — mg.	+400	+500	800	800	800	800	800	800	800	800
Iodine* — mcg.	125	150	90	90	90	90	90	90	90	90
Iron* — mg.	18	18	18	18	18	18	18	18	18	18
Magnesium — mg.	450	450	300	300	300	300	300	300	300	300
Phosphorus — mg.	+400	+500	800	800	800	800	800	800	800	800
Potassium — mg.			Average daily intake — 1950-5850 mg.							
Sodium — mg.			Average daily intake — 2300-6900 mg.							
Vitamins										
Vitamin A — I.U.	6000	8000	5000	5000	5000	5000	5000	5000	5000	5000
Vitamin B complex: Thiamine (B_1) —mg.	+0.1	+0.5	1.0	1.0	1.0	1.0	1.0	1.0	1.0	1.0
Riboflavin (B_2) — mg.	1.8	2.0	1.5	1.5	1.5	1.5	1.5	1.5	1.5	1.5
Pyridoxin (B_6) — mg.	2.5	2.5	2.0	2.0	2.0	2.0	2.0	2.0	2.0	2.0
Cyanocobalamin (B_{12})* — mcg.	8	6	6	6	6	6	6	6	6	6
Biotin — mcg.			Adequate daily intake — 150-300 mcg.							
Choline — mg.			Average daily intake — 500-900 mg.							
Folic Acid — mg.	0.8	0.5	0.4	0.4	0.4	0.4	0.4	0.4	0.4	0.4
Inositol — mg.[1]			Average daily intake — 1000 mg.							
Niacin — mg.	15	20	13	13	13	13	13	13	13	13
Para-Aminobenzoic Acid (PABA) — mg.			No Minimum Daily Requirement							
Pantothenic Acid — mg.			Adequate daily intake — 5-10 mg.							
Vitamin C (Ascorbic Acid) — mg.	60	60	55	55	55	55	55	55	55	55
Vitamin D — I.U.	400	400	Adequate daily intake — 400 I.U.							
Vitamin E — I.U.	30	30	25	25	25	25	25	25	25	25
Vitamin K — mg.[2]			Adequate daily intake — 300-500 mcg.							

[1]Goodhart, Robert S. and Shils, Maurice E. Modern Nutrition in Health and Disease. 5th ed., (Philadelphia: Lea and Febiger, 1973), p. 263.
[2]Ibid., p. 172.

CALORIE AND NUTRIENT ALLOWANCE CHART

WOMEN								BOYS			
65+								10-12	12-14	14-18	18-22
88	99	110	121	128	132	143	154	77	95	130	147
40	45	50	55	58	60	65	70	35	43	59	67
1300	1450	1500	1650	1700	1700	1850	1950	2500	2700	3000	2800
195	217	225	247	255	255	277	292	392	400	465	430
42	47	47	51	52	51	56	59	83	90	100	93
36	40	45	49	52	54	58	63	45	50	60	60
800	800	800	800	800	800	800	800	1200	1400	1400	800
90	90	90	90	90	90	90	90	125	135	150	140
18	18	18	18	18	18	18	18	10	18	18	10
300	300	300	300	300	300	300	300	300	350	400	400
800	800	800	800	800	800	800	800	1200	1400	1400	800
Average daily intake — 1950-5850 mg.											
Average daily intake — 2300-6900 mg.											
5000	5000	5000	5000	5000	5000	5000	5000	4500	5000	5000	5000
1.0	1.0	1.0	1.0	1.0	1.0	1.0	1.0	1.3	1.4	1.5	1.4
1.5	1.5	1.5	1.5	1.5	1.5	1.5	1.5	1.3	1.4	1.5	1.6
2.0	2.0	2.0	2.0	2.0	2.0	2.0	2.0	1.4	1.6	1.8	2.0
6	6	6	6	6	6	6	6	5	5	5	5
Adequate daily intake — 150-300 mcg.											
Average daily intake — 500-900 mg.											
0.4	0.4	0.4	0.4	0.4	0.4	0.4	0.4	0.4	0.4	0.4	0.4
Average daily intake — 1000 mg.											
13	13	13	13	13	13	13	13	17	18	20	18
No Minimum Daily Requirement Adequate daily intake — 5-10 mg.											
55	55	55	55	55	55	55	55	40	45	55	60
Adequate daily intake — 400 I.U.								400	400	400	400
25	25	25	25	25	25	25	25	20	20	25	30
Adequate daily intake — 300-500 mcg.											

CALORIE AND NUTRIENT ALLOWANCE CHART

	MEN								
Age:					**22-45**				
Weight (in pounds)	110	121	132	143	**154**	165	176	187	198
Weight (in kilograms)	50	55	60	65	**70**	75	80	85	90
Calories required for:									
Resting Metabolic Rate	1540	1620	1720	1820	**1880**	1970	2020	2110	2210
Light Activity	2200	2350	2500	2650	**2800**	2950	3050	3200	3350
Carbohydrate grams	330	352	375	397	**420**	442	457	480	502
Fats in grams	78	83	87	92	**96**	101	103	108	112
Protein in grams	45	49	54	58	**63**	67	72	76	81
Minerals									
Calcium — mg.	800	800	800	800	**800**	800	800	800	800
Iodine — mcg.	140	140	140	140	**140**	140	140	140	140
Iron — mg.	10	10	10	10	**10**	10	10	10	10
Magnesium — mg.	350	350	350	350	**350**	350	350	350	350
Phosphorus — mg.	800	800	800	800	**800**	800	800	800	800
Potassium — mg.	Average daily intake — 1950-5850 mg.								
Sodium — mg.	Average daily intake — 2300-6900 mg.								
Vitamins									
Vitamin A — I.U.	5000	5000	5000	5000	**5000**	5000	5000	5000	5000
Vitamin B complex:									
Thiamine (B_1) — mg.	1.4	1.4	1.4	1.4	**1.4**	1.4	1.4	1.4	1.4
Riboflavin (B_2) — mg.	1.7	1.7	1.7	1.7	**1.7**	1.7	1.7	1.7	1.7
Pyridoxin (B_6) — mg.	2.0	2.0	2.0	2.0	**2.0**	2.0	2.0	2.0	2.0
Cyanocobalamin (B_{12}) — mcg.	5	5	5	5	**5**	5	5	5	5
Biotin — mcg.	Average daily intake — 150-300 mg.								
Choline — mg.	Average daily intake — 500-900 mg.								
Folic Acid — mg.	0.4	0.4	0.4	0.4	**0.4**	0.4	0.4	0.4	0.4
Inositol — mg.[1]	Average daily intake — 1000 mg.								
Niacin — mg.	18	18	18	18	**18**	18	18	18	18
Para-Aminobenzoic Acid (PABA) — mg.	No Minimum Daily Requirement								
Pantothenic acid — mg.	Adequate daily intake — 5-10 mg.								
Vitamin C (Ascorbic Acid) — mg.	60	60	60	60	**60**	60	60	60	60
Vitamin D — I.U.	Adequate daily intake — 400 I.U.								
Vitamin E — I.U.	30	30	30	30	**30**	30	30	30	30
Vitamin K — mg.[2]	Adequate daily intake — 300-500 mcg.								

[1]Goodhart, Robert S. and Shils, Maurice E. Modern Nutrition in Health and Disease. 5th ed., (Philadelphia: Lea and Febiger, 1973), p. 263.

[2]Ibid., p. 172.

CALORIE AND NUTRIENT ALLOWANCE CHART

MEN

22-45		45-65										
209	220	110	121	132	143	154	165	176	187	198	209	220
95	100	50	55	60	65	70	75	80	85	90	95	100
2290 3500	2380 3700	2000	2150	2300	2400	2600	2700	2800	2950	3100	3200	3400
525	555	300	322	345	360	390	405	420	442	465	480	510
117	124	109	74	78	81	87	90	92	97	102	104	111
85	90	45	49	54	58	63	67	72	76	81	85	90
800	800	800	800	800	800	800	800	800	800	800	800	800
140	140	125	125	125	125	125	125	125	125	125	125	125
10	10	10	10	10	10	10	10	10	10	10	10	10
350	350	350	350	350	350	350	350	350	350	350	350	350
800	800	800	800	800	800	800	800	800	800	800	800	800

Average daily intake — 1950-5850 mg.

Average daily intake — 2300-6900 mg.

22-45		45-65										
5000	5000	5000	5000	5000	5000	5000	5000	5000	5000	5000	5000	5000
1.4	1.4	1.3	1.3	1.3	1.3	1.3	1.3	1.3	1.3	1.3	1.3	1.3
1.7	1.7	1.7	1.7	1.7	1.7	1.7	1.7	1.7	1.7	1.7	1.7	1.7
2.0	2.0	2.0	2.0	2.0	2.0	2.0	2.0	2.0	2.0	2.0	2.0	2.0
5	5	6	6	6	6	6	6	6	6	6	6	6

Adequate daily intake — 150-300 mcg.

Average daily intake — 500-900 mg.

22-45		45-65										
0.4	0.4	0.4	0.4	0.4	0.4	0.4	0.4	0.4	0.4	0.4	0.4	0.4

Average daily intake — 1000 mg.

22-45		45-65										
18	18	17	17	17	17	17	17	17	17	17	17	17

No Minimum Daily Requirement
Adequate daily intake — 5-10 mg.

22-45		45-65										
60	60	60	60	60	60	60	60	60	60	60	60	60

Adequate daily intake — 400 I.U.

22-45		45-65										
30	30	30	30	30	30	30	30	30	30	30	30	30

Adequate daily intake — 300-500 mcg.

CALORIE AND NUTRIENT ALLOWANCE CHART

	MEN										
Age:	65+										
Weight (in pounds)	110	121	132	143	154	165	176	187	198	209	220
Weight (in kilograms)	50	55	60	65	70	75	80	85	90	95	100
Calories required for: Resting Metabolic Rate Light Activity	1850	1950	2100	2200	2400	2500	2600	2700	2800	2900	3100
Carbohydrate grams	277	292	315	330	360	375	390	405	420	435	465
Fats in grams	62	65	69	72	79	81	83	86	88	91	98
Protein in grams	45	49	54	58	63	67	72	76	81	85	90
Minerals											
Calcium — mg.	800	800	800	800	800	800	800	800	800	800	800
Iodine — mcg.	110	110	110	110	110	110	110	110	110	110	110
Iron — mg.	10	10	10	10	10	10	10	10	10	10	10
Magnesium — mg.	350	350	350	350	350	350	350	350	350	350	350
Phosphorus — mg.	800	800	800	800	800	800	800	800	800	800	800
Potassium — mg.	Average daily intake — 1950-5850 mg.										
Sodium — mg.	Average daily intake — 2300-6900 mg.										
Vitamins											
Vitamin A — I.U.	5000	5000	5000	5000	5000	5000	5000	5000	5000	5000	5000
Vitamin B complex: Thiamine (B_1) — mg.	1.2	1.2	1.2	1.2	1.2	1.2	1.2	1.2	1.2	1.2	1.2
Riboflavin (B_2) — mg.	1.7	1.7	1.7	1.7	1.7	1.7	1.7	1.7	1.7	1.7	1.7
Pyridoxin (B_6) — mg.	2.0	2.0	2.0	2.0	2.0	2.0	2.0	2.0	2.0	2.0	2.0
Cyanocobalamin (B_{12}) — mcg.	6	6	6	6	6	6	6	6	6	6	6
Biotin — mcg.	Adequate daily intake — 150-300 mcg.										
Choline — mg.	Average daily intake — 500-900 mg.										
Folic Acid — mg.	0.4	0.4	0.4	0.4	0.4	0.4	0.4	0.4	0.4	0.4	0.4
Inositol — mg.[1]	Average daily intake — 1000 mg.										
Niacin — mg.	14	14	14	14	14	14	14	14	14	14	14
Para-Aminobenzoic Acid (PABA) — mg.	No Minimum Daily Requirement										
Pantothenic Acid — mg.	Adequate daily intake — 5-10 mg.										
Vitamin C (Ascorbic Acid) — mg.	60	60	60	60	60	60	60	60	60	60	60
Vitamin D — I.U.	Adequate daily intake — 400 I.U.										
Vitamin E — I.U.	30	30	30	30	30	30	30	30	30	30	30
Vitamin K — mg.[2]	Adequate daily intake — 300-500 mcg.										

[1]Goodhart, Robert S. and Shils, Maurice E. Modern Nutrition in Health and Disease. 5th ed., (Philadelphia: Lea and Febiger, 1973), p. 263.

[2]Ibid., p. 172.

SOME RICH SOURCES OF NUTRIENTS

CARBOHYDRATES
Whole grains
Sugar, syrup, honey
Fruits
Vegetables

FATS
Butter, margarine
Vegetable oils
Whole milk and mllk products
Eggs
Fats in meat
Nuts and seeds

PROTEINS
Meat, fish, poultry
Eggs
Milk and milk products
Whole grains

WATER
Beverages
Fruit
Vegetables

VITAMIN A
Eggs
Yellow fruits and vegetables
Dark green fruits and vegetable
Whole milk and milk products

VITAMIN B$_1$
Whole grains
Organ meats
Meat, fish, poultry
Eggs
Legumes
Nuts
Brewer's yeast
Tiger's Milk

VITAMIN B$_2$
Organ meats
Milk
Milk products
Eggs
Brewer's yeast

VITAMIN B$_6$
Whole grains
Meat
Organ meats
Brewer's yeast
Tiger's Milk

VITAMIN B$_{12}$
Organ meats
Milk and milk products
Fish
Eggs
Tiger's Milk

BIOTIN
Organ meats
Whole grains
Brewer's yeast
Tiger's Milk

CHOLINE
Eggs
Organ meats
Whole grains
Legumes
Fish
Brewer's yeast

FOLIC ACID
Organ meats
Green leafy vegetables
Brewer's yeast

INOSITOL
Citrus fruit
Grains
Meat
Milk
Nuts
Vegetables
Tiger's Milk

NIACIN
Organ meats
Meat, poultry, fish
Whole grains
Milk and milk products
Brewer's yeast
Tiger's Milk

PARA-AMINOBENZOIC ACID
Organ meats
Green leafy vegetables

PANTOTHENIC ACID
Organ meats
Eggs
Legumes
Whole grains
Brewer's yeast
Tiger's Milk

VITAMIN C
Citrus fruits
Vegetables
Rose hips
Acerola cherries

VITAMIN D
Eggs
Organ meats
Vitamin D-fortified
    milk and milk products
Fish liver oils
Bone meal

VITAMIN E
Oils
Margarine
Eggs
Organ meats

VITAMIN K
Green leafy vegetables
Fats
Fruits
Vegetables

BIOFLAVONOIDS
Citrus fruits
Fruits
Vegetables

CALCIUM
Milk and milk products
Green leafy vegetables
Bone meal
Dolomite

CHLORINE
Table salt
Seafoods
Meat

COBALT
Green leafy vegetables
Cereals
Fruits
Meat

COPPER
Organ meats
Nuts
Legumes

FLUORIDE
Tea
Seafoods
Fluoridated water

IODINE
Iodized salt
Seafoods

IRON
Organ meats, meat
Eggs
Green leafy vegetables
Whole grains
Dried fruit

MAGNESIUM
Nuts
Whole grains
Dark green vegetables
Seafoods
Dolomite

MANGANESE
Tea
Whole grains
Green leafy vegetables
Legumes
Nuts

PHOSPHORUS
Milk and milk products
Meat, fish, poultry
Eggs
Legumes
Nuts
Bone meal

POTASSIUM
Dried fruits
Legumes
Whole grains
Vegetables
Lean meats

SODIUM
Table salt
Baking powder and
    baking soda
Milk products
Processed food

SULFUR
Meat
Fish
Legumes
Nuts

ZINC
Organ meats
Seafoods

TABLE OF FOOD COMPOSITION

The foods in this table have been divided according to food groups and similar types of foods that do not belong to any one group. The chart runs alphabetically according to food groups, with the items in each group also being alphabetized. The first group analyzed is Beverages; the second is Breads, Flours, Cereals, Grains, and Grain Products, and so on. If you are unable to locate a particular food in a group, this does not necessarily mean that it has not been included. Check the Index in the back of the book, and look for the name indicated by an asterisk.

Food values have been calculated so as to permit easy computation. All figures are, of necessity, averages of different food samples. *The blank spaces on the chart do not indicate an absence of a particular nutrient, but rather that meaningful analysis of the food for that nutrient is lacking.* Only the zero confirms the absence of a nutrient.

There are three major factors that influence the nutrient content of foods—first, the inherent characteristics of the plant or animal; second, environmental conditions affecting the plant or animal; and third, the method of handling, processing, and cooking the plant or animal material. The content of trace minerals such as selenium, copper, and zinc depends on the soil in which they are grown and where they are grown, and will therefore vary significantly in foods from area to area.

Vitamin E values have been given in milligrams. To approximate the value in IUs, multiply milligrams by 1.5. For example, if 3 milligrams of vitamin E are present, multiply 3 by 1.5, which makes 4.5 IU of vitamin E.

See page 220 for the abbreviations and symbols used in the chart.

CONTENTS: TABLE OF FOOD COMPOSITION

Food Item	Measure	Weight g	Calories	Carbohydrate g	Protein g	Fiber g	Saturated fat g	Unsaturated fat g	Total fat g	Cholesterol mg	Vitamin A IU	Vitamin B$_1$ mg	Vitamin B$_2$ mg	Vitamin B$_6$ mg
BEVERAGES														
Alcoholic														
Beer, 4.5% alcohol	1 cup	240	101	9.1	.72				0			.01	.07	.2
Daiquiri	3.5 oz	100	122	5.2	.1							.014	.001	
Gin, rum, vodka, whiskey,														
86 proof	1 oz	28	70	t	0				0		0	0	0	
Martini	3.5 oz	100	140	.3	.1						4	t	t	
Tom Collins	10 oz	300	180	9	.3						0	.03	t	
Wines														
Sweet, 18.8% alcohol	1 cup	240	329	18.4	.24				0			.02	.05	.1
Dry, 12.2% alcohol	1 cup	240	204	9.6	.24				0			t	.02	.1
Common														
Club soda	1 cup	240	0	0	0	0			0		0	0	0	
Coffee, clear	1 cup	240	5	.8	.3	0			.1		0	.02	.02	t
Cola drinks	1 cup	240	94	19	0				0		0	0	0	
Fruit-flavored drinks	1 cup	240	110	29	0	0			0		0	0	0	
Diet drinks	1 cup	240	t		0	0			0		0	0	0	
Ginger ale	1 cup	240	74	19	0	0			0		0	0	0	
Root beer	1 cup	240	98	25	0	0			0		0	0	0	
Tea, clear	1 cup	240	4	.9	.1	t			t		0	0	.04	
BREADS, FLOURS, CEREALS, GRAINS, AND GRAIN PRODUCTS														
Barley														
Pearled, pot or Scotch, dry	1 cup	200	696	154	19.2	2.14	.48	1.52	2.2		0	.42	.14	
Pearled, light, dry	1 cup	200	698	158	16.4	.7	t	2	2		0	.24	.1	.448
Bran, wheat, raw	1 cup	57	121	35.4	9	5.2	.42	1.76	2.6		0	.41	.2	.468
Bran flakes, 40%, fortified	1 cup	35	106	28.2	3.6	1			.6		1650	.41	.49	.134
Bulgur (parboiled wheat), dry	1 cup	170	602	129	19	3	.34	1.48	2.5		0	.48	.24	.38
Breads														
Biscuit, enr.	2″ diam	28	103	12.8	2.1	.1	1	3	4.8		t	.06	.06	
Cornbread, whl grd	2″ sq	45	93	13.1	3.3	.2	.81	2.25	3.2	30	68	.06	.09	
Cracked wheat, enr	1 slice	23	60	12	2	.1	.1	.4	.6		t	.03	.02	.02
Cracked wheat, enr, toasted	1 slice	19	60	11.8	2	.1	.1	.4	.6		t	.02	.02	
English muffin, enr[1]	1 avg	130	27	4				1			t	.23	.136	
French or Vienna, enr	1 slice	20	58	11.1	1.8	t	.14	.45	.64		t	.06	.04	.01
Italian, enr	1 slice	20	55	11.3	1.8	t	t	.17	.3			.06	.05	
Pita, whole wheat, sesame	1 avg	42.5	140	24	6				2		t	.2	.068	
Pumpernickel	1 slice	32	79	17	2.9	.4			.4			.07	.04	.05
Raisin, enr	1 slice	23	60	12.3	1.5	.2	.18	.46	.64		t	.01	.02	
Rye, American	1 slice	23	56	12	2.1	.1			.3			.04	.02	.02
White, enr	1 slice	23	62	11.6	2	t	.16	.53	.79		t	.06	.05	.009
White, enr, toasted	1 slice	20	62	11.6	2	t	.1	.5	.7		t	.05	.05	
Whole wheat	1 slice	23	56	11	2.4	.4	.11	.42	.7		t	.06	.02	.04
Whole wheat, toasted	1 slice	19	55	11	2.4	.4	.1	.4	.7		t	.04	.02	
Breadcrumbs, enr, dry	1 cup	100	392	73.4	12.6	.3	1	3	4.6		t	.22	.3	
Buns (hamburger, hot dog), enr	1 avg	40	119	21.2	3.3		.5	1.6	2.2		t	.11	.07	
Cornflakes, fortified	1 cup	25	97	21	2				.1		1180	.29	.35	.016
Corn-grits (hominy), degermed, enr, ckd	1 cup	245	125	27	2.9	.2	.03	.17	.25		150[2]	.1	.07	t
Corn meal, whl grd, dry	1 cup	118	427	88	10.6	1.2	.46	3	4		566[2]	.35	.09	.29
Corn meal, degermed, enr, ckd	1 cup	238	119	25.5	2.4	.2	.05	.33	.5		142[2]	.14	.1	
Cornstarch	1 tbsp	8	29	7	t	t	t		.04	.05		0		.006	t
Crackers														
Graham, plain	1 lg	14.2	55	10.4	1.1	.22	.3	.9	1.3		0	.01	.03	
RyKrisp, Ralston	2 avg	12.6	42	9.6	1.6	.3			.15			.04	.03	
Soda	1 avg	2.8	12.5	2	.26	.008	.075	.225	.37		0	t	.001	
Soup or oyster	10	7.5	33	5.3	.7				1		0	t	t	
Whole wheat, Ak-Mak	4 pieces	28	117	18.9	4.64				2.33	14		.06	.04	
Zwieback	1 piece	7	31	5.4	.9	.02	.2	.4	.6	3		.004	.005	

[1]Thomas

[2]Based on yellow corn; the white variety has only a trace.

[3]No added salt. Added salt specified by manufacturer is 264 mg/cup cornmeal; 708 mg/cup cream of wheat; 353 mg/cup farina; 523 mg/cup oatmeal; 519 mg/cup wheat-meal cereal.

Vitamin B12 mcg	Biotin mcg	Folic Acid mg	Niacin mg	Pantothenic Acid mg	Vitamin C mg	Vitamin E mg	Sodium mg	Phosphorus mg	Potassium mg	Calcium mg	Iron mg	Magnesium mg	Copper mg	Manganese mg	Selenium mcg	Zinc mg
0	t		1.44	.19			17	72	60	12	t		.3		.46	.07
			t		8			3		4	.1					
			0		0		t	0	1	0	0					
			t					1		5	.1					
			t		21			6		6	t					
0			.48	.07			10		184	16		24		.72		
0		.002	.24	.07			12	24	221	22	.96	12	.3	.72	12	.24
0			0		0		59		t							
			.9	.008	0		2.3	5	83	4.6	.23	21.8	.05	.22	.3	.05
			0		0		2									.05
			0		0		18									
			0		0		18		.1							
			0		0		18									.02
			.1		1		1.6	4	58	5	.2	8	1.13	1.66	.1	.04
0		.04	7.4		0			580	592	68	5.4	71.4				
0			6.2	1	0		6	378	320	32	4	71.4	.8	3.36		
0		.147	12	1.65	0	5.13		727	639	67.8	8.49	279	.9		35.9	5.59
0		.04	4.1	.31	12		207	125	137	19	12.4		.213			1.26
0		7.7	7.8	1.12	0			575	389	49	6.3					
			.5			t	175	49	33	34	.4					
			.3			t	283	95	71	54	.5					
0		.01	.3	.14	t		122	29	31	20	.3	8				
			.3		t		120	29	30	20	.2	8				
			2		t					20	1.08		.1			
0		.002	.5	.08	t		116	17	18	9	.4	4				
			.5	.1			117	15	15	3	.4					.01
			2.4		t					40	1.8					
0			.4	.16			182	73	145	27	.8	23				.365
			.2		t		84	20	54	16	.3	6				
0		.006	.3	.1			128	34	33	17	.4	10	.06	.3		.4
t	.2	.009	.6	.1	t	.23	117	22	24	20	.6	5	.05	.07	6.44	.2
			.6		t		117	22	24	19	.5	5	.03			
0	.46	.013	.6	.174	t	.3	121	52	63	23	.5	18	.06		15.5	.5
			.6		t		119	52	62	22	.5	18				
			3.5		t		736	141	152	122	3.6		.2			.38
			.9		t		202	34	38	30	.8	14				.21
0		.003	2.9	.048	9		251	9	30	17	.6	3	.043	.012	.6	.08
0			1				502	25	27	2	.7	7				
0	t	.019	2.2	.65			1	263	293	20	2.1	125	.156			2.1
0			1.2			.354	t[3]	33	38	2	1	16				.3
			.002		0		.32	2.4		.32	0	.04	.16	.004		
			.2		0		95	21	55	6	.2	5.68	.03			
			.15				111	49		7	.5		.042			
0			.03		0	.1	31	2.5	3.4	.6	.04	.81	.001			
			.1		0		83	7	9	2	.1					
	3.29	.012	1.05	.18	1.6	.33		.01		21.3	.45	41	.08			.9
			.1				18.2	5.04	11	.95	.04					

Food Item	Measure	Weight g	Calories	Carbohydrate g	Protein g	Fiber g	Saturated fat g	Unsaturated fat g	Total fat g	Cholesterol mg	Vitamin A IU	Vitamin B$_1$ mg	Vitamin B$_2$ mg	Vitamin B$_6$ mg
Cream of wheat, ckd	1 cup	200	133	28.2	4.5	.1			.4		0	.11	.07	
Farina, enr, ckd	1 cup	245	103	21.3	3.2	.2	.074	.25	.49		0	.1	.07	
Flour														
Buckwheat, dark, sftd	1 cup	100	333	72	11.7	1.6	.47	1.76	2.5		0	.58	.15	.578
Buckwheat, light, sftd	1 cup	100	347	79.5	6.4	.5	.24	.83	1.2		0	.08	.04	
Carob (St. John's bread)	1 tbsp	8	14	6.5	.4	.64			.1					
Corn	1 cup	117	431	89.9	9.1		.35	2.34	3		400	.23	.07	
Gluten, wheat	1 cup	140	529	66.1	58	.6			2.7		0			
Pastry, wheat, sftd	1 cup	100	364	79.4	7.5	.2			.8		0	.03	.03	.045
Peanut, defatted	1 cup	60	223	18.9	28.7	1.62	1.2	4	5.5			.45	.13	
Potato	1 cup	110	386	87.9	8.8	1.76			.88		t	.46	.15	.008
Rice, granulated	1 cup	125	479	107	7.5	.2			.4		0	.52	.14	.2
Rye, dark, sftd	1 cup	128	419	87.2	20.9	3.07	.42	1	3.3			.78	.28	.384
Rye, light, sftd	1 cup	80	286	62.3	7.5	.3			.8			.12	.05	.07
Soy, full-fat, stirred	1 cup	72	303	21.9	26.4	1.7	2.5	10.6	14.2		79	.61	.22	.48
Soy, low-fat, stirred	1 cup	100	356	36.6	43.4	2.5	1.02	4.88	6.7		80	.83	.36	.68
Soy, defatted, stirred	1 cup	138	450	52.6	64.9	3.2	1.17	23	2.76		55	1.5	.47	1
Wheat, all purpose, sftd	1 cup	110	400	83.7	11.6	.3			1.1		0	.07	.06	.066
Wheat, all purpose, enr, sftd	1 cup	110	400	83.7	11.6	.3			1.1		0	.48	.28	.066
Wheat, whole, stirred	1 cup	120	400	85.2	16	2.8	t	2	2.4		0	.66	.14	.41
Granola[1]	1 cup	85	390	57	9				15			.09	.034	
Macaroni, enr, ckd	1 cup	140	151	32.2	4.8	.1			1		0	.2	.11	.029
Millet, whl grain, dry	1 cup	228	746	166	22.6	7.3	1.96	4.1	6.8		0	1.66	.87	
Muffins														
Plain, enr	1 avg	40	118	16.9	3.1	.1	1	3	4		40	.07	.09	
Bran, enr	1 avg	40	104	17.2	3.1	.72	1.2	2.4	3.9		90	.06	.1	
Corn meal, whl grd	1 med	45	130	19.1	3.2	.2	2.3	2.2	4.6		140	.08	.08	
Whole wheat	1 avg	40	103	20.9	4	.6			1.1		t	.14	.05	
Noodles, egg, enr, ckd	1 cup	160	200	37.3	6.6	.2	1	1	2.4	50	112	.22	.13	.04
Oat flakes, fortified	1 cup	37	147	26.7	6.67	.5			2.1			.5	.57	.67
Oatmeal (rolled oats), ckd	1 cup	240	132	23.3	4.8	.5	.4	1.76	2.4		0	.19	.05	.024
Pancakes														
Plain, enr	4" diam	27	62	9.2	1.9	.1	.5	1.3	1.9		30	.05	.06	
Buckwheat, from mix	4" diam	27	54	6.4	1.8	.2	.8	1.5	2.5		60	.03	.04	
Whole wheat[3]	4" diam	45	74	8.8	3.4				3.2		80	.09	.07	
Pasta, whole wheat, dry[6]	4 oz	113	400	78	20				1		200	.6	.85	
Pizza, cheese, 14" diam	1/8	65	153	18.4	7.8	.2	2	3	5.4		410	.04	.13	
Popcorn, plain	1 cup	14	54	10.7	1.8	.3	t	.6	.7			.055	.02	.03
Pretzel, twisted	1 avg	16	62	12.1	1.6	.05			.7		0	.003	.008	.003
Rice														
Brown, raw	1 cup	196	704	152	14.8	1.6			3.6		0	.68	.08	1
Brown, ckd w/salt	1 cup	150	178	38.2	3.8	.45	.31	.94	1.2		0	.14	.03	
Instant, enr, ckd w/salt	1 cup	165	180	39.9	3.6	.1			t		0	.21		
Parboiled, enr, ckd w/salt	1 cup	175	186	40.8	3.7	.2	.1	.24	.4		0	.19	.02	
White, ckd w/salt	1 cup	205	223	49.6	4.1	.2	.1	.24	.4		0	.04	.02	
White, enr, dry	1 cup	195	708	157	13.1	.4	.4	.9	1.5		0	.86	.06	.3
White, enr, ckd w/salt	1 cup	205	223	49.6	4.1	.2	.1	.24	.4		0	.23	.02	
Wild, raw	1 cup	160	565	121	22.6	.12			1.1		0	.72	1.01	
Rice, puffed, fortified w/o salt, sugar	1 cup	15	60	13.4	.9	.1			.1		0	.07	.01	.01
Rice polish or bran	1 cup	105	278	60.6	12.7	2.4	2.44	9.34	12.8		0	1.93	.19	
Rolls														
Danish, enr	1 avg	42	179	19.4	3.1	t	3.25	6.5	10		130	.03	.06	
Dinner, enr	1 avg	38	113	20.1	3.1	.1	.54	1.49	2.2		t	.11	.07	
Hard, enr	1 avg	50	156	29.8	4.9	.1	.28	.77	1.6		t	.13	.12	
Whole wheat	1 avg	35	90	18.3	3.5	.6			1		t	.12	.05	
Shredded wheat, biscuit	1 avg	25	89	20	2.5	.5	.09	.38	.5		0	.06	.03	.06
Spaghetti, enr, ckd	1 cup	140	155	32.2	4.8	.2			.6		0	.2	.11	
Tapioca, dry	1 cup	152	535	131	.9	.15			.3		0	0	.15	
Tortilla, yellow corn	6" diam	30	63	13.5	1.5	.3			.6		6	.04	.015	.022

[1] Nature Valley; made with oats, brown sugar, honey, and sesame seeds.

[3] 25% soya powder; prepared with egg, milk, and oil.

[6] Erewhon, made with 96% durum flour and 4% vegetable flour.

Vitamin B12 mcg	Biotin mcg	Folic Acid mg	Niacin mg	Pantothenic Acid mg	Vitamin C mg	Vitamin E mg	Sodium mg	Phosphorus mg	Potassium mg	Calcium mg	Iron mg	Magnesium mg	Copper mg	Manganese mg	Selenium mcg	Zinc mg
0			.85		0		3.7[3]	110		13	1.4	8				
0			1.3		0		2[3]	29	22	10	2–12	8	.25			.2
0			2.9	1.5	0		1	347	656	33	5		.7	2.09		
			.4		0		1	88	320	11	1	48				
								6		28	.33					
			1.6		0		1	92		7	2.1					
					0		3	196	84	56						
0			.7	.32	0		2	73	95	17	.5	26				.3
			16.7		0		5	432	712	62	2.1	216				
0			3.74		19		37.4	196	1747	36.3	18.9					
0			7.2		0			120		11	6.8	35				
0			3.5	1.7	0		1	686	1101	69	5.8	147			.54	
0		.069	.5	.58	0		1	148	125	18	.9	58	.3			
0	49	.311	1.5	1.22	0		1	402	1195	143	6	178				
0			2.6	2.08	0		1	634	1859	263	9.1	289				
0			3.6	3.06	0		1	904	2512	366	15.3	428				
0	1.1	.024	1	.51	0	1.87	2	96	105	18	.9	28	.21		21.7	.77
0	1.1	.024	3.9	.51	0	1.87	2	96	105	18	3.2	28	.21		21.7	.77
0	6	.065	5.2	1.32	0	3.12	4	446	444	49	4	136	.6		77.4	2.88
			t					80		20	1.08	32	.08			.6
0			1.5		0		1[3]	70	85	11	1.2	25	.028			.7
			5.24		0	4		709	980	45.6	15.5	369				
			.6		t		176	60	50	42	.6	11				
			1.6		t		179	162	172	57	1.5					
			.5		t		223	97	59	50	.6	48				
			1.2		t		226	112	117	42	1	45				
t			1.9		0		3[3]	94	70	16	1.4		.27			
2		.13	3.2			.09	420	133	133	53	3.1	53.7	.274	1.81		
0			.2	.236	0		.8[3]	137	146	22	1.4	50	.07			1.18
			.4		t		115	38	33	27	.4	6.59	.02			.37
			.2		t		125	91	66	59	.4	13.2				
			.4		t					50	.54					
			8		10.8			400		20	5.4					
			.7		5		456	127	85	144	.7					.79
0			.3		0		t	39	33.6	2	.4		.04			.574
t			.1	.09	0	t	269	21	21	4	.2		.024			.173
0	18	.032	9.2	2.1	0	3	16	432	420	64	3.2	172	.4	3.2	77.2	3.6
			2.1		0		423	110	105	18	.8	45				.9
			1.7		0		450	31	t	5	1.3					.33
			2.1		0		627	100	75	33	1.4		.47			.526
			.8		0		767	57	57	21	.4	12	.04			.8
0	5.86	.02	6.8	1.26	0	.7	10	183	179	47	5.7	13	.2	2.1	65.1	2.5
			2.1		0		767	57	57	21	1.8	12	.04			.8
0			9.9	1.63	0		11	542	352	30	6.7	144				
0		.003	.7	.049	0		t	14	15	3	.3		.051		.403	.18
		.039	29.6		0		t	1161	750	72	16.9					
			.3		t		156	46	48	21	.4	8				.35
			.8		t		192	32	36	28	.7	14				.46
			1.4		t		313	46	49	24	1.2	8				.4
			1.1		t		197	98	102	37	.8	40				
0		.011	1.1	.155	0		1	97	87	11	.9	33			1.1	.62
0			1.5		0		1[3]	70	85	11	1.3	27				
		.012	0		0		5	27	27	15	.6	3	.14	1.04		
0			.3	.016	0			42		60	.9	32				

Food Item	Measure	Weight g	Calories	Carbohydrate g	Protein g	Fiber g	Saturated fat g	Unsaturated fat g	Total fat g	Cholesterol mg	Vitamin A IU	Vitamin B$_1$ mg	Vitamin B$_2$ mg	Vitamin B$_6$ mg
Waffles, plain, enr	5½″ diam	75	209	28.1	7	.1	2	5	7.4		248	.13	.19	
Wheat germ														
Raw	1 cup	100	363	46.7	26.6	2.5	1.88	8.18	10.9	0	2	.68	.92	
Toasted[7]	1 cup	96	368	48	29	1.7	1.59	8	11.2	110	1.76	.8	1.1	
Wheat flakes, fortified	1 cup	30	106	24.2	3.1	.5	.11	.47	.72	1410	.35	.42	.088	
Wheat, puffed, fortified w/o sugar, salt	1 cup	15	54	11.8	2.3	.2			.2	0	.08	.03	.02	
Wheatmeal cereal														
Dry	1 cup	125	423	90.4	16.9	.75	.325	.94	2.75	0	.64	.16	.489	
Cooked	1 cup	245	110	23	4.4				.7	0	.15	.05		

DAIRY PRODUCTS

Cheese

Food Item	Measure	Weight g	Calories	Carbohydrate g	Protein g	Fiber g	Saturated fat g	Unsaturated fat g	Total fat g	Cholesterol mg	Vitamin A IU	Vitamin B$_1$ mg	Vitamin B$_2$ mg	Vitamin B$_6$ mg
American, pasteurized, processed	1 oz	28	107	.5	6.5	0	5.58	2.82	8.86	27	340	.006	.11	.02
Blue	1 oz	28	103	.66	6	0	5.3	2.44	8.15	21	204	.008	.108	.047
Brick	1 oz	28	103	.79	6.59	0	5.32	2.66	8.4	27	307	.004	.1	.018
Brie	1 oz	28	95	.13	5.88	0			7.85	28	189	.02	.147	.067
Camembert, domestic	1 oz	28	84	.5	5.6	0	4.33	2.19	6.9	20	262	.01	.21	.064
Cheddar, American	1 oz	28	112	.36	7	0	5.98	2.93	9.4	30	300	.008	.106	.021
Cheddar, American, grated, not packed	1 cup	113	455	1.45	28	0	23.8	11.7	37.4	119	1197	.03	.424	.084
Cheese spread, American, pasteurized, processed	1 oz	28	81	2.3	4.5	0	3.78	1.94	6	16	223	.003	.122	.033
Colby	1 oz	28	112	.73	6.74	0	5.73	2.9	9.1	27	293	.004	.106	.022
Cottage, creamed, not packed	1 cup	210	217	5.6	26.2	0	5.99	3	9.47	31	342	.044	.342	.141
Cottage, 2% fat, not packed	1 cup	226	203	8.2	31	0	2.76	1.37	4.36	19	158	.054	.418	.172
Cottage, dry, not packed	1 cup	145	123	2.68	25	0	.396	.182	.61	10	44	.036	.206	.119
Cream	1 oz	28	105	.6	2.2	0	5.88	3.64	10.6	31	430	.006	.06	.013
Edam	1 oz	28	101	.4	7.7	0	4.98	2.49	7.8	25	260	.01	.11	.022
Gjetost	1 oz	28	132	12.09	2.74	0	5.43	2.5	8.37					
Gouda	1 oz	28	101	.63	7.07	0	4.99	2.39	7.78	32	183	.009	.095	.023
Gruyere	1 oz	28	115	15	8.45	0	5.36	3.34	9.17	31	346	.017	.079	.023
Limberger	1 oz	28	93	.14	5.68	0	4.75	2.58	7.72	26	363	.023	.143	.024
Monterey	1 oz	28	106	.19	6.94	0			8.58		269		.11	
Mozzarella	1 oz	28	80	.63	5.51	0	3.73	2.08	6.12	22	225	.004	.069	.018
Mozzarella, part skim, low moisture	1 oz	28	79	.89	7.79	0	3.08	1.52	4.85	15	178	.006	.097	.022
Muenster	1 oz	28	104	.32	6.64	0	5.42	2.66	8.52	27	318	.004	.091	.016
Parmesan, hard	1 oz	28	110	.8	10	0	4.65	2.29	7.3	19	300	.011	.094	.026
Parmesan, grated	1 tbsp	5	23	.19	2.08	0	.95	.47	1.5	4	35	.002	.019	.005
Port du Salut	1 oz	28	100	.16	6.74	0	4.73	2.86	8	35	378		.068	.015
Provolone	1 oz	28	100	.61	7.25	0	4.84	2.32	7.55	20	231	.005	.091	.021
Ricotta, whl milk	1 cup	246	428	7.48	27.7	0	20.4	9.87	31.9	124	1205	.032	.48	.11
Ricotta, part skim	1 cup	246	340	12.6	28	0	12.1	6	19.5	9	1063	.052	.455	.049
Roquefort	1 oz	28	105	.57	6.1	0	5.46	2.77	8.69	26	297	.011	.166	.035
Swiss	1 oz	28	107	.96	8.06	0	5.04	2.34	7.78	26	240	.006	.103	.024
Swiss, pasteurized, processed	1 oz	28	95	.6	7.01	0	4.55	2.18	7.09	24	229	.004	.078	.01
Cheese souffle, cheddar	1 cup	95	207	5.9	9.4		8.57	6.67	16.2	159	760	.05	.23	

Cream

Food Item	Measure	Weight g	Calories	Carbohydrate g	Protein g	Fiber g	Saturated fat g	Unsaturated fat g	Total fat g	Cholesterol mg	Vitamin A IU	Vitamin B$_1$ mg	Vitamin B$_2$ mg	Vitamin B$_6$ mg
Half and half	1 cup	242	315	10.4	7.16	0	17.3	9.07	27.8	89	1050	.085	.361	.094
Half and half	1 tbsp	15	20	.64	.44	0	1.07	.56	1.72	6	65	.005	.022	.006
Coffee or table	1 tbsp	15	29	.55	.4	0	1.8	.96	2.9	10	108	.005	.022	.005
Sour, cultured	1 cup	230	493	9.8	7.27	0	30	15.7	48.7	102	1817	.081	.343	.037
Whipping, lt	1 cup	239	699	7.07	5.19	0	46.2	23.8	73.9	265	2694	.057	.299	.067
Whipping, hvy	1 cup	238	821	6.64	4.88	0	54.8	28.7	88.1	326	3499	.052	.262	.062

Eggs

Food Item	Measure	Weight g	Calories	Carbohydrate g	Protein g	Fiber g	Saturated fat g	Unsaturated fat g	Total fat g	Cholesterol mg	Vitamin A IU	Vitamin B$_1$ mg	Vitamin B$_2$ mg	Vitamin B$_6$ mg
Raw, ext lge	1	64	94	.5	7.4	0	2.18	2.67	7.24	351	680	.06	.17	.077
Raw, lge	1	57	82	.5	6.5	0	1.94	2.37	6.44	312	590	.05	.15	.068
Raw, med	1	50	72	.4	5.7	0	1.75	2.08	5.65	274	520	.05	.13	.06
Raw, sm	1	40	65	.4	5.2	0	1.36	1.66	4.5	219	470	.04	.12	.048

[7]Used mainly as a ready-to-eat cereal.

Vitamin B$_{12}$ mcg	Biotin mcg	Folic Acid mg	Niacin mg	Pantothenic Acid mg	Vitamin C mg	Vitamin E mg	Sodium mg	Phosphorus mg	Potassium mg	Calcium mg	Iron mg	Magnesium mg	Copper mg	Manganese mg	Selenium mcg	Zinc mg
			1	.5	t		356	130	109	85	1.3	19				
		.328	4.2	2.2	0	15	3	1118	827	72	9.4	336	1.3		83.3	14.3
0		.42	4.8	1.15	10		2	1080	912	48	8					14.8
0			3.5		11		310	83	81	12	1.3		.132		3.3	.691
0			1.2		0		1	48	51	4	.6		.052			.312
			5.9				3	498	463	56	4.6	128	.32		30	4.5
			1.5		0		t[3]	127	118	17	1.2					
.197		.002	.02	.137	0	.28	406	216	46	174	.11	6	.017	.004	2.52	.85
.345		.01	.288	.490	0		396	110	73	150	.09	7	.011	.003		.75
.28		.006	.033	.081	0		159	127	38	191	.1	7	.007	.003		.74
.468		.018	.108	.196	0		178	53	43	52	.14					
.367	1	.018	.2	.387	0		239	98	53	110	.1	6	.022	.011		.68
.234	1	.005	.023	.117	0		176	145	28	211	.19	8	.031	.003		.88
.935		.021	.09	.467	0		701	579	111	815	.77	31				3.51
.113		.002	.037	.194	0		381	202	67	158	.09	8	.009	.005		.73
.234			.026	.06	0		171	129	36	194	.22	7	.012	.003		.87
1.31		.026	.265	.447	t		850	277	177	126	.29	11	.04	.007	11.3	.78
1.61		.03	.325	.547	t		918	340	217	155	.36	14				.95
1.2	3	.021	.225	.236	0		19	151	47	46	.33	6				.68
.12		.004	t	.077	0		70	23	21	17	.1	2	.011	.001		.15
.435		.005	.023	.08	0		274	136	53	225	.12	8	.008	.003		1.06
		.001	.23		0		170	126		113						
		.006	.018	.096	0		232	155	34	198	.07	8				1.11
.454		.003	.03	.159	0		95	172	23	287	.3	12				
.295		.016	.045	.334	0		227	111	36	141	.2	6				.6
					0		152	126	23	212	.2	8	.009	.003		.85
.185		.002	.024	.018	0		106	105	19	147	.05	5				.63
.262		.003	.034	.026	0		150	149	27	207	.07	7	.008	.003		.89
.418		.003	.029	.054	0		178	133	38	203	.12	8	.009	.002		.8
.002			.077	.128	0		205	197	42	320	.23	13	.101	.006		.78
		t	.016	.026	0		93	40	5	69	.05	3	.018			.16
.425		.005	.017	.06	0		151	102		184						
.415		.003	.044	.135	0		248	141	39	214	.15	8	.007	.003		.92
.831			.256		0		207	389	257	509	.94	28	.085	.024		2.85
.716			.192		0		307	449	308	669	1.08	36				3.3
.182	.8	.014	.208	.491	0		513	111	26	188	.16	8	.01	.009		.59
.475		.002	.026	.122	0	.098	74	171	31	272	.3	10	.036	.005	2.83	1.11
.348			.011	.074	0		388	216	61	219	.17	8				1.02
			.2		t		346	185	115	191	1					
.796		.006	.189	.699	2.08		98	230	314	254	.17	25				1.23
.049		t	.012	.043	.13		6	14	19	16	.01	2				.08
.033		t	.009	.041	.11		6	12	18	14	.01	1	.033		.075	.04
.690		.025	.154	.828	1.98		123	195	331	268	.14	26				.62
.466	.119	.009	.1	.619	1.46	1.4	82	146	231	166	.07	17				.6
.428	.071	.009	.093	.607	1.38	3	89	149	179	154	.07	17				.55
.99	13	.041	.039	1.11	0	.64	70	118	74	31	1.3	7.68	.13	.032	14.8	.922
.88	11	.036	.035	.986	0	.57	61	103	65	27	1.2	6	.1	.029	13.2	.84
.773	10	.032	.031	.864	0	.5	54	90	57	24	1	5	.09	.025	11.6	.72
.618	8	.026	t	.69	0	.4	49	82	52	22	.9	4	.05	.02	9.24	.576

Food Item	Measure	Weight g	Calories	Carbohydrate g	Protein g	Fiber g	Saturated fat g	Unsaturated fat g	Total fat g	Cholesterol mg	Vitamin A IU	Vitamin B$_1$ mg	Vitamin B$_2$ mg	Vitamin B$_6$ mg
Raw, white	1 lg	33	17	.3	3.6	0	0	0		0	0	.002	.094	.001
Raw, yolk	1 lg	17	59	.1	2.79	0	1.72	3	5.7	312	580	.043	.074	.053
Fried[8]	1 lg	46	99	.53	5.37	0	2.41	1	6.4	312	640	.033	.126	.05
Hard cooked	1 lg	57	82	.5	6.5	0	1.9	3.36	5.8	312	590	.04	.14	.065
Omelet or scrambled[9]	1 egg	64	111	1.5	7.2	0	2.82	3.31	7.08	314	690	.05	.18	.058
Poached	1 lg	50	82	.5	6.5	0	1.67	2.94	5.8	312	590	.04	.13	.051
Dried, whole	2 tbsp	10	60	.48	4.58	0	1.26	2.22	4.18	210	600	.03	.118	.04
Eggnog[10]	1 cup	254	342	34.4	9.68	0	11.3	6.53	19	149	894	.086	.483	.127
Ice cream, hard	1 cup	133	269	31.7	4.8	0	8.92	4.67	14.3	59	543	.052	.329	.061
Ice milk, hard	1 cup	131	184	29	5.16	0	3.51	1.84	5.63	18	214	.076	.347	.085
Milk														
Buttermilk	1 cup	244	99	11.7	8.1	0	1.34	.7	2.16	9	81	.083	.337	.083
Chocolate, whole	1 cup	250	208	25.9	7.92	.3	5.26	2.79	8.48	30	500[11]	.092	.405	.1
Condensed, sweetened	1 cup	306	982	166	24.8	0	16.8	8.46	26.6	104	1004	.275	1.27	.156
Dried, whole	1 cup	128	635	49.2	33.7	0	21.4	11	34.2	124	1180	.362	1.54	.387
Dried, whole, instant	1 cup	68	527	40.1	27.7			28.9	65	1190	.3	1.53		
Dried, nonfat	1 cup	120	435	62.4	43.4	0	.6	.28	.92	24	43[12]	.498	.1.86	.433
Dried, nonfat, instant	1 cup	68	244	35.5	23.9	0	.32	.15	.49	12	18.4[12]	.281	1.19	.235
Evaporated, whole, unsw	1 cup	252	338	25.3	17.2	0	11.6	6.5	19.1	74	612	.118	.796	.126
Evaporated, skim, unsw	1 cup	256	198	28.9	19.3	0	.31	.174	.52	10	1000	.114	.788	.14
Goat, whole	1 cup	244	168	10.9	8.69	0	6.5	3.07	10.1	28	451	.117	.337	.112
Human	1 oz	30.8	21	2.12	.32	0	.62	.66	1.35	4	74	.004	.011	.003
Low-fat	1 cup	244	121	11.7	8.12	0	2.92	1.52	4.68	18	500[11]	.095	.403	.105
Malted[13]	1 cup	265	236	26.6	10.8	.13	5.96	3.46	9.94	37	376	.204	.538	.18
Skim	1 cup	245	86	11.8	8.35	0	.287	.132	.44	4	500[11]	.088	.343	.098
Whole	1 cup	244	159	11.4	8.5	0	5.07	2.65	8.15	33	350	.093	.395	.102
Sherbet	1 cup	193	270	58.7	2.16	t	2.38	1.24	3.82	14	185	.033	.089	.025
Whey, sweet, dry	1 tbsp	7.5	26	5.56	.96	0	.05	.02	.08	.t	3	.039	.165	.044
Yogurt														
Whole milk, plain	8 oz	227	139	10.6	7.88	0	4.76	2.24	7.38	29	279	.066	.322	.073
Low-fat, plain, 12 g protein[14,15]	8 oz	227	144	16	11.9	0	2.27	1.07	3.52	14	150	.1	.486	.11
Skim, plain, 13 g protein[15]	8 oz	227	127	17.4	13	0	.264	.124	.41	4	16	.109	.531	.12
Low-fat, fruit, 9 g protein[14,15,16]	8 oz	227	225	42.3	9.04	.27	1.68	.79	2.61	10	111	.077	.368	.084
Low-fat, fruit, 11 g protein[14,15,16]	8 oz	227	239	42.2	11	.27	2.06	.97	3.2	12	136	.093	.449	.102
DESSERTS AND SWEETS														
Apple or brown Betty[17]	1 cup	215	325	63.9	3.4	1.4	2.15	2.2	7.5		220	.13	.09	
Apple butter	1 tbsp	17.6	33	8.2	.1	.2			.1		0	t	t	
Boston cream pie, ⅛ cake	1 piece	103	311	51.4	5.2	0	3	5	9.7		220	.03	.11	
Brownies, enr, 2 × 2 × ¾"	1 piece	30	146	15.3	2	.2	1.5	6	9.4	25.5	60	.05	.03	
Cake														
Angel food, 1/10 cake	1 piece	45	121	27.1	3.2	▸0			.1		0	.004	.06	
Chocolate, devils food, no icing, 2 × 3 × 2"	1 piece	45	165	23.4	2.2	.1			7.7		68	.009	.045	

[8]Made with ½ tsp fat and dash of salt.

[9]Made with 1½ tbsp milk, ½ tsp fat, and dash of salt.

[10]Made with 8 oz whole milk, one egg, and 3 tsp sugar.

[11]Value if vitamin A is added.

[12]Value based on data without added vitamin A. If vitamin A is added, each cup of reconstituted milk contains 500 IU.

[13]Made with 8 oz whole milk, 3 heaping tsp malt powder.

[14]Fat content may vary with resultant variation in vitamin A and fat constituents.

[15]Contains nonfat milk solids.

[16]Carbohydrate and calorie content may vary because of amount of sugar or honey added, and/or the level and solids content of added flavoring material.

[17]Made with enriched bread.

Vitamin B$_{12}$ mcg	Biotin mcg	Folic Acid mg	Niacin mg	Pantothenic Acid mg	Vitamin C mg	Vitamin E mg	Sodium mg	Phosphorus mg	Potassium mg	Calcium mg	Iron mg	Magnesium mg	Copper mg	Manganese mg	Selenium mcg	Zinc mg
.021	2	.005	.029	.08	0		48	5	46	3	.01	2.97	.025	.013	1.88	.01
.647	9	.026	.012	.753	0	.51	9	97	17	24	.95	2.72	.045	.015	2.96	.58
.581		.022	.026	.763	0		144	80	58	26	.92	5	.023			.64
.749		.027	.034	.985	0		61	103	65	27	1.2	6.84				.821
.638		.022	.042	.819	0		164	121	93	51	1.1	8	.032			.7
.616		.024	.026	.86	0		61	103	65	27	1.2	6	.015			.72
.001			.024	.638	0		52	68	48	22	.78	4	.018			.54
1.14		.002	.267	1.06	3.8		138	278	420	330	.51	47				1.17
.625		.003	.134	.654	.7	.399	116	134	257	176	.12	18	.2			1.4
.875		.003	.118	.662	.76		105	129	265	176	.18	19				.55
.537	5		.142	.674	2.4	.118	257	219	371	285		27	.047			1.03
.835		.012	.313	.738	2.28		149	251	417	280	.6	33				1.02
1.36	9	.034	.643	2.3	7.96		389	775	1136	868	.58	77	.66			2.88
4.16	17	.047	.827	2.91	11.1		475	993	1702	1168	.6	108	.4			4.28
			.7		6		425	743	1397	954	.5					
4.84	19	.06	1.14	4.28	8.1		642	1162	2153	1508	.38	132				4.9
2.72		.034	.606	2.2	3.79		373	670	1160	837	.21	80				3
.41	7	.02	.488	1.61	4.74	.75	266	510	764	658	.48	60	.075		3.02	1.94
.61		.022	.444	1.88	2.16		294	496	846	738	.74	68				2.3
.159	5	.001	.676	.756	3.15		122	270	499	326	.12	34	.095	.019		.73
.014	t	.002	.055	.069	1.54	.069	5	4	16	10	.01	1	.015	t		.05
.888		.012	.21	.78	2.32		122	232	377	297	.12	33				.95
1.04		.022	1.28	.766	2.31		215	307	529	347	.29	52				1.14
.926	5	.013	.216	.806	2.4	t	126	247	406	302	.1	28	.1		11	.98
.871	5	.012	.205	.766	2.29	.293	120	228	351	291	.12	33	.5	.005	3.17	.93
.158		.014	.131	.062	3.86		88	74	198	103	.31	15				1.33
.177		.001	.094	.419	.11		80	70	155	59	.07	13				.15
.844		.017	.17	.883	1.2		105	215	351	274	.11	26				1.34
1.28		.025	.259	1.34	1.82		159	326	531	415	.18	40				2.02
1.39		.028	.281	1.46	1.98		174	355	579	452	.2	43				2.2
.967		.019	.195	1.01	1.36		121	247	402	314	.14	30				1.5
1.18		.024	.238	1.24	1.68		147	301	491	383	.16	37				1.86
		.9			2		329	47	215	39	1.3	14	.774			
		t			t		t	6	44	2	.1		.065			
		.2			t		192	104	92	69	.5					
		.2			t		75	44	57	12	.6					
		.1			0		127	10	40	4	.1	6.76				
		.1	.1		t		132	62	63	33	.4		.144			

Food Item	Measure	Weight g	Calories	Carbohydrate g	Protein g	Fiber g	Saturated fat g	Unsaturated fat g	Total fat g	Cholesterol mg	Vitamin A IU	Vitamin B₁ mg	Vitamin B₂ mg	Vitamin B₆ mg
Gingerbread, enr, 3 × 3 × 2″	1 piece	117	371	60.8	4.4	t			12.5		110	.14	.13	
Pound, old-fashioned, 3 × 3 × ½″	1 piece	30	142	14.1	1.7	t			8.8		84	.009	.03	
Pound, low-fat, 3 × 3 × ½″	1 piece	30	123	16.4	1.9	t			5.6		87	.01	.03	
Sponge, 1/10 cake	1 piece	50	149	27	3.8	0	1	1	2.85	123	225	.03	.07	
White, no icing	1 piece	50	188	27	2.3	.1	2	5	8		15	.005	.04	.025
Cake icing														
Chocolate	1 cup	275	1034	185	8.8	t	21	15	38.2		580	.06	.28	
White, boiled	1 cup	94	297	75.5	1.3	0			0		0	t	.03	
Candied citron	1 oz	28	89	22.7	.1	.39			.1					
Candy														
Caramel, plain or chocolate	1 piece	5	20	3.88	.2	.01	.357	.179	.536		t	.002	.009	
Chocolate milk bar, plain	1 oz	28	147	16.1	2.2	.112	5	3	9.2		80	.02	.1	
Chocolate fudge	1″ cube	21	84	15.8	.6	.04	1.5	.752	3		t	t	.02	
Mint patty, chocolate-covered	1¼″ diam	11	45	8.9	.2	t			1.2		t	t	.01	
Peanut brittle	1 oz	25	119	23	1.6	.125	.5	1.75	2.6		0	.05	.01	
Chocolate														
Bitter or baking	1 oz	28	143	8.2	3	.7	8	6	15		20	.01	.07	
Bittersweet	1 oz	28	135	13.3	2.2	.5			11.3		10	.01	.05	
Semisweet	1 oz	28	144	16.2	1.2	.28	5.6	3.79	10.1		10	t	.02	
Chocolate syrup	1 tbsp	18.7	46	11.7	.45	.1	t	t	.49		t	.005	.015	
Cookies														
Chocolate chip, enr, 2¼″ diam	1	10	51	6	.55	t	1	2	3		10	.01	.01	
Fig bar	1	14	50	10.5	.55	.238	.14	.42	.775		15	.005	.01	
Gingersnap, 2″ diam	1	7	29.4	5.59	.39	t			.62		5	.003	.004	
Macaroon	1 med	14	67	9.3	.7	.3	2.24	.84	3.2		0	.006	.02	
Oatmeal w/raisin, 3″ diam	1	14	63	10.3	.9	.1			2.2		7	.015	.011	
Vanilla wafer	1	3.67	17	2.73	.2	t			.6		4.67	.067	.027	
Custard, baked	1 cup	265	305	29.4	14.3	0	7	6	14.6	278	930	.11	.5	
Doughnut														
Cake, plain	1 avg	32	125	16.4	1.5	t	1	4	6		26	.05	.05	
Raised, plain	1 avg	30	124	11.3	1.9	.1	1.8	5.69	8		18	.05	.05	
Eclair, custard, choc-olate icing	1 avg	100	239	23.2	6.2	0	4	8	13.6		340	.04	.16	
Honey	1 tbsp	21	64	17.3	.1	0			0		0	.002	.014	.004
Jams, preserves	1 tbsp	20	54	14	.1	.1			t		t	t	.01	.005
Jellies	1 tbsp	18	49	12.7	t	0			t		t	t	.01	
Molasses														
Blackstrap	1 tbsp	20	43	11	0							.02	.04	.054
Light	1 tbsp	20	50	13	0							.01	.01	
Pie														
Apple, 1/6 of 9″ pie	1 piece	160	410	61	3.4	.6	4.74	11.8	17.8	156	48	.03	.03	
Meringue, lemon, 1/6 of pie	1 piece	140	357	52.8	5.2	t	4.67	8.33	14.3	130	238	.05	.11	
Pecan, 1/6 of pie	1 piece	160	668	82	8.2	.8	5.36	28	36.6		256	.25	.11	
Pumpkin, 1/6 of pie	1 piece	150	317	36.7	6	.8	5.77	9.23	16.8	91	3700	.04	.15	
Piecrust, baked, enr, 9″	1	135	675	59.1	8.2	.3	12	30	45.2		0	.27	.19	
Pudding														
Bread w/raisins, enr	1 cup	265	496	75.3	14.8	.2	7.95	5.3	16.2	170	800	.16	.5	
Chocolate, cornstarch	1 cup	260	385	66.8	8.1	.2	7	4	12.2	30	390	.05	.36	
Rice w/raisins	1 cup	265	387	70.8	9.5	.133	5.3	2.65	8.2	29	290	.08	.37	
Tapioca cream	1 cup	165	221	28.2	8.3	0	4	3	8.4		480	.07	.3	
Sugar														
Beet or cane, granulated	1 cup	200	770	199	0	0			0		0	0	0	
Beet or cane, granulated	1 tbsp	12	46	11.9	0	0			0		0	0	0	
Brown, packed	1 cup	220	821	212	0	0			0		0	.02	.07	
Powdered	1 cup	120	462	119	0	0			0		0	0	0	
Raw, brown	1 tbsp	14	14	12.7	.06				.07		t	.003	.016	
Syrup														
Maple	1 tbsp	20	50	12.8	0	0			0		0			
Corn	1 tbsp	20	57	14.8	0	0			0		0	0	.002	

Vitamin B$_{12}$ mcg	Biotin mcg	Folic Acid mg	Niacin mg	Pantothenic Acid mg	Vitamin C mg	Vitamin E mg	Sodium mg	Phosphorus mg	Potassium mg	Calcium mg	Iron mg	Magnesium mg	Copper mg	Manganese mg	Selenium mcg	Zinc mg
			1.1		0		277	76	531	80	2.7					
			.1		0		33	24	18	6	.2					
			.1		t		53	31	23	12	.2		.027			
		.003	.1		t		84	56	44	15	.6					
			.1	.15	t	4.21	162	46	38	32	.1					.1
			.6		1		168	305	536	165	3.3					
			t		0		134	2	17	2	t					
							82	7	34	24	.2					
			.018		t		11.4	6.25	9.64	7.5	.071					
		.002	.1		t	.308	27	65	109	65	.3	16.2	.137			.129
			t		t		40	18	31	16	.2					.192
			t		t		20	6	10	6	.1		.004			.038
			1		0		9	27	43	10	.7					
			.4		0	3.12	1	109	235	22	1.9	81.8	.748			
			.3		0		1	81	174	16	1.4					
			.1		t		1	43	92	9	.7					
			.1		0		10	17	53	3	.3	11.8	.08			.15
		.001	.1		t		34.8	10	11.8	3.5	.2					.096
			.05		t		35.3	8.5	27.8	11	.15					
			.03		t		40	3.3	32.3	5.1	.16					
			.1		0		5	12	65	4	.1					
			.1		t		23	14	52	3	.4		.015			.183
			t		0	.009	9.33	2.33	2.67	1.33	t	.588	.027			.011
			.3		1		209	310	387	297	1.1					
		.003	.4	.12	t	.81	160	61	29	13	.4	7	.035			2
		.007	.4		0		70	23	24	11	.5	6				
0		.001	.1	.04	t		82	112	122	80	.7	.6	.008	.006		.016
0		.002	t	t	0		2	2	18	4	.2	1	.062			.006
			t		1		3	1	14	4	.3	.72	.016			
0	1.8	.002	.4	.1			19	17	585	137	3.2	51.6	.284			
			t				3	9	183	33	.9	9.2	.2		5.2	
0		.006	.6	.176	2	.32	482	35	128	1	.5		.096			.143
			.3		4		395	69	70	20	.7					
			.5		t		354	165	197	75	4.5					
			.8	.778	t		321	104	240	76	.8					
			2.4		0	1.17	825	67	67	19	2.3					.715
			1.3		3		533	302	570	289	2.9		.212			
			.3		1	1.79	146	255	445	250	1.3					
		.013	.5		t		188	249	469	260	1.1		.08			.82
		.003	.2		2		257	180	223	173	.7		.066			
			0		0		2	0	6	0	.2		.04			.1
			0		0		t	0	t	0	t		.002			.006
			.4		0		66	42	757	187	7.5		.77			
			0		0		1	0	4	0	.1		.024			
			.04		.3			6		7	.6		.059			
					0		3	3	26	33	.2		.09			
			t		.1			3		9	.8		.072		2.8	

FISH, SEAFOOD, AND SEAWEED[18]

Food Item	Measure	Weight g	Calories	Carbohydrate g	Protein g	Fiber g	Saturated fat g	Unsaturated fat g	Total fat g	Cholesterol mg	Vitamin A IU	Vitamin B₁ mg	Vitamin B₂ mg	Vitamin B₆ mg
Abalone	1 lb	453	445	15.4	84.8	0			2.3				.83	.62
Agar-agar		100		74.6	2.3	0			.1		0	0	0	
Anchovy, canned	3 fillets	12	21	t	2.3	0	.2	.45	.767					.014
Bass	1 lb	453	472	0	85.7	0	2.04	5.8	9.5				.46	.13
Bluefish	1 lb	453	531	0	93	0			15				.52	.43
Carp	1 lb	453	522	0	81.6	0	3.44	13.1	19.1		770		.04	.18
Catfish	1 lb	453	467	0	79.8	0	3.9	9.29	14.1				.18	.13
Caviar, sturgeon, granular	1 rd tsp	10	26	3.3	2.7				1.5	30				
Clams														
Fresh	4 lg or 9 sm	100	82	1.3	14				1.9	120		.1	.19	.08
Canned	1 cup	200	104	5.6	15.8				1.4	240		.02	.22	.166
Cod	1 lb	453	354	0	79.8	0	.544	1.54	3.31	227	0	.27	.33	1.02
Crab														
Steamed	1 lb	453	422	2.3	78.5				8.6	453	9830	.72	.38	1.36
Canned, drained, packed	1 cup	160	162	1.8	27.8				4	161		.13	.13	.48
Dulse		100				.7			3					
Eel	1 lb	453	1057	0	72.1	0	19	30	83	227	7300	1	1.66	1.04
Flounder, sole, or sandabs	1 lb	453	358	0	75.8	0	1.26	2.54	5.44	227		.24	.23	.77
Frog's legs	4 lg	100	73	0	16.4	0			.3	40	0	.14	.25	.12
Haddock	1 lb	453	358	0	83	0	.498	1.22	2.99	272		.19	.29	.80
Halibut	1 lb	453	454	0	94.8	0	.91	2.72	4.98	227	2000	.29	.3	1.95
Herring														
Fresh	1 lb	453	798	0	78.5	0	8.7	16.2	28.1	386	520	.1	.68	1.68
Canned	1 cup	200	416	0	39.8	0							.36	.32
Hijiki		100		42.8	5.6	13			.8		150	.01	.2	
Kelp	1 tbsp	14.2		5.53	1.03	.97			.157				.046	
Kombu		100		54.9	7.3	3			1.1		430	.08	.32	
Lobster	1 lb	453	413	2.3	76.7	0			8.6	900	t	1.84	.23	
Mackerel														
Fresh	1 lb	453	866	0	86.2	0	11	27.5	44.4	431	2040	.66	1.49	2.99
Canned, drained	1 cup	210	384	0	40.4	0			12.4	199	920	.12	.44	.54
Nori		100		44.3	35.6	4.7			.7		11,000	.25	1.24	
Oysters														
Fresh	1 lb	453	299	15.4	38.1				8.2	227	1410	.64	.82	.23
Canned	1 cup	240	158	8.2	20.2		1.97	2.02	4.3	108	740	.34	.43	.089
Perch														
Ocean	1 lb	453	431	0	86.2	0	1.86	7.57	11.3		136	.41	.36	1.04
Yellow	1 lb	453	413	0	88.5	0			4.1	317	136	.27	.77	1.04
Pike, walleye	1 lb	453	422	0	87.5	0	.725	2.08	5.4			1.13	.73	.52
Pollock, fillet	1 lb	453	431	0	92.5	0	.544	2.49	4.1			.23	.46	.56
Salmon														
Fresh	1 lb	453	984	0	102	0	22	23	60.8	272	1359	.45	.36	3.18
Pink, canned	1 cup	220	310	0	45.1	0	4	2	13	77	150	.07	.4	.66
Sockeye, canned	1 cup	220	376	0	44.7	0	1.65	9.94	14.7	77	510	.09	.35	.66
Sardines, canned in oil, drained	1 oz	28	58		6.8				3.1	20	60	.01	.06	.05
Scallops	1 lb	453	367	15	69.4				.9	159		.18	.29	
Shad	1 lb	453	771	0	84.4	0			45.4			.68	1.09	
Shrimp														
Fresh	1 lb	453	413	6.8	82.1				3.6	680	40.5	.09	.14	.45
Canned, drained	1 cup	128	148	.9	31				1.4	192	66.8	.01	.04	.077
Smelt	1 lb	453	445	0	84.4	0			9.5			.04	.56	
Snails	3.5 oz	100	90	2	16.1				1.4					

[18]Values are for raw flesh only unless stated otherwise. One lb fish steaks = 4 svgs. One lb fish fillets = 5 svgs.

[19]The flesh of some oysters is high in vitamin C, containing from 22 to 38 mg/100 gr.

[20]Based on frozen scallops, possibly brined.

Vitamin B$_{12}$ mcg	Biotin mcg	Folic Acid mg	Niacin mg	Pantothenic Acid mg	Vitamin C mg	Vitamin E mg	Sodium mg	Phosphorus mg	Potassium mg	Calcium mg	Iron mg	Magnesium mg	Copper mg	Manganese mg	Selenium mcg	Zinc mg
			0		0			866		168	10.9					
								8		400	5					
								25		20						
			9.6	2.32			308	871	1160							
			8.8				336	1102		104	2.7					
t			6.7	.68	5		227	1148	1297	227	4.1	68				
.01			7.7	2.12			272		1497		1.8			.77		
							220	36	18	28	1.2					
.098		.003	1.5	.3			36	183	235	12	3.4	63			55	1.5
			2					274	280	110	8.2					
3.6	.91	.005	10	.544	9		318	880	1733	45	1.8	127	2.27	.045	186	
45.4	22.7	.018	12.7	2.72	9			794		195	3.6	154	5.89			19.5
16	8	t	8.6	.959			1600	291	176	72	1.3	61	1.66		81.6	
								22		567	6.3					
4.5			6.2	.68	6.43		353	916	1119	82	3.2	81.5	.136	.14		
5.4			7.6	3.86			354	885	1551	54	3.6	136	.815	.091	152	3.2
			1.2	.37			55	147	308	18	1.5					
5.9	1.36	.005	13.6	.59	0	2.72	277	894	1379	104	3.2	109	1.04	.091		
4.5	9.06	.009	37.8	1.25	t		245	957	2037	59	3.2		1.04	.045		3.2
40.5			16.4	4.4	2.27	9.06	535	1161	1436	258	5	118	1.36	.091		
16				1.4				594		294	3.6					
			4		0			56		1400	29					
				.784			429	34.3	753	156	.014	104	t			
			1.8		11		2500	150		800	10					
2.3	22.7	.002	6.6	6.8	t		1359	830	1178	132	2.7	77.9	9.97	.18	471	8.2
40	9.06	.005	37.1	3.86	t	7.25	652	1084	1622	23	4.5	127	.725	.091		
			12	.94				574		388	4.4					
			10		10		600	510		260	12					
81.6	4.53	.018	11.3	1.13	t[19]		331	649	549	426	24.9	145	5.44	.906	222	338
			6				175	343	290	226	13.2					
4.5			11.3	1.63	13.6		286	960	1769	208	4.53					
4.5			7.9	1.63			308	816	1043	90.6	2.7					
			10.5			.906	231	971	1447	90.6	1.8	136	1.13	.091		
4.5			7.1	1.36			218		1588							
18.1	4.53	.009	32.6	5.9	41		217	844	1771	358	4.1	131	.906	.045		
15.2		.001	17.6	1.07			851	629	794	431	1.8	65	.154	.15		
15		.001	16.1	1			1148	757	757	570	2.6	63.8	.11			
2.8	5.6	t	1.5	.238	t		233	141	167	124	.8		.011			
5.4	1.36	.002	5.8	.6			1155[20]	943	1796[20]	118	8.2		.544		349	
			38.1	2.76			245	1179	1497	91	2.3					
4.1			14.5	1.27	t		635	753	998	286	7.3	190	1.95		906	
		.003	2.3	.269	t		80	337	156	147	4		218		557	
			6.1					1234			1.8					
										170	3.5	250	.4	1.6		

Food Item	Measure	Weight g	Calories	Carbohydrate g	Protein g	Fiber g	Saturated fat g	Unsaturated fat g	Total fat g	Cholesterol mg	Vitamin A IU	Vitamin B₁ mg	Vitamin B₂ mg	Vitamin B₆ mg
Snapper	1 lb	453	422	0	89.8	0	1.09	2.9	5.44			.78	.11	
Swordfish	1 lb	453	535	0	87.1	0			18.1		7170	.24	.23	
Trout, rainbow	1 lb	453	885	0	97.5	0	11	13	51.7	249	t	.34	.92	3.13
Tuna														
Canned in oil, drained	1 cup	160	315	0	46.1	0	4.8	6.4	13.1	104	130	.08	.19	.39
Canned in water	1 cup	200	254	0	56	0			1.6	126			.2	.85
Wakame		100		51.4	12.7	3.6			1.5		140	.11	.14	
Whitefish	1 lb	453	703	0	85.7	0	3.9	15.7	37.2		10,250	.64	.54	

FRUITS AND FRUIT JUICES

Food Item	Measure	Weight g	Calories	Carbohydrate g	Protein g	Fiber g	Saturated fat g	Unsaturated fat g	Total fat g	Cholesterol mg	Vitamin A IU	Vitamin B₁ mg	Vitamin B₂ mg	Vitamin B₆ mg
Acerola (Barbados cherry)														
Raw	10 fruits	100	23	5.6	.3	.4			.2			.02	.05	.009
Juice	1 cup	242	56	11.6	1	.73			.7			.05	.15	.01
Apple														
Raw	1 med	180	96	24	.3	1.8			1		150	.05	.03	.05
Dried	1 cup	85	234	61	.9	2.6			1.4			.05	.1	.115
Juice, unsw	1 cup	248	117	29.5	.2	.26			t			.02	.05	.075
Applesauce, unsw	1 cup	244	100	26.4	.5	1.3			.5		100	.05	.02	.07
Apricot														
Raw	3 avg	114	55	13.7	1.1	.7			.2		2890	.03	.04	.077
Canned, hvy syrup	1 cup	258	222	56.8	1.5	1			.3		4490	.05	.05	.139
Dried	1 cup	130	338	86.5	6.5	3.9			.7		14,170	.01	.21	.22
Nectar	1 cup	251	143	36.6	.8	.5			.3		2380	.03	.03	
Avocado, raw, pitted	1 avg	200	334	12.6	4.2	3.2			32.8		580	.22	.4	.84
Banana, raw	1 avg	150	127	33.3	1.6	.8			.3		270	.08	.09	.76
Blackberries														
Raw	1 cup	144	84	18.6	1.7	5.9			1.3		290	.04	.06	.07
Canned, hvy syrup	1 cup	256	233	56.8	2	6.5			1.5		330	.03	.05	.06
Juice, unsw	1 cup	245	91	19.1	.7	t			1.5			.05	.07	
Blueberries														
Raw	1 cup	145	90	22.2	1	2.2			.7		150	.04	.09	1
Canned, hvy syrup	1 cup	240	242	62.4	1	2.16			.4		96	.02	.02	
Frozen, sweetened, unthawed	1 cup	230	242	61	1.4	2			.7		70	.09	.12	.124
Boysenberries, frozen, unsw	1 cup	126	60	14.4	1.5	3.38			.4		210	.03	.16	.071
Cantaloupe, raw	¼ avg	100	30	7.5	.7	.3			.1		3400	.04	.03	.086
Casaba melon, raw	1/10 avg	245	38	9.1	1.7	1.2			t		40	.06	.04	
Cherries														
Sour, raw, pitted	1 cup	155	90	22.2	1.9	.4			.5		1550	.08	.09	.095
Sour, canned, hvy syrup	1 cup	270	119	29.6	2.2	.2			.5		150	.05	.05	.118
Sweet, raw	1 cup	130	82	20.4	1.5	.52			.4		130	.06	.07	.041
Sweet, canned, hvy syrup	1 cup	279	208	52.6	2.3	.2			.5		150	.05	.05	.084
Crabapple, raw	3.5 oz	100	68	17.8	.4	.6			.3		40	.03	.02	
Cranberry, raw	1 cup	100	46	10.8	.4	1.4			.7		40	.03	.02	.035
Cranberry sauce														
Home-prepared[23]	1 cup	277	493	126	.6	1.94			.8		60	.03	.03	
Canned	1 cup	277	404	104	.3	.55			.6		60	.03	.03	.06
Currants														
Black, raw	3.5 oz	100	54	13.1	1.7	2.4			.1		230	.05	.05	.066
Red or white, raw	1 cup	133	67	16	1.87	4.5			.267		160	.05	.07	.049
Dates, pitted	10 med	100	274	72.9	2.2	2.3			.5		50	.09	.1	.153
Elderberries, raw	3.5 oz	100	72	16.4	2.6	7			.5		600	.07	.06	.23
Figs														
Raw	2 lg	100	80	20.3	1.2	1.2			.3		80	.06	.05	.113
Canned, hvy syrup	1 cup	259	218	56.5	1.3	1.7			.5		80	.08	.08	

[21]Applies to dietary low-sodium pack. Regular water pack with salt added is 1733 mg/cup.
[22]Range may be from 2400–5300 mg.
[23]Made with 1 lb cranberries and 2 cups sugar.

Vitamin B₁₂ mcg	Biotin mcg	Folic Acid mg	Niacin mg	Pantothenic Acid mg	Vitamin C mg	Vitamin E mg	Sodium mg	Phosphorus mg	Potassium mg	Calcium mg	Iron mg	Magnesium mg	Copper mg	Manganese mg	Selenium mcg	Zinc mg
4.5			36.4	.85			304	971	1465	73	3.6	127				
								885		86	4.1	86				
22.7			38	8.85	t		177		2129	86	4.53		1.5	.136		
1.6	.8	.024	19	.32				374		13	3		.192			1.76
4.4	1	.03	26.3	.64			82[21]	380	558	32	3.2		.24			
			1		15		2500	260		1300	13					
			13.6		t		236	1225	1356		1.8			.861		
0			.3		1066		7	9	68	10	.2					
0			1	.49	3872[22]		7	22		24	1.2					
0	1.8	.014	.2	.19	7	1.33	2	17	182	12	.5	14.4	.16	.126	.9	.09
0			.4		9		4	44	484	26	1.4	18.7	.2			
0	1.2	.002	.2	.05	2		2	22	250	15	1.5	10	.5			
0		.003	.1	.2	2		5	12	190	10	1.2	12.2	.85		.488	.24
0		.003	.6	.26	11		1	25	301	18	.5	13.7	.12	.2		
0			1	.237	10		3	39	604	28	.8	17	.13	.2		
0		.018	4.3	.98	16		34	140	1273	87	7.2	80.6	.455	.36		
0			.5		8		t	30	379	23	.5					
0		.102	3.2	2.14	28		8	84	1208	20	1.2	90	.8	4		.7
0	6	.042	1	.39	15	.6	2	39	550	12	1	49	.24	.96	1.5	.3
0	.6	.018	.6	.345	31		1	27	245	46	1.3	43	.23	.9		
0			.5	.195	18		3	31	279	54	1.5					
0			.7	.2	25		2	29	417	29	2.2	51.5				
0		.009	.7	.231	20		1	19	117	22	1.5	8.7	.22	.4		
			.4		14		2	20	132	22	1.4	9.6				
0			.9	.278	18		2	25	152	14	.9	9.2				
0			1.3	.269	16		1	30	193	32	2	22.5				
0	3	.03	.6	.25	33	.14	12	16	251	14	.4	17	.05	.04		.06
			.8		18		17	22	351	20	.6					
0	.6	.012	.6	.213	16		3	29	296	34	.6	21	.18	.045		
0			.5	.28	7		2	32	323	37	.7		.16			
0	.52	.01	.5	.339	12		2	22	223	26	.5	18	.156	.039		
0			.5		8		3	33	323	39	.8	25.2	.168			
			.1		8		1	13	110	6	.3					
0		.002	.1	.219	11		2	10	82	14	.5	8	.11	.3		
			.3		6		3	14	105	19	.6	5.5				.017
0			.1		6		3	11	83	17	.6	5.5				.017
0	2.4		.3	.398	200		3	40	372	60	1.1	10	.13			
0	3.46		.3	.085	54.7		2.68	30.7	343	42.7	1.3	21	.17	.78		
0		.021	2.2	.78	0		1	63	648	59	3	58	.22	.15		
0	2	.017	.5	.14	36			28	300	38	1.6					
0		.01	.4	.3	2		2	22	194	35	.6	20	.07	.128		
0			.5	.179	3		5	34	386	34	1					

Food Item	Measure	Weight g	Calories	Carbohydrate g	Protein g	Fiber g	Saturated fat g	Unsaturated fat g	Total fat g	Cholesterol mg	Vitamin A IU	Vitamin B₁ mg	Vitamin B₂ mg	Vitamin B₆ mg
Dried	5 med	100	274	69.1	4.3	5.6			1.3		80	.1	.1	.175
Fruit cocktail, canned, hvy syrup	1 cup	255	194	50.2	1	1			.3		360	.05	.03	.3
Gooseberries														
Raw	1 cup	150	59	14.6	1.2	2.9			.3		440	.22	.045	.018
Canned, hvy syrup	1 cup	200	180	46	1	2.4			.2		380			
Granadilla (passion fruit), raw	3.5 oz	100	90	21.2	2.2				.7		700	t	.13	
Grapefruit														
Raw	½ med	100	41	10.8	.5	.2			.1		10	.04	.02	.034
Canned in syrup	1 cup	254	178	45.2	1.5	.5			.3		30	.08	.05	.05
Juice, unsw	1 cup	250	98	23	1.2	t			.2		200	.1	.05	.027
Grapes														
American (slip skin), raw	1 cup	153	106	24	2	.9			1.5		150	.08	.05	.12
European (adherent skin), raw	1 cup	160	107	27.7	1	.8			.5		160	.08	.05	.13
Thompson seedless, canned, hvy syrup	1 cup	256	197	51.2	1.3	.4			.3		180	.1	.03	
Juice, unsw	1 cup	253	167	42	.5	t			t			.1	.05	.1
Guava, raw	1 med	100	62	15	.8	5.6			.6		280	.05	.05	
Honeydew melon, raw	2" wide	150	49	11.5	1.2	.9			.5		60	.06	.05	.084
Kumquat, raw	1 med	20	12	3.2	.2	.74			t		110	.01	.02	
Lemon														
Raw, peeled	1 med	110	20	6	.8	.4			.2		10	.03	.01	.08
Juice, unsw	1 tbsp	15.2	4	1.2	.1	t			t		t	t	t	.007
Peel, grated	1 tbsp	6		1	.1				t		t	t	t	
Lemonade, frozen concentrate, diluted	1 cup	248	107	28.3	.1	t			t		10	.01	.02	.012
Lime														
Raw	1 sm	80	19	6.4	.5	.5			.1		10	.02	.01	
Juice, unsw	1 tbsp	15.4	4	1.4	t	t			t		t	t	t	
Loganberries, raw	1 cup	144	89	21.5	1.4	4			.9		290	.04	.06	
Loquats, raw	10 fruits	160	59	15.3	.5	.8			.2		830			
Lychees														
Raw	10 fruits	150	58	14.8	.8	.45			.3				.05	
Dried	3.5 oz	100	277	70.7	3.8	1.4			1.2					
Mango, raw	1 fruit	300	152	38.8	1.6	2.7			.9		11,090	.12	.12	
Nectarine, raw	1 avg	150	88	23.6	.8	.6			t		2280			
Olives														
Green	2 med	13	15	.2	.2	.2			1.6		40	.004	.01	.003
Ripe	2 lg	20	37	.6	.2	.3			4		14	t	t	.003
Greek (salt-cured)	3 med	20	67	1.7	.4	.8			7.1					
Orange														
Raw	1 avg	180	64	16	1.3	.9			.3		260	.13	.05	.108
Juice, unsw	1 cup	248	112	25.8	1.7	.3			.5		500	.22	.07	1
Juice, frozen concentrate, diluted, unsw	1 cup	249	122	28.9	1.7	t			.2		540	.23	.03	.07
Papaya														
Raw	½ med	150	58	15	.9	1.8			.15		2625	.06	.06	
Juice, canned	1 cup	250	120	30.2	1				0		5000	.04	.02	
Peach														
Raw	1 med	115	38	9.7	.6	.69			.1		1330	.02	.05	.026
Canned, hvy syrup	1 cup	256	200	51.5	1	1			.3		1100	.03	.05	.06
Dried	1 cup	160	419	109	5	5			1.1		6240	.02	.3	.16
Pear														
Raw	1 avg	200	122	30.6	1.4	2.8			.8		40	.04	.08	.034
Canned, hvy syrup	1 cup	255	194	50	.5	1.5			.5		10	.03	.05	.038
Dried	1 cup	180	482	121	5.6	6.2			3.2		130	.02	.32	

Vitamin B$_{12}$ mcg	Biotin mcg	Folic Acid mg	Niacin mg	Pantothenic Acid mg	Vitamin C mg	Vitamin E mg	Sodium mg	Phosphorus mg	Potassium mg	Calcium mg	Iron mg	Magnesium mg	Copper mg	Manganese mg	Selenium mcg	Zinc mg
0		.03	.7	.435	0		34	77	640	126	3	71	.28	.35		
0			1	.92	5		13	31	411	23	1	17	.075			
0	.7		.45	.429	50		2	23	233	27	.8	13.5	.12	.06		
					20		2	18	196	22	.6					
			1.5		30		28	64	348	13	1.6	·29				
0	3	.011	.2	.283	38	.26	1	16	135	16	.4	12	.04	.01		
0			.5	.3	76		3	36	343	33	.8	27	.1			
0	1.7	.052	.5	.32	95	.1	2	38	405	22	.5	30	.05			.075
0	3	.011	.5	.112	6		5	18	242	24	.6	19.5	.135	.124		
0	3.2	.011	.5	.119	6		5	32	278	19	.6	9.6	.15	.13		
			.5		5		10	33	269	20	.8					
0	.9	.005	.5	.175	t		5	30	293	28	.8	32.5	.22		10	
0			1.2	.15	242		4	42	289	23	.9	13				
0			.9	.31	35		18	24	377	21	.6	6.7	.09	.027		
					7		1	4	44	12	.1					
0		.012	.1	.19	39		1	12	102	19		9	.15	.04		
0		t	t	.015	7		t	2	21	1	t	.12	.012	.001		.002
		t			8		t	1	10	8	t					
0		.012	.2	.027	17		1	3	40	2	.1	2.5				.025
0		.003	.1	.217	25		1	12	69	22	.4					
0			t	.047	5		t	2	16	1	t	.81	.005	.001		
			.6		35		1	24	245	50	1.7	36	.21			
					1			44	429	25	.5					
					38		3	38	153	7	.4					
							3	181	1100	33	1.7					
0			2.5	.48	81	3	16	30	437	23	.9	54	.36	.078		1.41
0		.007		.025	18		8	33	406	6	.7	19.5	.12	.057		
0		t	.065	.002	0		312	2	7	8	.2	2.86	.06	.007		.007
0				.003			150	3	5	21	.3					.06
							658	6								
0	1.8	.083	.5	.45	66	.43	1	26	263	54	.5	19.8	.11	.045	2.5	.26
0	.8	.136	1	.47	124		2	42	496	27	.5	49	.2		14.9	.09
0		.136	.9	.41	120		2	42	503	25	.2	25	.025			.09
0			.45	.327	84		4.5	24	351	30	.45	11.4	.015	.013		
		.008	.2		111			24		44	.8					
0	2	.004	1	.177	7		1	19	202	9	.5	11.5	.09	.11	.46	.2
0	.5	.001	1.5	.15	8		5	31	333	10		15	.15	.1	.512	.25
0			8.5		29		26	187	1520	77		76.7	.48	1.07		
0	.2	.028	.2	.14	8		4	22	260	16	.6	14	.3	.12	1.2	
0			.3	.055	3		3	18	214	13	.5	13	.1		.51	
			1.1		13		13	86	1031	63	2.3	55.8				

Food Item	Measure	Weight g	Calories	Carbohydrate g	Protein g	Fiber g	Saturated fat g	Unsaturated fat g	Total fat g	Cholesterol mg	Vitamin A IU	Vitamin B$_1$ mg	Vitamin B$_2$ mg	Vitamin B$_6$ mg
Persimmon														
Japanese, raw	1 med	100	77	19.7	.7	1.6			.4		2710	.03	.02	
Native, raw	1 med	100	127	33.5	.8	1.5			.4					
Pineapple														
Diced, raw	1 cup	155	81	21.2	.6	.5			.3		110	.14	.05	.132
Canned, hvy syrup	1 cup	255	189	49.5	.8	.7			.3		130	.2	.05	.185
Juice, unsw	1 cup	250	138	33.8	1	.2			.3		130	.13	.05	.24
Plantain (baking banana), raw	1 lg	365	313	82	2.9	1.4			1.1		[24]	.16	.11	
Plums														
Damson, raw	2 med	100	66	17.8	.5	.4			t		300	.08	.03	.052
Prune type, raw	3 med	100	75	19.7	.8	.4			.2		300	.03	.03	.052
Purple, canned, hvy syrup	1 cup	272	214	55.8	1	.8			.3		3130	.05	.05	
Pomegranate, raw	1 lg	275	97	25.3	.8	.5			.5		t	.05	.05	
Pricklypear, raw		100	42	10.9	.5	1.6			.1		60	.01	.03	
Prunes														
Dehydrated, nugget type	1 cup	100	344	91.3	3.3	2.2			.5		2170	.12	.22	.5
Dried, softenized	1 cup	185	411	108	3.4	1.96			1		2580	.14	.27	.44
Cked, unsw	1 cup	250	253	66.7	2.1	2			.6		1590	.07	.15	
Juice, unsw	1 cup	256	197	48.6	1	t			.3			.03	.03	
Quince, raw	3.5 oz	100	57	15.3	.4	1.7			.1		40	.02	.03	
Raisins, packed	1 cup	165	477	128	4.1	1.4			.3		30	.18	.13	.396
Raspberries														
Black, raw	1 cup	134	98	21	2	7.65			1.9		t	.04	.12	.08
Red, raw	1 cup	123	70	16.7	1.5	4			.6		100	.04	.11	.072
Frozen, sweetened, un-thawed	1 cup	250	245	61.5	1.8	5.5			.5		180	.05	.15	.095
Juice, unsw	1 cup	120	49	12.8	t	t			0		120	.02		.04
Rhubarb, diced, raw	1 cup	122	20	4.5	.7	.7			.1		120	.04	.09	.036
Strawberries														
Raw	1 cup	150	56	12.6	1	2			.8		90	.04	.1	.082
Frozen, sweetened, un-thawed	1 cup	255	278	70.9	1.3	2			.5		80	.05	.15	.112
Tangelo, raw	1 med	170	39	9.2	.5				.1					
Tangerine, raw	1 med	116	39	10	.7	.5			.2		360	.05	.02	.08
Watermelon														
Slice	6" × 1½"	600	156	38.4	3	1.8			1.2		3540	.18	.18	
Balls or cubes	1 cup	100	26	6.4	.5	.3			.2			.03	.03	.068
Meat and Poultry [25]														
Beef [26]														
Chuck roast	1 lb	454	905	0	78.8	0	36	34	75	270	130	.34	.7	1.27
Club steak	1 lb	454	1443	0	58.9	0	63.4	60.7	132	261	260	.25	.52	1.27
Corned, boneless	1 lb	454	1329	0	71.7	0	54	52	113			.14	.68	.56
Dried, chipped	3 oz	85	173	0	29.1	0	2.55	2.55	5.4			.06	.272	
Flank steak	1 lb	454	653	0	98	0	12.4	11.9	25.9	261	50	.42	.87	1.27
Ground beef, lean	1 lb	454	812	0	93.9	0	22	21	45.4	295	90	.4	.83	1.97
Ground beef, regular	1 lb	454	1216	0	81.2	0	48	44	96.2	307	160	.35	.72	1.5
Heart	1 lb	454	490	3.2	77.6	0	5	7.72	16.3	680	90	2.42	3.98	1.13
Kidney	1 lb	454	590	4.1	69.9	0			30.4	1700	3130	1.61	11.57	1.95
Liver	1 lb	454	635	24	90.3	0	6.8	5	17.3	1360	199,130[27]	1.16	14.79	3.8

[24]Value varies with color; white varieties have 10 IU/100 gms, deep yellow varieties up to 1200 IU/100 gms.

[25]Values are for raw meat only, unless stated otherwise. If meats are cooked at low temperatures, proteins are not altered. However, high temperatures and overcooking can harm some of the essential amino acids and decrease their health-promoting value. With the possible exception of folic acid, the B vitamins are not depleted at low temperatures except at the surface of the meat. Above the boiling point, the B vitamins are destroyed in proportion to the temperature. The B vitamins and minerals dissolve in water and can be lost if meats are soaked or boiled and the cooking water is not used. Juices that seep from frozen meats during thawing and those that drip into the broiling pan can be used in gravy or added to soup stock.

[26]Beef steak contains .63 mg vitamin E/100 gms; beef has approx. 13.6 mcg biotin/lb; lean beef contains 19 mg zinc/lb.

[27]Values vary widely in all kinds of liver, ranging from 450 IU/lb.

Vitamin B12 mcg	Biotin mcg	Folic Acid mg	Niacin mg	Pantothenic Acid mg	Vitamin C mg	Vitamin E mg	Sodium mg	Phosphorus mg	Potassium mg	Calcium mg	Iron mg	Magnesium mg	Copper mg	Manganese mg	Selenium mcg	Zinc mg
			.1		11		6	26	174	6	.3	8				
					66		1	26	310	27	2.5					
0		.017	.3	.24	26		2	12	226	26	.8	20	.09	1.57	.93	
0		.002	.5	.25	18		3	13	245	28	.8	20	.25		2.04	
0		.003	.5	.25	23		.3	23	373	38	.8	30	.15			
0		.058	1.6	.86	37		13	79	1012	18	1.8					
0	t	.006	.5	.186	6		2	17	299	18	.5	9	.1	.1		
0	t	.002	.5	.186	4		1	18	170	12	.5	9	.15	.1		
		1			5		3	26	367	23	2.3					
0			.5	1.64	6		5	12	399	5	.5					
			.4		22		2	28	166	20	.3					
0		.005	2.1	.35	4		11	107	940	90	4.4	32	.16		.18	
0		.007	2.6	.85	5		13	127	1117	82	6.3	74	.52			
			1.5		2		9	79	695	51	3.8	50	.42			.79
			1		5		5	51	602	36	10.5	25.6	.05			.025
			.2		15		4	17	197	11	.7	6	.13	.04		
0	7	.007	.8	.074	2		45	167	1259	102	5.8	57.7	.41	.47		.3
0	2.5	.007	1.2	.324	24		1	29	267	40	1.2	40.5	.24	.68		
0	2.28	.006	1.1	.288	31		1	27	207	27	1.1	24	.22	.61		
0			1.5	.317	53		3	43	250	33	1.5	27.5				
0					18			14		29	1	21				
0		.009	.4	.102	11		2	22	306	117	1	19	.02			.44
0	1.6	.024	.9	.51	88		2	32	246	32	1.5	18	.11	.09		.12
0			1.3	.337	135	.48	3	43	286	36	1.8	23				
					26											
0		.021	.1	.24	27		2	15	108	34	.3	11	.08	.04		
			1.2		42		6	60	600	42	3	48	.24			
0	4	.008	.2	.3	7		1	10	100	7	.5	8	.04	.02		
5.4		.032	18.9	1.81	0		276	731	1261	49	11.8	80	.45			
5.4		.032	14.1	1.81			206	539	942	34	8.7	81				
3.9			7.7		0		5897	567	272	41	10.9					9
1.56			3.2		0		3660	343	170	17	4.3					
5.4		.032	23.5	1.81	0		343	912	1568	59	14.5	100	.09			
8.2		.032	22.5	2.81	0			871		54	14.1	95				15
6.4		.032	19.5	2.13	0			708	1070	45	12.2	77	.27		94	
50	36	.014	34.1	11.3	9		390	885	875	23	18.1	82	1.32			
141	40.9	.363	29.2	17.5	68		798	993	1021	50	33.6	50	1.14	.36	640	
363	454	.99	61.6	35	140	6.36	617	1597	1275	36	29.5	59	12.7	1.23	206	17

Food Item	Measure	Weight g	Calories	Carbohydrate g	Protein g	Fiber g	Saturated fat g	Unsaturated fat g	Total fat g	Cholesterol mg	Vitamin A IU	Vitamin B₁ mg	Vitamin B₂ mg	
Porterhouse steak	1 lb	454	1603	0	60.8	0	71	68	148	261	300	.26	.55	1.27
Rib roast	1 lb	454	1673	0	61.8	0	74.9	71.8	156	261	310	.27	.55	1.27
Round steak	1 lb	454	863	0	88.5	0	26	25	53.9	261	110	.38	.79	1.27
Rump roast	1 lb	454	1167	0	67	0	47	46	97.4	261	190	.29	.6	1.27
Sirloin steak	1 lb	454	1316	0	71	0	52	50	112	261	220	.3	.63	1.27
T-bone steak	1 lb	454	1596	0	59	0	70	89	168	261	300	.25	.53	1.27
Tongue	1 lb	454	714	1.4	56.5	0			52		0	.42	.99	.43
Brains, all kinds	1 lb	454	567	3.6	47.2	0			39	320	0	1.05	1.18	.68
Chicken[28]														
Back	1 lb	454	385	0	40.4	0	11.1	24	39	368	760	.13	.55	2.27
Breast	1 lb	454	394	0	74.5	0	5.3	11	18	239	270	.18	.57	3.1
Canned	1 cup	205	406	0	44.5	0	8	12	24		470	.08	.25	.6
Drumstick	1 lb	454	313	0	51.2	0	8.67	18.8	30.7	239	340	.18	.87	1.47
Gizzard	1 lb	453	513	3.2	91.2	0			12.2	658		.12	.89	
Heart	10 med	100	157	1.6	20.5	0			7	170	30	.12	.91	.363
Liver	1 lb	454	585	13.2	89.4	0	7.54	9.44	20.4	2517	54,890[27]	.86	11.3	3.4
Neck	1 lb	454	329	0	33.7	0			20.5	368	660	.1	.53	1.47
Thigh	1 lb	454	435	0	61.6	0	9.49	20.6	33.5	368	620	.2	1.13	1.47
Wing	1 lb	454	325	0	41.1	0	15.3	32.9	52.7	368	530	.09	.32	3.1
Chili con carne w/beans	1 cup	255	339	31	19	1.5	7.5	7.5	15.6		150	.08	.18	
Corned beef hash w/potato	1 cup	220	398	23.5	19.4	1.25	11	11	24.9		t	.02	.2	.165
Duck, ready to cook	1 lb	454	1213	0	59.5	0	31	80	130	318		.29	.71	
Frankfurter	1 lb	454	1402	8.2	56.7	0	51	72	131	295		.71	.9	.64
Goose, ready to cook	1 lb	454	1172	0	54.3	0	41	88	153			.25	.63	2.72
Lamb[29]														
Leg	1 lb	454	845	0	67.7	0	35	24	61.7	265		.59	.82	1.05
Chops	1 lb	454	1146	0	63.7	0	54.3	37.8	97	270		.57	.79	1.05
Liver	1 lb	454	617	13.2	95.3	0	6.9	6.63	19.6	1361	229,070[27]	1.81	14.9	1.36
Shoulder	1 lb	454	1082	0	59	0	52	36	92	270		.53	.73	1.05
Liver pate	1 tbsp	13	60	.6	1.5	0			5.7			.01	.04	
Pheasant, ready to cook	1 lb	454	596	0	95.9	0	16	31	52					
Pork[30]														
Bacon, sliced	1 lb	454	3016	4.5	38.1	0	101	179	314	999	0	1.64	.52	.57
Bacon, Canadian	1 lb	454	980	1.4	90.7	0	23	33	65.3		0	3.75	1.01	
Boston butt	1 lb	454	1220	0	65.9	0	37	53	104	232	0	3.2	.77	1.3
Chops	1 lb	454	1065	0	61	0	32	45	89	260	0	2.97	.71	1.3
Feet, pickled	1 lb	454	903	0	75.8	0	24	34	67.1					
Ham, cured	1 lb	454	1535	1.2	66.7	0	50	70	138	318	0	3.36	.817	1.25
Ham, deviled	1 cup	225	790	0	31.3	0	30	39	72.7		0	.32	.23	
Ham, minced	1 lb	454	1034	20	62.1	0	28	38	76.7		0	1.68	1	
Picnic	1 lb	454	1083	0	59	0	33	47	92.2	232	0	2.87	.69	1.3
Spareribs	1 lb	454	976	0	39.2	0	32	46	89.7	232	0	1.91	.46	2.18
Potted meat, all kinds	1 cup	225	558	0	39.4	0			43.2			.07	.5	
Rabbit, ready to cook	1 lb	454	581	0	75	0	11	13	29	295	136	.29	.2	1.58
Sausage														
Blood	1 lb	454	1787	1.4	64	0			167					.17
Bologna	1 lb	454	1379	5	54.9	0	54	69	133			.72	.98	.45
Braunschweiger	1 lb	454	1447	10.4	67.1	0	45	63	124		29,620	.78	6.55	
Brown and serve	1 lb	454	1783	12.2	61.2	0			163					
Cervelat	1 lb	454	2046	7.7	112	0	50	50.4	123		0	1.22	1.04	.64
Country-style	1 lb	454	1565	0	68.5	0	51	72	141			1	.87	
Headcheese	1 lb	454	1216	4.5	70.3	0	36	51	99.8		0	.18	.45	
Knockwurst	1 lb	454	1261	10	64	0	45.5	70.5	123			.77	.95	
Liverwurst	1 lb	454	1393	8.2	73.5	0			116		28,800	.91	5.9	.86

[28] Whole chicken per lb contains 15 gms total fat, 5 gms sat. fat, and 9 gms uns. fat. Chicken contains .25 mg vitamin E/100 gms and approx. 4.54 mcg biotin/lb.
[29] Lamb contains 13.6 mg zinc/lb in lean meat only, no fat. Lamb contains approx. 13.6 mcg biotin/lb.
[30] Lean meat only, no fat.

Vitamin B12 mcg	Biotin mcg	Folic Acid mg	Niacin mg	Pantothenic Acid mg	Vitamin C mg	Vitamin E mg	Sodium mg	Phosphorus mg	Potassium mg	Calcium mg	Iron mg	Magnesium mg	Copper mg	Manganese mg	Selenium mcg	Zinc mg
5.4		.032	14.6	1.81			213	559	973	33	9	71	.54			
5.4		.032	14.8	1.81			216	630	989	38	9.2	71				
5.4		.032	21.3	1.81			310	890	1416	53	13.1	97	.318		165	
5.4		.032	16.1	1.81			235	616	1072	39	10	71				
5.4		.032	17.1	1.81			249	652	1138	42	10.5	71	.182			
5.4		.032	14.2	1.81			207	543	946	32	8.8	100	.545			
13.6	13.6		17.2	6.89	0		252	627	679	28	7.2	41	.32			
18.1	31.8	.055	20.1	11.8	82		567	1415	993	45	10.9	54.5	.95			
		.014	10.5	3.6	11.4		377	453	1630	29	4.2	168	1	.091		8.17
2		.027	28.3	3.63	11.4		377	767	1630	39	4.3	82	.636	.091	48	3.18
1.58			9	1.7	8			506	283	43	3.1		.22			
1.8		.05	11.7	4.54	11.4		377	506	1630	35	4.4	168	1	.091	55	8.17
			20.3				295	476	1089	45	13.2	59	.363	.499		13
4	8	.003	5.2	2.56	6		79	142	158	23	1.7	14	.23			2.9
113		1.65	49	27.2	79		318	1070	780	54	35.8	91	.27	1.18		11
1.8		.05	6.5	4.54	11.4		377	396	1630	24	4.1	168	1	.091		12.3
1.8		.05	19.3	4.54	11.4		377	633	1630	41	5.4	168	1	.091		8.17
2		.027	9.1	3.63	11.4		377	451	1630	22	3.3	82	.636	.091		7.26
			3.3				1354	321	594	82	4.3					4.1
			4.6				1188	147	440	29	4.4					
			24.8		36		386	655	1294	37	6		1.86	.136		
5.9		.018	12.2	1.95			4990	603	998	32	8.6		.36			9.1
			22.1				386	583	1907	33	5.3		1.5	.227		
8.2		.018	19	2		3.6	237	593	1083	39	5.1	61	.27			
8.2		.018	18.5	2		3.5	223	567	1019	35	4.7	55	.73		78	
472	454	.99	76.5	32.7	152		236	1583	916	45	49.4	64	25	1.04		
8.2		.018	17.1	2		3.6	206	516	942	35	3.9	50				
			.3													
3.2	31.8		8.3	1.5		1.82	3084	490	590	59	5.4	54	.726			
			21.2		0		8578	816	1778	54	13.6	91				
2	18.2	.036	17.1	2.23		3.18	231	735	1054	38	9.8					14.5[30]
2	18.2	.036	15.9	2.23	0	3.2	214	690	978	36	9.3	68	1.41		98.5	10[30]
2	22.7	.036	18.2	2.05	0		3415	763	1067	41	10.4	62	.136	.27		12.7[30]
			3.6					207			18	4.7				
			15.4					404		36	9.5					
2	18.2	.036	15.4	2.23		3.18	207	664	944	34	9	67				12.7[30]
4.54	22.7	.036	10.2	2.95	9.08	2.7	137	432	627	22	5.9	86.3		.27		
			2.7										.158			
			45.9	2.8		4.5	154	1261	1379	72	4.7					
		.023	12				5897	581	1043	32	8.2		.091			8.2
			37					1111		45	26.8					12.7
								971		50	12.7					
			24.9					1334		64	12.2					
			14					762		41	10.4					
		.009	4					785		41	10.4					
			11.8					699		36	9.5					
63.1		.136	25.9	12.6				1080		41	24.5					

Food Item	Measure	Weight g	Calories	Carbohydrate g	Protein g	Fiber g	Saturated fat g	Unsaturated fat g	Total fat g	Cholesterol mg	Vitamin A IU	Vitamin B1 mg	Vitamin B2 mg	Vitamin B6 mg
Polish-style	1 lb	454	1379	5.4	71.2	0	41	64.4	117		0	1.54	.86	.75
Pork, link or bulk	1 lb	454	2259	t	42.6	0	83		118	230	0	1.95	.76	.56
Salami	1 lb	454	2041	5.4	108		53.5	89.5	151			1.68	1.13	.56
Thuringer	1 lb	454	1393	7.3	84.4	0			111			.51	1.17	
Vienna, canned	7 saus	113	271	.3	15.8	0			22.4			.09	.15	.083
Turkey														
Dark meat, ckd	1 lb	454	921	0	136	0	10.9	24.1	37.6	458	t	.18	1.04	
Light meat, ckd	1 lb	454	798	0	149	0	5.1	11.3	17.7	349	t	.23	.64	
Canned	1 cup	205	414	0	42.8	0	8	16	25.6		270	.04	.29	
Veal (calf)[31]														
Breast	1 lb	454	828	0	65.6	0	29.3	28	61	254		.48	.87	1.22
Chuck	1 lb	454	628	0	70.4	0	17	17	36	320		.52	.94	1.22
Cutlet	1 lb	454	681	0	72.3	0	19.7	18.8	41	254		.53	.96	1.22
Liver	1 lb	454	635	18.6	87.1	0			21.3	1361	102,060[27]	.9	12.3	3.04
Rib roast	1 lb	454	723	0	65.7	0	23.5	22.6	49	254		.48	.87	1.22
Rump roast	1 lb	454	573	0	68	0	14.9	14.2	31	254		.5	.9	1.22
Sweetbreads (pancreas)	1 lb	454	426	0	80.7	0			9.1	1135		.37	.76	
Venison (deer)	1 lb	454	572	0	95	0	11	5	18			1.03	2.19	
NUTS, NUT PRODUCTS, AND SEEDS[32]														
Almonds														
Raw	1 cup	142	849	27.7	26.4	3.85	6.2	67	77		0	.34	1.31	.142
Roasted and salted	1 cup	157	984	30.6	29.2	3.85	7.3	78.8	90.6		0	.08	1.44	.149
Almond meal	1 oz	28	116	8.2	11.2	.64	.4	4.5	5.2		0	.09	.48	
Brazil nuts, raw	1 cup	140	916	15.3	20	4.2	18.7	69.3	93.7		t	1.34	.17	.238
Cashews, roasted	1 cup	140	785	41	24.1	1.96	10.9	49.3	64		140	.6	.35	
Chestnuts														
Fresh	1 cup	160	310	67.4	4.6	1.66	.44	2.04	2.7		0	.35	.35	.527
Dried	1 cup	100	377	78.6	6.7	2.5			4.1			.34	.39	
Coconut														
Fresh, shredded, not packed	1 cup	80	277	7.5	2.8	2.7	24.3	2	28.2		0	.04	.02	.035
Dried, shredded, sweetened	1 cup	62	344	33	2.24	2.55			24.2		0	.025	.019	
Milk[33]	1 cup	240	605	12.5	7.7		51.4	4.2	59.8		0	.07	t	
Water (liquid from coconuts)	1 cup	240	53	11.3	.7	t			.5		0	t	t	.045
Hazelnuts (filberts), raw	1 cup	135	856	22.5	17	1.05	4.2	59	84.2		144	.62	.738	.735
Hickory nuts, raw	15 sm	15	101	2	2.1	.3	.9	8.8	10.1			.08		
Lychee nuts, dried	6 avg	15	45	10.5	.5	.48			.1					
Macadamia nuts, roasted	6 avg	15	109	1.5	1.4	.375	1.64	8.9	11.7		0	.032	.018	
Peanuts, roasted	1 cup	144	838	29.7	37.7	3.89	15.4	50.5	70.1		t	.46	.19	.576
Peanut butter	1 tbsp	15	86	3.2	3.9	.33	1.5	6.1	8.1		0	.018	.02	.05
Pecans, halves, raw	1 cup	108	742	15.8	9.9	2.3	5.4	63.8	76.9		140	.93	.14	.183
Pine nuts, raw	1 oz	28	180	5.8	3.7	.31	1.7	11.7	14.3		10	.36	.07	
Pistachio nuts, shelled	30 avg	15	88	2.8	2.9	.3	1.1	6.5	8		34.4	.1		
Pumpkin and squash seeds, dried, hulled	1 cup	140	774	21	40.6	2.66	11.8	51	65.4		100	.34	.27	
Sesame seeds, dried, hulled	1 cup	150	873	26.4	27.3	3.6	11.2	64	80			.27	.2	.126
Sunflower seeds, dried, hulled	1 cup	145	812	28.9	34.8	5.5	8.2	56.9	68.6		70	2.84	.33	1.8
Walnuts														
Black, chopped, raw	1 cup	125	785	18.5	25.6	2.13	4.5	61.6	74.1		380	.28	.14	
English, halves, raw	1 cup	100	651	15.8	14.8	2.1	4.5	49.5	64		30	.33	.13	.73

[31]Veal contains 12.7 mg zinc/lb lean meat only, no fat.

[32]All nuts and seeds are unsalted, unless stated otherwise. For salted nuts, the sodium content is approx. 280 mg/cup.

[33]Liquid from mixture of coconut meat and water.

Vitamin B$_{12}$ mcg	Biotin mcg	Folic Acid mg	Niacin mg	Pantothenic Acid mg	Vitamin C mg	Vitamin E mg	Sodium mg	Phosphorus mg	Potassium mg	Calcium mg	Iron mg	Magnesium mg	Copper mg	Manganese mg	Selenium mcg	Zinc mg
2.4		.064	14.1	3.09			3357	798	635	41	10.9	41				15
6.4			10.4					417		23	6.4					
			24					1284		64	16.3					
			19.2					971		50	12.7					
			2.9					173		9	2.4					
		.032	19.1	5			449	962	1805	36	10.4		.545	.136		14.1
		.023	50.3	2.68			372	962	1864	36	5.4		.454	.136		7.26
			9.6							21	2.9					
5.7	22.7	.023	22	3.23			230	652	1050	39	9.7					
5.7	22.7	.023	23.6	3.23			246	722	1126	40	10.5					
5.7	22.7	.023	24.2	3.23			253	734	1157	41	10.9	73	1.14			
272			51.8	36.3	161		331	1510	1275	36	39.9	73	36			17
5.7	22.7	.023	22	3.23	0		230	664	1051	38	9.8	52	1.14		.136	
5.7	22.7	.023	22.8	3.23			238	699	1090	38	10					
63.6	63		11.7				281	1521	1130	41	4.54	68	.27			
			28.6		0		318	1129	1525	45	22.7	150				
0	25	.136	5	.668	t	21.3	6	716	1098	332	6.7	386	1.18	2.7	2.8	
0			5.5	.393	0		311	791	1214	369	7.4					4.02
			1.8		0		2	259	397	120	2.4					
0		.006	2.2	.323	14	9.1	1	970	1001	260	4.8	351	2.14	3.9	144	7.1
0		.095	2.5	1.82			21	522	650	53	5.3	374				6.1
0	2.1		1	.756	9.6	.8	10	141	726	43	2.7	65.6	.67		5.9	
			.8		0		4	170	875	57	3.3					
0		.031	.4	.16	2	.8	18	76	205	10	1.4	37	.368	1.05		
0			.248		2.5		11	69.6	219	9.94	1.24	46	.33			
			1.9		5		240			38	3.8					
0			.2	.12	5		60	31	353	48	.7	67				
0		.097	1.2	1.54	t	28	3	455	950	282	4.6	313	1.72	5.67	2.7	4
					0				165	4	.4	24	.214			
			.2		5		36			8	.3					
0	49	.153	24.6	3		9.36	7	586	1009	104	3.2	252	.62	2.17		
0	5.8	.013	2.4		0		18	59	123	11	.3	26	.085			
0		.026	1	1.7	2	1.5	t	312	651	79	2.6	142	1.14	1.54		3.24
			1.3		t			171		3	1.5					
		.009	.21		0			75	145	19.6	1.09	23.7	.168			
		.144	3.4				1602			71	15.7					
0			8.1		0		888			165	3.6	270	2.39			
0			7.8	2			1214		1334	174	10.3	57	2.57			
			.9				4	713	575	t	7.5	238	1.74			2.82
0	37	.066	.9	.9	2	1.5	2	380	450	99	3.1	131	1.39	1.8		2.26

Food Item	Measure	Weight g	Calories	Carbohy-drate g	Protein g	Fiber g	Satu-rated fat g	Unsatu-rated fat g	Total fat g	Choles-terol mg	Vitamin A IU	Vitamin B$_1$ mg	Vitamin B$_2$ mg	Vitamin B$_6$ mg
OILS, FATS, AND SHORTENING														
Bacon fat	1 tbsp	14	126		0	t			14					
Butter	1 tbsp	14.2	102	.1	.1	0	6.3	4.1	11.5	35	470	t	.001	t
Butter	1 cup	227	1625	.9	1.4	0	101	66.2	184	570	7500	t	.02	.006
Chicken fat	1 tbsp	14	126	0	0				14					
Lard	1 tbsp	13	117	0	0	0	4.9	7.3	13	12	0	0	0	.003
Margarine														
Regular	1 tbsp	14.2	102	.1	.1	0	2.1	9	11.5	0[34]	470	t	t	
Whipped	1 tbsp	9.4	68	t	.1	0	1.4	6	7.6	0[34]	310	t	t	
Oils														
Cod-liver	1 tbsp	14	126	0	0	0			14	119	11,900		0	
Corn	1 tbsp	14	126	0	0	0	1.4	11	14	t	t	t	t	
Cottonseed	1 tbsp	14	126	0	0	0	3.4	9.7	14	0	0	0	0	
Olive	1 tbsp	14	124	t	t	0	1.5	11.2	14	t	0	0	0	
Peanut	1 tbsp	14	124	t	t	0	2.4	10.2	14	t	0	0	0	
Safflower	1 tbsp	14	124	0	0	0	1.1	11.8	14	t	t	t	t	
Soybean	1 tbsp	14	124	t	t	0	2	9.8	14	t	0	0	0	
Sesame	1 tbsp	14	120	t	t	0	1.9	10.9	14	t	0	0	0	
Sunflower	1 tbsp	14	124	t	t	0	1.8	12	14	t	0	0	0	
Wheat germ	1 tbsp	14	124	t	t	0	2.34	8.8	14	t	0	0	0	
Vegetable shortening	1 tbsp	12.5	111	0	0	0	3.1	9	12.5			0	0	
SALAD DRESSINGS AND SAUCES														
Barbecue sauce	1 tbsp	15	14	1.25	.238	.09	.106	.875	1.08		56	.002	.002	
Catsup, tomato	1 tbsp	15	16	3.8	.3	.075			.1		210	.01	.01	.016
Chili sauce	1 tbsp	17	16	4	.5	.126			.1		210	.02	.01	
Hollandaise sauce	1 tbsp	12.5	45	.1	.55				4.6		257	.007	.011	
Horseradish, prepared	1 tbsp	15	6	1.4	.2	.108			t					.022
Mayonnaise	1 tbsp	14	101	.3	.2	t	2	8	11.2	10	40	t	.01	
Miso, takka		100	249	42.8	9	2			5.2		0	.1	.15	
Mustard	1 tbsp	15	15	.9	.9	.3			.9					
Salad dressings														
Blue or Roquefort cheese, regular	1 tbsp	15	76	1.1	.7	t	1.6	5.5	7.8		30	t	.02	
Blue or Roquefort cheese, low calorie	1 tbsp	16	12	.7	.5	.01	.5	.3	.9		30	t	.01	
Caesar	1 tbsp	15	73	.6	.3				8					
French, regular	1 tbsp	16	66	2.8	.1	.04	1.1	4.5	6.2					
French, low calorie	1 tbsp	16	15	2.5	.1	.04	.1	.5	.7					
Green goddess	1 tbsp	15	72	.8	.1				7.4					
Italian	1 tbsp	15	83	1	t	t	1.6	6.6	9		t	t	t	
Russian	1 tbsp	15	74	1.6	.2	.045	1.4	5.5	7.6		100	.01	.01	
Thousand Island, regular	1 tbsp	16	80	2.5	.1	.04	1.4	5.7	8		50	t	t	
Thousand Island, low calorie	1 tbsp	15	27	2.3	.1	.04	.4	1.4	2.1		50	t	t	
Soy sauce	1 tbsp	18	12	1.7	1	0			.2		0	t	.05	
Tartar sauce	1 tbsp	14	31	.9	.1	.042			3.1	7	30	t	t	
Umeboshi		100	17	3.4	.3	.3			.8		0	.06	.09	
Vinegar	1 tbsp	15	2	.9	t	0			0					t
White sauce, medium	1 tbsp	16	27	1.5	.65	t	1	.71	2.05	2.06	82	.005	.025	
Worcestershire sauce	1 tbsp	15	12	2.7	.3				0					
SOUPS[35]														
Asparagus, cream of	1 cup	240	65	10.1	2.4	.8			1.7		310	.05	.1	
Bean and pork	1 cup	250	168	21.8	8	1.8	1.3	3.9	5.8		650	.13	.08	
Beef														
Consomme or bouillon	1 cup	240	31	2.6	5	.14			0		t	t	.02	
Noodle	1 cup	245	140	14.2	7.8	.15	.8	1.6	2.6		120	.1	.12	

[34]Value for all vegetable fat; ⅔ animal fat and ⅓ vegetable fat has 7 mg/tbsp.

[35]All soups are diluted with water.

Vitamin B12 mcg	Biotin mcg	Folic Acid mg	Niacin mg	Pantothenic Acid mg	Vitamin C mg	Vitamin E mg	Sodium mg	Phosphorus mg	Potassium mg	Calcium mg	Iron mg	Magnesium mg	Copper mg	Manganese mg	Selenium mcg	Zinc mg
t					0	.35	140	2	3	3	0	.28	.004	.006		.01
t					0	5.2	2240	36	52	45	0	4.5	.067	.09		.2
0		0			0	.14	.039	.39	.026	.129	.013		.004			.03
		t	t		0	1.25	140	2	3	3	0		.006			.03
		t	t		0	.89	93	2	2	2	0		.004			.03
			0			3.6	.014									
		t			t	11	t	0	0	t	t					.025
		0			0	10.9	0	0	0	0	0					.025
		0			0	.714	.001	0	t	.07	.01		.01			.025
		0			0	1.8	t	0	0	t	0		.001			.025
		t			t	10.5	t	0	0	t	t					.025
		0			0	7.9	t	0	0	t	0		.056			.025
		0			0	2.3	t	0	0	t	0					
		0			0	1.3	t	0	0	t	0					
		0			0	21.5	t	0	0	t	0					
		0			0	0	0	0	0	0	0					
		.001	.05	.8			127	3	27	3.3	.125					.005
0		.001	.2	2			156	8	54	3	.1		.089			.039
			.2	2			201	3	56	2	.1					
			t	t				19.5		6	.225					
0		t	t		0		14	5	44	9	.1	5	.021			.16
			1.5		0		84	4	5	3	.1	.28	.034			.022
								250		150	60					
							195	21	21	18	.3	7.2	.06			.032
		t			t		164	11	6	12	t					.038
		t			t		177	8	5	10	t					
						236										
						1.3	219	2	13	2	.1	1.4				.012
						.2	126	2	13	2	.1					
						1.54	140									
		t				1.8	314	1	2	2	t		.105			.017
		.1		1		1.34	130	6	24	3	.1					.065
		t			t	1.5	112	3	18	2	.1					.021
		t			t	.33	105	3	17	2	.1					
		.005	.1		0		1319	19	66	15	.9					
		t			t		99	4	11	3	.1					
			.6		0		9400	26		6.1	2					
0			.05	.125			t	1	15	1	.1	.2	.014		13.3	.015
							59	15	21.7	18	.05					
									9	15	.9					
		.047	.7				984	38	120	26	.7					
			1		3		1008	128	395	63	2.3					
		.01	1.2				782	31	130	t	.5		1.85			
			2.2		2		1872	98	157	15	1.7		.09			3

Food Item	Measure	Weight g	Calories	Carbohy-drate g	Protein g	Fiber g	Satu-rated fat g	Unsatu-rated fat g	Total fat g	Choles-terol mg	Vitamin A IU	Vitamin B mg	Vitamin B₂ mg	Vitamin B₆ mg
Celery, cream of	1 cup	240	86	8.9	1.7	.84	.9	3.7	5		190	.02	.05	
Chicken														
Consomme or bouillon	1 cup	240	22	1.9	3.4	t			t					
Cream of	1 cup	240	94	7.9	2.9	.3	.9	4.3	5.8		410	.02	.05	
Gumbo	1 cup	240	55	7.4	3.1	.1			1.4		220	.02	.05	
Noodle	1 cup	240	62	7.9	3.4	.25			1.9		50	.02	.02	
w/rice	1 cup	240	48	5.8	3.1	.12			1.2		140	t	.02	
Chili beef	1 cup	250	168	23.4	7.9	1.1			4.7		851	.09	.08	
Clam chowder														
Manhattan	1 cup	245	81	12.3	2.2	.4			2.5		880	.02	.02	
New England	1 cup	240	130	10.5	4.3	.25			7.7		48	.05	.1	
Minestone	1 cup	245	105	14.2	4.9	.9			3.4		2350	.07	.05	
Mushroom, cream of	1 cup	240	134	10.1	2.4	.12	1.3	7.3	9.6		70	.02	.12	
Onion	1 cup	240	65	5.3	5.3	.5			2.4		t	t	.02	
Oyster stew	1 cup	240	120	8	5.88	.1			8		240	.07	.19	
Pea, split	1 cup	245	145	20.6	8.6	.5	1	1.8	3.2		440	.25	.15	
Potato, cream of	1 cup	260	115	12	3.6	.45	3	2	5.7		442	.05	.07	
Tomato	1 cup	245	88	15.7	2	.7	.4	1.7	2.5		1000	.05	.05	
Turkey noodle	1 cup	240	79	8.4	4.3	.12	.8	1.8	2.9		190	.05	.05	
Vegetable														
Beef	1 cup	245	78	9.6	5.1	.65			2.2		2700	.05	.05	
Vegetarian	1 cup	245	78	13.2	2.2	.9			2		2940	.05	.05	
SPICES AND HERBS														
Allspice, grd	1 tsp	1.9	5	1.37	.12	.41	.05	.05	.17	0	10	.002	.001	
Anise seed	1 tsp	2.1	7	1.05	.37	.31		.28	.33	0				
Basil, grd	1 tsp	1.4	4	.85	.2	.25			.06	0	131	.002	.004	
Bay leaf, crumbled	1 tsp	.6	2	.45	.05	16	.01	.02	.05	0	37	t	.003	
Caraway seed	1 tsp	2.1	7	1.05	.42	.27	.01	.22	.31	0	8	.008	.008	
Cardamom, grd	1 tsp	2	6	1.37	.21	.23	.01	.03	.13	0		.004	.004	
Celery seed	1 tsp	2	8	.83	.36	.24	.04	.39	.5	0	1			
Chervil, dried	1 tsp	.6	1	.3	.14	.07			.02	0				.007
Chili powder	1 tsp	2.6	8	1.42	.32	.58			.44	0	908	.009	.021	
Cinnamon, grd	1 tsp	2.3	6	1.84	.09	.56	.01	.02	.07	0	6	.002	.003	
Cloves, grd	1 tsp	2.1	7	1.29	.13	.2	.09		.42	0	11	.002	.006	
Coriander leaf, dried	1 tsp	.6	2	.31	.13	.06			.03	0		.008	.009	
Coriander seed	1 tsp	1.8	5	.99	.22	.52	.02	.27	.32	0		.004	.005	
Cumin seed	1 tsp	2.1	8	.93	.37	.22			.47	0	27	.013	.007	
Curry powder	1 tsp	2	6	1.16	.25	.33			.28	0	20	.005	.006	
Dill seed	1 tsp	2.1	6	1.16	.34	.44	.02	.22	.31	0	1	.009	.006	
Dill weed, dried	1 tsp	1	3	.56	.2	.12			t	0		.004	.003	.015
Fennel seed	1 tsp	2	7	1.05	.32	.31	.01	.23	.3	0	3	.008	.007	
Fenugreek seed	1 tsp	3.7	12	2.16	.85	.37			.24	0		.012	.014	
Garlic powder	1 tsp	2.8	9	2.04	.47	.05			.02	0		.013	.004	
Ginger, grd	1 tsp	1.8	6	1.27	.16	.11	.03	.04	.11	0	3	.001	.003	
Mace, grd	1 tsp	1.7	8	.86	.11	.08	.16	.26	.55	0	14	.005	.008	
Marjoram, dried	1 tsp	.6	2	.36	.08	.11			.04	0	48	.002	.002	
Mustard seed, yellow	1 tsp	3.3	15	1.15	.82	.22	.05	.83	.95	0	2	.018	.013	
Nutmeg, grd	1 tsp	2.2	12	1.08	.13	.09	.57	.08	.8	0	2	.008	.001	
Onion powder	1 tsp	2.1	7	1.69	.21	.12			.02	0		.009	.001	
Oregano, grd	1 tsp	1.5	5	.97	.17	.22	.04	.09	.15	0	104	.005		
Paprika	1 tsp	2.1	6	1.17	.31	.44	.04	.2	.27	0	1273	.014	.037	
Parsley, dried	1 tsp	.3	1	.15	.07	.03			.01	0	70	.001	.004	.003
Pepper														
Black	1 tsp	2.1	5	1.36	.23	.28	.03	.03	.07	0	4	.002	.005	
Red or cayenne	1 tsp	1.8	6	1.02	.22	.45	.06	.2	.31	0	749	.006	.017	

*Present, but approximate value in milligrams unavailable.

Vitamin B$_{12}$ mcg	Biotin mcg	Folic Acid mg	Niacin mg	Pantothenic Acid mg	Vitamin C mg	Vitamin E mg	Sodium mg	Phosphorus mg	Potassium mg	Calcium mg	Iron mg	Magnesium mg	Copper mg	Manganese mg	Selenium mcg	Zinc mg
			t	1.1	t		955	36	108	48	.5					
							722	72		12	1.2		.02			
			.5		t		970	34	79	24	.5					
			1.2		5		950	24	108	19	.5		.27			
			.7		t		979	36	55	10	.5					
			.7				917	24	98	7	.2					
			1.4				1102	151		28.5	3.3					
		.018	1				938	47	184	34	1					1.42
			.5				104	82	221	91	.96					
			1				995	59	314	37	1					
		.007	.7		t		955	50	98	41	.5					1.25
			t				1051	26	103	29	.5					
			.5		t		512	148	246	158	1.4					
			1.5		1		941	149	270	29	1.5					
			.53	.878			1274	68	239	62	1.04					
0			1.2		12		970	34	230	15	.7	22	.27			.17
			1.2		t		998	43	77	14	.7					
		.015	1				1046	49	162	12	.7		.09			3.87
			1	.34			838	39	172	20	1	24	.32			1.8
			.054		.75		1	2	20	13	.13	3	*	*	.06	.02
0							t	9	30	14	.78	4				.11
0			.097		.86		t	7	48	30	.59	6	*	*		.08
0			.012		.28		t	1	3	5	.26	1	*	*		.02
0			.076				t	12	28	14	.34	5			.18	.12
0			.022				t	4	22	8	.28	5	*	*		.15
0					.34		3	11	28	35	.9	9	*	*		.14
0							t	3	28	8	.19	1				.05
0			.205		1.67		26	8	50	7	.37	4			.65	.07
0			.03		.65		1	1	11	28	.88	1	*	*	.5	.05
0			.031		1.7		5	2	23	14	.18	6	*	*		.02
0			.064		3.4		1	3	27	7	.25	4	*	*		
0			.038				1	7	23	13	.29	6	*	*		.08
0			.096		.16		4	10	38	20	1.39	8	*	*		.1
0			.069		.23		1	7	31	10	.59	5	.021			.08
0			.059				t	6	25	32	.34	5	*	*		.11
0			.029				2	5	32	18	.49	5	*	*		.03
0			.121				2	10	34	24	.37	8	*	*		.07
0		2.11	.061		.11		2	11	28	6	1.24	7				.09
0			.019				1	12	31	2	.08	2	*	*		.07
0			.093				1	3	24	2	.21	3	.01	*		.08
0			.023				1	2	8	4	.24	3	*			.04
0			.025		.31		t	2	9	12	.5	2	*	*		.02
0			.26				t	28	23	17	.33	10	*	*		.19
0			.029				t	5	8	4	.07	4	*	*	.4	.05
0			.014		.31		1	7	20	8	.05	3	*	*		.05
0			.093				t	3	25	24	.66	4	*	*		.07
0			.322		1.49		1	7	49	4	.5	4	*	*	.22	.08
0			.024		.37		1	1	11	4	.29	1	*	*		.01
0			.024				1	4	26	9	.61	4	.012	*	.02	.03
0			.157		1.38		1	5	36	3	.14	3	*	*		.05

Food Item	Measure	Weight g	Calories	Carbohydrate g	Protein g	Fiber g	Saturated fat g	Unsaturated fat g	Total fat g	Cholesterol mg	Vitamin A IU	Vitamin B₁ mg	Vitamin B₂ mg	Vitamin B₆ mg
White	1 tsp	2.4	7	1.65	.25	.1			.05	0		.001	.003	
Poppy seed	1 tsp	2.8	15	.66	.5	.18	.14	1.04	1.25	0		.024	.005	.012
Poultry seasoning[36]	1 tsp	1.5	5	.98	.14	.17			.11	0	39	.004	.003	
Pumpkin pie spice[37]	1 tsp	1.7	6	1.17	.1	.25			.21	0	4	.002	.002	
Rosemary, dried	1 tsp	1.2	4	.77	.06	.21			.18	0	38	.006		
Saffron	1 tsp	.7	2	.46	.08	.03			.04	0				
Sage, grd	1 tsp	.7	2	.43	.07	.13	.05	.02	.09	0	41	.005	.002	
Salt	1 tsp	5.5	0	0	0				0	0	0	0	0	
Savory, grd	1 tsp	1.4	4	.96	.09	.21			.08	0	72		.005	
Tarragon, grd	1 tsp	1.6	5	.8	.36	.12			.12	0	67	.004	.021	
Thyme, grd	1 tsp	1.4	4	.89	.13	.26	.04	.03	.1	0	53	.007	.006	
Turmeric, grd	1 tsp	2.2	8	1.43	.17	.15			.22	0		.003	.005	

VEGETABLES, LEGUMES, SPROUTS, AND VEGETABLE JUICES[38]

Food Item	Measure	Weight g	Calories	Carbohydrate g	Protein g	Fiber g	Saturated fat g	Unsaturated fat g	Total fat g	Cholesterol mg	Vitamin A IU	Vitamin B₁ mg	Vitamin B₂ mg	Vitamin B₆ mg
Alfalfa, sprouts, raw	1 cup	100	41		5.1	1.7			.6			.14	.21	
Artichoke, globe, boiled[39]	1 avg	100	44	9.9	2.8	2.4			.2		150	.07	.04	
Asparagus														
Cut pieces, raw	1 cup	135	35	6.8	3.4	.945			.3		1220	.24	.27	.2
Spears, ckd	4 lg	100	20	3.6	2.2	.7			.2		900	.16	.18	.1[40]
Spears, canned, drained	4 avg	80	17	2.7	1.9	.4			.3		640	.05	.08	.044
Bamboo shoots, raw	1 cup	125	36	6.9	3.47	.932			.4		26.7	.02	.093	
Beans														
Azuki, dry		100	326	58.4	21.5	4.3			1.6		6	.5	.1	
Black, dry	1 cup	200	678	122	44.6				3		60	1.1	.4	
Black-eye peas, ckd	1 cup	165	178	29.9	13.4				1.3		580	.5	.18	.18[40]
Canned w/pork	1 cup	250	304	47.6	15.2	3.6	2.3	3.3	6.4		324	.2	.08	
Canned w/o pork	1 cup	250	300	57.6	15.8	3.6			1.2		150	.18	.1	
Chickpeas (garbanzos), dry	1 cup	200	720	122	41	10	.9	8.3	9.6		100	.62	.3	
Green, snap, raw	1 cup	110	35	7.8	2.1	1.1			.2		660	.09	.12	.08
Green, snap, ckd	1 cup	125	31	6.8	2	1.2			.3		680	.09	.11	.087[40]
Green, snap, canned, drained	1 cup	135	32	7	1.9	1.2			.3		630	.04	.07	.054
Lentils, ckd	1 cup	200	212	38.6	15.6	2.4			t		40	.14	.12	
Lentil sprouts, raw	1 cup	100	104		8.4	1.1			.3			.21	.09	
Lima, ckd	1 cup	190	262	48.6	15.6	3			1.1			.25	.11	.3[40]
Lima, canned, drained	1 cup	170	163	31	9.2	3			.5		320	.05	.09	.15
Mung, sprouts, raw	1 cup	105	37	6.9	4	.7			.2		20	.14	.14	
Pinto, dry	1 cup	190	663	121	43.5	8			2.3			1.6	.4	1
Red kidney, ckd	1 cup	185	218	39.6	14.4	2.78			.9		10	.2	.11	
Red kidney, canned	1 cup	255	230	41.8	14.5	2.3			1		10	.13	.1	
Soybeans, ckd	1 cup	180	234	19.4	19.8	3			10.3		50	.38	.16	
Soybeans, canned, drained	1 cup	150	153	11.1	13.5	2.1			7.5		510	.09		
Soybean curd (tofu)	3.5 oz	100	72	2.4	7.8	.1			4.2		0	.06	.03	
Soybeans, fermented, miso		100	776	107	47.6				20.9		180	.29	.44	
Soybeans, fermented, natto		100	758	52.2	76.7				33.6		0	.32	2.27	
Soybean granules	1 cup	152	480	48	76				8		t	2.4	.68	
Soybean milk	1 cup	226	75	5	7.7				3.4		90	.18	.065	
Soybean sprouts, raw	1 cup	105	48	5.6	6.5	2.3			1.5		80	.24	.21	
Yellow wax, ckd	1 cup	125	28	5.8	1.8	1			.3		290	.09	.11	.098[40]
Yellow wax, canned, drained	1 cup	135	32	7	1.9	1			.4		140	.04	.07	.056
White, ckd	1 cup	190	224	40.3	14.8	3			1.1		0	.27	.13	

*Present, but approximate value in milligrams unavailable.

[36]Mixture of white pepper, sage, thyme, marjoram, savory, ginger, allspice, nutmeg.

[37]Mixture of cinnamon, ginger, nutmeg, allspice, cloves.

[38]Most of the vegetables are cooked, unsalted, in small amount of water for a short time.

[39]Base and soft ends of leaves.

[40]Based on frozen product.

Vitamin B$_{12}$ mcg	Biotin mcg	Folic Acid mg	Niacin mg	Pantothenic Acid mg	Vitamin C mg	Vitamin E mg	Sodium mg	Phosphorus mg	Potassium mg	Calcium mg	Iron mg	Magnesium mg	Copper mg	Manganese mg	Selenium mcg	Zinc mg
0		.005					t	4	2	6	.34	2	*	*		.03
0		.027					1	24	20	41	.26	9	*	*		.29
0		.045		.18			t	3	10	15	.53	3				.05
0		.038		.4			1	2	11	12	.34	2				.04
0		.012		.74			1	1	11	15	.35	3	*	*		.04
0							1	2	12	1	.08					
0		.04		.23			t	1	7	12	.2	3	*	*		.03
		0		0			2132		t	14	t		.022			.22
0		.057					t	2	15	30	.53	5	*	*		.06
0		.143					1	5	48	18	.52	6	*	*		.06
0		.069					1	3	11	26	1.73	3	*	*	.075	.09
0		.113		.57			1	6	56	4	.91	4	*	*		.1
			1.6		16					28	1.4					1
			.7		8		30	69	301	51	1.1		.2	.36		.35
0	.675	.086	2	.837	45	2.59	3	84	375	30	1.4	27	.148	.256		1.31
0			1.4	.4[40]	26		1	50	183	21	.6		.1			
0	1.6	.005	.6	.156	12		189	42	133	15	1.5		.12			
			.8		5.32			78.7	708	17.3	.667					
			2.5		0		7	350		75	4.8					
			4.4				50	840	2076	270	15.8					
0		.168	2.3	.66[40]	28		2	241	625	40	3.5	90.7				3
		.061	1.6	.23	4		1158	230	526	136	4.4	100	.55			
			1.6		4		844	302	670	170	5	146				
		.398	4		t		52	662	1594	300	13.8					5.4
0		.048	.6	.19	21	.1	8	48	267	62	.9	35	.26	.45	.66	.4
0		.05	.6	.168[40]	15		5	46	189	63	.8		.125			.4
0	1.35	.016	.4	.1	5		319	34	128	61	2	28	.054		1.2	.4
			1.2		0			238	498	50	4.2		.54			2
			1.1		24					12	3					1.5
0		.082	1.3	.48[40]			4	293	-1163	55	5.9		.32			1.7
0		.022	.9	.22	10		401	119	377	48	4.1					
		.012	.8		20		5	67	234	20	1.4					.9
0		.41	4.2	1.23			19	868	1870	257	12.2					
		.068	1.3				6	259	629	70	4.4		.647			
			1.5				8	278	673	74	4.6					
			1.1		0		4	322	972	131	4.9					
					3		354	176		100	5.2					
			.1		0		7	126	42	128	1.9	111				
			1.3		0		13.381	1402	1515	308	7.7					
			5		0			826	1129	467	16.8					
			1.6		t		8			240	10.8					
			.5		0			109		47.5	1.8					
			.8		14			70		50	1.1					1.6
0		.042	.6	.172[40]	16		4	46	189	63	.8					
0			.4		7		319	34	128	61	2					
			1.3		0		13	281	790	95	5.1					1.8

Food Item	Measure	Weight g	Calories	Carbohydrate g	Protein g	Fiber g	Saturated fat g	Unsaturated fat g	Total fat g	Cholesterol mg	Vitamin A IU	Vitamin B$_1$ mg	Vitamin B$_2$ mg	Vitamin B$_6$ mg
Beets, diced														
Raw	1 cup	135	58	13.4	2.2	1.1			.1		30	.04	.07	.074
Cooked	1 cup	170	54	12.2	1.9	.94			.2		30	.05	.07	
Canned, drained	1 cup	170	63	15	1.7	.94			.2		30	.02	.05	.068
Beet greens														
Raw	3.5 oz	100	24	4.6	2.2	1.3			.3		6100	.1	.22	.05
Cooked	1 cup	145	26	4.8	2.5	1.4			.3		7400	.1	.22	
Broccoli														
Raw, 5½" long	1 piece	100	32	5.9	3.6	1.5			.3		2500[41]	.1	.23	.195
Cooked	1 cup	155	40	7	4.8	2			.5		3800	.14	.31	
Brussels sprouts														
Raw	9 med	100	45	8.3	4.9	1.6			.4		550	.1	.16	.23
Cooked	1 cup	155	56	9.9	6.5	2.1			.6		810	.12	.22	.262[40]
Cabbage														
Common, sliced, raw	1 cup	70	17	3.8	.9	.8			.1		90	.04	.04	.112
Common, sliced, ckd	1 cup	145	29	6.2	1.6	1			.3		190	.06	.06	
Red, sliced, raw	1 cup	70	22	4.8	1.4	1			.1		30	.06	.04	.14
Savoy, sliced, raw	1 cup	70	17	3.2	1.7	.5			.1		140	.04	.06	.133
Chinese, raw	1 cup	75	11	2.3	.9	.6			.1		110	.04	.03	
Chinese, ckd	1 cup	160	16	2.6	2.4						80	.14	.14	
Carrots														
Raw	1 lg	100	42	9.7	1.1	1			.2		11,000	.06	.05	.15
Cooked	1 cup	155	48	11	1.4	1.5			.3		15,750	.08	.08	
Canned, drained	1 cup	155	47	10.4	1.2	1			.5		22,500	.03	.05	.045
Juice	1 cup	227	96	22.2	2.47						24,750	.13	.12	.5
Cauliflower, flower buds														
Raw	1 cup	100	27	5.2	2.7	1			.2		60	.11	.1	.21
Cooked	1 cup	125	28	5.1	2.9	1.25			.3		80	.11	.1	.22[40]
Celeriac root, raw	4 roots	100	40	8.5	1.8	1.3			.3			.05	.06	.165
Celery														
Raw	1 cup	120	20	4.7	1.1	.7			.1		320	.04	.04	.072
Cooked	1 cup	150	21	4.7	1.2	.9			.2		390	.03	.05	
Chard, Swiss														
Raw	3.5 oz	100	25	4.6	2.4	.8			.3		6500	.06	.17	
Cooked	1 cup	145	26	4.8	2.6	1			.3		7830	.06	.16	
Chives, chopped, raw	1 tbsp	10	3	.6	.2	.1			t		580	.008	.013	.018
Collards														
Raw	3 oz	100	40	7.2	3.6	.9			.7		6500	.2	.31	
Cooked	1 cup	145	42	7.1	3.9	1.15			.9		7830	.2	.29	
Corn														
Cooked	1 cup	165	137	31	5.3				1.7		660	.18	.17	.47[40]
Canned, drained	1 cup	165	139	32.7	4.3	1.1			1.3		580	.05	.08	.33
Cream-style canned	1 cup	256	210	51.2	5.4				1.5		840	.08	.13	.1
Cress, sprigs														
Raw	5–8	10	3	.6	.3	.1			.1		930	.008	.026	.025
Cooked	1 cup	135	31	5.1	2.6	1.2			.8		10,400	.08	.22	
Cucumber, sliced, un-pared, raw	1 cup	105	16	3.6	.9	.6			.1		260	.03	.04	.042
Dandelion greens														
Raw	3.5 oz	100	45	9.2	2.7	1.6			.7		14,000	.19	.26	
Cooked	1 cup	105	35	6.7	2.1	1.3			.6		12,290	.14	.17	
Dock (sorrel), raw	3.5 oz	100	28	5.6	2.1	.8			.3		12,900	.09	.22	
Eggplant														
Raw	1 cup	200	50	11.6	2.4	1.8			.4		20	.1	.1	.162
Cooked	1 cup	200	38	8.2	2	1.8			.4		20	.1	.08	
Endive, raw	1 cup	50	10	2.1	.9	.45			.1		1650	.04	.07	
Garlic, raw	1 clove	3	4	.9	.2				t		t	.01	t	
Ginger root, fresh	3.5 oz	100	49	9.5	1.4	1.1			1		10	.02	.04	

[41]Value for leaves is 16,000 IU/100 gr, flower clusters 3000 IU, stalks 400 IU.

Vitamin B12 mcg	Biotin mcg	Folic Acid mg	Niacin mg	Pantothenic Acid mg	Vitamin C mg	Vitamin E mg	Sodium mg	Phosphorus mg	Potassium mg	Calcium mg	Iron mg	Magnesium mg	Copper mg	Manganese mg	Selenium mcg	Zinc mg
0		.126	.5	.2	14		81	45	452	22	.9	31	.297	1.27		.068
		.133	.5		10		73	39	354	24	.9		.34			
0			.2	.17	5		401	31	284	32	1.2	25.5	.238			
0	3	.05	.4	.1	30		130	40	570	119	3.3	106	.09	1.3		
			.4		22		110	36	481	144	2.8					
0		.069	.9	1.17	113		15	78	382	103	1.1	24	.03	.15		
		.073	1.2		140		16	96	414	136	1.2		.15			.23
0	.4	.078	.9	.723	102	1	14	80	390	36	1.5	29	.05	.27		.38
0		.056	1.2	.63[40]	135		16	112	423	50	1.7		.12			.54
0	.07	.046	.2	1.143	33	.2	14	20	163	34	.3	13	.091		1.54	.3
		.026	.4			.48	20	29	236	64	.4		.13			.6
0	1.4	.031	.3	.226	43	.14	18	25	188	29	.6	12.6	.042	.07		
0			.2		39		15	38	188	47	.6					
		.062	.5		19		17	30	190	32	.5	10.5				
			1.6		52			64		52	.4					
0	3	.032	.6	.28	8	.45	47	36	341	37	.7	23	.15	.1	2.2	.4
		.037	.8		9		51	48	344	51	.9		.12			.5
0	2	.002	.6	.195	3		366	34	186	47	1.1	7	.06		2.02	.5
.023	0		1.35		20		105	81	767	8.3	1.5	51				
0	1.5	.055	.7	1	78	.15	13	56	295	25	1.1	24	.13	.17	.7	.37
0		.042	.8	.64[40]	69		11	53	258	26	.9		.07			
0			.7		8		100	115	300	43	6					
0	.12	.014	.4	.514	11	.57	151	34	409	47	.4	26	.17	.19		.16
			.5		9		132	33	359	47	.3		.18			
0		.03	.5	.172	32	1.5	147	39	550	88	3.2	65	.11	.3		
			.6		23		125	35	465	106	2.6					
0			.1		6		t	4	25	7	.2	3	.011			
		.102	1.7		92		43	63	401	203	1	57				
			1.7		67		36	57	339	220	.9					
0		.035	2.1	.725[40]	12		t	147	272	5	1					.7
0	1.95	.013	1.5	.363	7		389	81	160	8	.8	34			.495	.7
			2.6		13		604	143	248	8	1.5					1.06
0			1		7		1	8	61	8	.1					
			1.1		46		11	65	477	82	1.1					
0	1	.015	.2	.25	12	8.4	6	28	168	26	1.2	12	.09	.15		.22
					35		76	66	397	187	3.1	36	.15	.3		
					19		46	44	244	147	1.9					
			.5		119		5	41	338	66	1.6					
0		.062	1.2	.44	10		4	52	428	24	1.4	32	.2	.22		
		.032	1		6		2	42	300	22	1.2					
		.024	.3		5		7	27	147	41	.9	5	.045	.11		
			t		t		1	6	16	1	t	1.08	.008		.008	.038
			.7		4		6	36	264	23	2.1					

Food Item	Measure	Weight g	Calories	Carbohydrate g	Protein g	Fiber g	Saturated fat g	Unsaturated fat g	Total fat g	Cholesterol mg	Vitamin A IU	Vitamin B₁ mg	Vitamin B₂ mg	Vitamin B₆ mg
Jerusalem artichoke, raw	4 sm	100	42	16.7	2.3	.8			.1		20	.2	.06	.071
Kale														
Raw	3.5 oz	100	38	6	4.2	1.3			.8		8900	.16	.26	.3
Cooked	1 cup	110	43	6.7	5	1.4			.8		9130	.11	.2	.19[40]
Kohlrabi, diced														
Raw	1 cup	150	43	9.9	3	1.5			.15		30	.09	.06	.22
Cooked	1 cup	165	40	8.7	2.8	1.5			.2		30	.1	.05	
Leeks, raw, 5" long	3–4	100	52	11.2	2.2	1.3			.3		40	.11	.06	.2
Lettuce														
Boston or bib, raw	1 cup	55	8	1.4	.7	.25			.1		530	.03	.03	.028
Cos or romaine, raw	1 cup	55	10	1.9	.7	.35			.2					
Iceberg, raw	1 cup	75	10	2.2	.7	.35			.1		250	.05	.05	.028
Looseleaf, raw	1 cup	55	10	1.9	.7	.35			.2		1050	.03	.04	.028
Lotus root, 1 segment	⅔ avg	100	69	15.7	2.8				.1		0	.146	.011	
Mushrooms														
Raw	1 cup	70	20	3.1	1.9	.56			.2		t	.07	.32	.087
Canned, drained	1 cup	270	51	6.9	3.3				.6		0	.06	.66	.16
Sauteed	4 med	70	78	2.8	1.7	.7			7.4		173	.055	.275	
Mustard greens														
Raw	3.5 oz	100	31	5.6	3	1.1			.5		7000	.11	.22	
Cooked	1 cup	180	29	5	3.1	1.82			.4		14,760	.144	.25	.139[40]
Okra														
Raw	1 cup	100	36	7.6	2.4	1			.3		520	.17	.21	.075
Cooked	1 cup	160	46	9.6	3.2	1.5			.5		780	.21	.29	.07[40]
Onions														
Raw	1 cup	170	65	14.8	2.6	1			.2		70	.05	.07	.22
Cooked	1 cup	210	61	13.7	2.5	1.2			.2		80	.06	.06	
Dehydrated, flakes	3.5 oz	100	350	82	8.7	4.4			1.3		200	.25	.18	.5
Scallions, bulb and tops, raw	1 cup	100	36	8.2	1.5	1			.2		2000	.05	.05	
Parsley, chopped, raw	1 cup	60	26	5.1	2.2	.9			.4		5100	.07	.16	.098
Parsnips														
Raw	½ lg	100	76	17.5	1.7	2			.5		30	.08	.09	.09
Cooked	1 cup	155	102	23.1	2.3	3			.8		50	.11	.12	
Peas														
Raw	1 cup	145	122	20.9	9.1	2.9			.6		930	.51	.2	.23
Cooked	1 cup	160	114	19.4	8.6	3.2			.6		860	.45	.18	.2[40]
Canned, drained	1 cup	170	150	28.6	8	3.9			.7		1170	.15	.1	.085
Split, ckd	1 cup	200	230	41.6	16	.8			.3		80	.3	.18	
Peppers														
Green, sliced, raw	1 cup	80	18	3.8	1	1.12			.2		340	.06	.06	.208
Green, sliced, ckd	1 cup	135	24	5.1	1.4	1.89			.3		570	.08	.09	
Red, sliced, raw	1 cup	100	31	7.1	1.4				.3		4450	.08	.08	
Hot chili, green, canned	1 cup	245	49	12.3	1.7	3			.2		1490	.07	.07	
Hot chili, red, canned	1 cup	245	51	9.6	2.2				1.5		23,500	.02	.22	
Pickles														
Dill	1 lg	100	11	2.2	.7	.5			.4		100	t	.02	.007
Sour	1 lg	105	10	2	.5	.5			.2		100	t	.02	
Sweet (gherkins)	1 lg	35	51	12.8	.2				.1		30	t	.01	
Pimientos, canned	3 med	100	27	5.8	.9	.6			.5		2300	.02	.06	
Potato														
Raw, diced	1 cup	150	114	25.7	3.2				.2		t	.15	.06	
Baked in skin	1 lg	202	145	32.8	4	1.2			.2		t	.15	.07	
Boiled in skin	1 med	100	76	17.1	2.1	.5			.1		t	.09	.04	
Dehydrated flakes, dry	1 cup	45	164	37.8	3.2	.5			.3		t	.1	.03	.216
Dehydrated flakes, prepared	1 cup	210	195	30.5	4				6.7		270	.08	.08	
French fries	10 pieces	50	137	18	2.1	.5	2	4	6.6		t	.06	.04	.09[40]

[42]Values range from 7/100 gm for freshly harvested to 75 after long storage.

Vitamin B$_{12}$ mcg	Biotin mcg	Folic Acid mg	Niacin mg	Pantothenic Acid mg	Vitamin C mg	Vitamin E mg	Sodium mg	Phosphorus mg	Potassium mg	Calcium mg	Iron mg	Magnesium mg	Copper mg	Manganese mg	Selenium mcg	Zinc mg
0			1.3		4			78		14	3.4	11				
0	.5	.06	2.09	1	125	8	75	73	318	179	2.2	37	.09	.5		
0			1.8	.38[40]	102		47	64	243	206	1.8	31				
0		.015	.45	.247	99		12	75	558	61	.53	55	.21	.16		
			.3		71		10	68	429	54	.5					
0	1.4		.5	.12	17	1	5	50	347	52	1.1	23	.09	.07		
0	.35	.02	.2	.1	4	.22	5	14	145	19	1.1	5	.08	.4		.3
0	.35	.02	.2	.1	5		7	17	131	15	.4	5	.035		.675	.3
0	.35	.02	.2	.1	10		5	14	145	37	.8		.035			.2
			.3		75			103		30	.6					
0	11.2	.016	2.9	1.54	2	.58	11	81	290	4	.6	7.7	1.08	.056	8.54	.91
0			5.4	2.7				243		21	2.1	21	.7		29.4	
			2.9		t			81		8	.7		.545			
0			.8	.21	97		32	50	377	183	3	27				
0			1.1	.295[40]	117		32	32	396	284	1.4					
0		.024	1	.26	31		3	51	249	92	.6	41	.11			
0			1.4	.34[40]	32		3	66	278	147	.8					
0	1.53	.042	.3	.22	17	.442	17	61	267	46	.9	20.4	.255	.61	2.55	.6
			.4		15		15	61	231	50	.8		.14			
0			1.4	1.2	35		88	273	1383	166	2.9	106				
0		.036	.4	.144	32		5	39	231	51	1					.3
0	.24	.07	.7	.18	103		27	38	436	122	3.7	24.5	.293	.563		
0	.1	.067	.2	.6	16		12	77	541	50	.7	32	.1	.2		
			.2		16		12	96	587	70	.9					
0		.029	4.2	1.1	39	3.1	3	168	458	38	2.8	50.7	.33			1.2
0			3.7	.5[40]	32		2	158	314	37	2.9		.24			1.2
0	3.4	.034	1.4	.255	14	.034	401	129	163	44	3.2	34	.289			1.3
			1.8				26	178	592	22	3.4		.5			
0		.015	.4	.184	102		10	18	170	7	.6	14.4	.128		.48	.048
			.6		130		12	22	201	12	.7					
0			.5	.271	204			30		13	.6					
0			1.7	1.68	167		10.4	34	462	12	1	28	.26	.31		
0		.15	1.5	2.65	74			39		22	1.2	418				
			t		6		1428	21	200	26	1	12				.27
			t		7		1353	15		17	3.2					
			t		2			6		4	.4		.35			.052
0			.4	.166	95			17		7	1.5		.6			
			2.3		30		5	80	611	11	.9					
			2.7		31		6	101	782	14	1.1		.26			
			1.5		16		3	53	407	7	.6		.1			.3
0			2.4	.065	14		40	78	720	16	.8	45	.08			
			1.9		11		485	99	601	65	.6					.76
0		.011	1.6	.27[40]	10		3	56	427	8	.6					.14
			4.8		32		379	172	1318	26	1.9		.459			

Food Item	Measure	Weight g	Calories	Carbohy-drate g	Protein g	Fiber g	Satu-rated fat g	Unsatu-rated fat g	Total fat g	Choles-terol mg	Vitamin A IU	Vitamin B₁ mg	Vitamin B₂ mg	Vitamin B₆ mg
Fried from raw	1 cup	170	456	55.4	6.8	1.6			24.1	t		.2	.12	
Hash browns	1 cup	155	355	45.1	4.8	1.2			18.1	t		.12	.08	.13[44]
Mashed w/milk[43]	1 cup	210	137	27.3	4.4	.8			1.5		40	.17	.11	.18[44]
Scalloped and au gratin w/o cheese	1 cup	245	255	36	7.4				9.6	14	390	.15	.22	
Scalloped and au gratin w/ cheese	1 cup	245	355	33.3	13				19.4	36	780	.15	.29	
Potato chips	10 chips	20	113	10	1.1	.3	2	6	8		t	.04	.014	
Pumpkin, canned	1 cup	245	81	19.4	2.5	3			.7		15,860	.07	.12	.139
Radish														
Red, raw	10 med	50	8	1.6	.5	.35			t		t	.01	.01	.037
Oriental, raw	3.5 oz	100	19	4.2	.9	.7			.1		10	.03	.02	
Rutabaga														
Raw	1 cup	140	64	15.4	1.5	1.4			.1		810	.1	.1	.14
Cooked	1 cup	170	60	13.9	1.5	2			.2		940	.1	.1	
Sauerkraut														
Canned	1 cup	235	42	9.4	2.4	1.6			.5		120	.07	.09	.31
Juice	1 cup	242	24	5.6	1.7				t			.07	.1	.605
Shallots, chopped, raw	1 tbsp	10	7	1.7	.3	1			t		t	.01	t	
Spinach														
Raw	1 cup	55	14	2.4	1.8	.3			.2		4460	.06	.11	.14
Cooked	1 cup	180	41	6.5	5.4	1			.5		14,580	.13	.25	.34[44]
Canned, drained	1 cup	205	49	7.4	5.5	1.6			1.2		16,400	.04	.25	.14
New Zealand, raw	3.5 oz	100	19	3.1	2.2	.7			.3		4300	.04	.17	
New Zealand, cooked	1 cup	180	23	3.8	3.1	1.1			.4		6480	.05	.18	
Squash														
Summer, raw	1 cup	130	25	5.5	1.4	.75			.1		530	.07	.12	.186
Summer, ckd	1 cup	180	25	5.6	1.6	.8			.2		700	.09	.14	.113[44]
Winter, baked	1 cup	205	129	31.6	3.7	2.6			.8		8610	.1	.27	.18[44]
Sweet potato														
Baked	1 avg	146	161	37	2.4	1.8			.6		9230[45]	.1	.08	
Candied, 2″ × 4″	2 halves	100	168	34.2	1.3	.6			3.3		6300[45]	.06	.04	
Canned	1 cup	200	216	49.8	4	2			.4		15,600[45]	.1	.08	.132
Tomato														
Raw	1 med	150	33	7	1.6	.8			.3		1350	.09	.06	.15
Canned	1 cup	241	51	10.4	2.4	.8			.5		2170	.12	.07	.126
Juice	1 cup	243	46	10.4	2.2	.4			.2		1940	.12	.07	.366
Paste, canned	1 cup	262	215	48.7	8.9	2			1		8650	.52	.31	
Puree, canned	1 cup	249	97	22.2	4.2	1			.5		4000	.22	.12	.45
Turnips														
Raw	1 cup	130	39	8.6	1.3	1.15			.3		t	.05	.09	.117
Cooked	1 cup	155	36	7.6	1.2	1.35			.3		t	.06	.08	
Turnip greens														
Raw	3.5 oz	100	28	5	3	.8			.3		7600	.21	.39	.263
Cooked	1 cup	145	29	5.2	3.2	1			.3		9140	.22	.35	.14[44]
Vegetable juice cocktail	1 cup	242	41	8.7	2.2	.8			.2		1690	.12	.07	
Water chestnuts	4 avg	25	20	4.8	.4	.2			.1		0	.04	.05	
Watercress, raw	1 cup	35	7	1.1	.8	.35			.1		1720	.03	.06	.045
Yams, ckd in skin	1 cup	200	210	48.2	4.8	1.8			.4		t	.18	.8	
Yeast														
Bakers', dry (active)	1 oz	28	80	11	10.5	.1			.5		t	.66	1.53	.56
Bakers', compressed	1 oz	28	24	3.1	3.4				.1		t	.2	.47	.168
Brewer's, debittered	1 tbsp	8	23	3.1	3.1	.14			.1		t	1.25	.34	.2
Torula	1 oz	28	79	10.5	10.9	.92			.3		t	3.97	1.43	.84

[43]Made with 6 tbsp milk and ¾ tsp salt added to four med. potatoes.

[44]Amounts may vary significantly between brands.

[45]Varies with color of flesh; deep orange varieties average 10,000 IU/100 gm; lt yellow about 600 IU.

Vitamin B$_{12}$ mcg	Biotin mcg	Folic Acid mg	Niacin mg	Pantothenic Acid mg	Vitamin C mg	Vitamin E mg	Sodium mg	Phosphorus mg	Potassium mg	Calcium mg	Iron mg	Magnesium mg	Copper mg	Manganese mg	Selenium mcg	Zinc mg
0		.026	3.3	.47[40]	14		446	122	736	19	1.4					
0		.021	2.1	.48[40]	21		632	103	548	50	.8		.2			
			2.5		27		870	181	801	132	1					
			2.2		25		1095	299	750	311	1.2					
			1		3			28	226	8	.4	9.6	.06			.162
0		.047	1.5	1	12		5	64	588	61	1		.33			
0		.012	.1	.092	12		8	14	145	14	.5	7	.08	.025	2.1	.13
			.4		32			26	180	35	.6					
0		.038	1.5	.22	60		7	55	335	92	.6	20	.11	.056		
		.036	1.4		44		7	53	284	100	.5					
0			.5	.22	33		1755[44]	42	329	85	1.2		.235			1.88
0			.5	.29	44		1905[44]	34		90	2.7					
			t		t		1	6	33	4	.1					
0	3.5	.106	.3	.15	28	1.25	39	28	259	51	1.7	44	.32	.42		.5
0		.164	.9	.23[40]	50		90	68	583	167	4		.252			1.3
0	4	.1	.6	.13	29		484	53	513	242	5.3	112				1.6
0			.6	.312	30		159	46	795	58	2.6	40				
			.9		25		166	50	833	86	2.7					
0		.04	1.3	.468	29		1	38	263		.5	21	.22	.182		
0			1.4	.3[40]	18		2	45	254		.7					.324
0			1.4	.56[40]	27		2	98	945		1.6					.28
		.026	.8		25		14	66	342	46	1		.22			
			.4		10		42	43	190	37	.9					
0			1.2	.86	28		96	82	400	50	1.6		.12			
0	2	.012	1	.48	34	.54	4	40	366	20	.8	21	.24	.27	.75	.2
0	4.32	.007	1.7	.55	41		3.3	46	523	14	1.2	24	.5	.1	2.41	.5
0		.017	1.9	.607	39		486	44	552	17	2.2	20				.1
			8.1		128		100	183	2237	71	9.2	50				
0			3.2		82		1000	85	1060	32	4.2	50				
0	.13	.026	.8	.26	47	.026	64	39	348	51	.7	25	.09	.052	.78	
			.5		34		53	37	291	54	.6		.06			
0		.095	.8	.38	139	2.3	10	58	440	246	1.8	58	.09	1.4		
0			.9	.2[40]	100			54		267	1.6					
			1.9		22		484	53	535	29	1.2					
			.2		1		5	16	125	1	.2	2.4				
0	.14	.017	.3	.108	28		18	19	99	53	.6	6.5	.032	.189		
			1.2		18			100		8	1.2		.44			
0		1.15	10.4	3.08	t		15	366	566	12	4.6		1.96			
0	112	.14	3.2	.98	t		5	112	173	4	1.4	16.5				
0	64	.192	3	1	t		10	140	152	17	1.4	18.5	.266	.042		
0	28	.84	12.6	3.08	t		4	486	580	120	5.5	46				

Composition of Foods, Agric. Handbook no. 8, Dept. of Agric.
Nutritive Value of American Foods, Agric. Handbook no. 456, Dept. of Agric.
Food Values, Bowes and Church, J.B. Lippincott, New York.
Scientific Tables, 6th ed., Geigy Pharmaceuticals, Ardsley, New York.
The Composition of Foods, McCance and Widdowson, Medical Research Council Special Report Series no. 297, Her Majesty's Stationery Office, London, England.
Selected articles from *The Journal of the American Dietetic Association, Cereal Chemistry, British Journal of Nutrition,* and the *Journal of Nutrition.*

WEIGHTS AND MEASURES

Weights

1 microgram	=	1/1,000,000 gram
1,000 micrograms	=	1 milligram
1 milligram	=	1/1,000 gram
1,000 milligrams	=	1 gram
1.00 ounce	=	28.35 grams
3.57 ounces	=	100.00 grams
0.25 pound	=	113.00 grams
0.50 pound	=	227.00 grams
1.00 pound	=	16.00 ounces
1.00 pound	=	453.00 grams

Capacity Measurements

1 quart	=	4 cups
1 pint	=	2 cups
1 cup	=	½ pint
1 cup	=	8 fluid ounces
1 cup	=	16 tablespoons
2 tablespoons	=	1 fluid ounce
1 tablespoon	=	½ fluid ounce
1 tablespoon	=	3 teaspoons

Approximate Equivalents

1 average serving	=	about 4 ounces
1 ounce fluid	=	about 28 grams
1 cup fluid		
Cooking oil	=	200 grams
Water	=	220 grams
Milk, soups	=	240 grams
Syrup, honey	=	325 grams

1 cup dry		
Cereal flakes	=	50 grams
Flours	=	100 grams
Sugars	=	200 grams
1 tablespoon fluid		
Cooking oil	=	14 grams
Milk, water	=	15 grams
Syrup, honey	=	20 grams
1 tablespoon dry	=	1/6 ounce
Flours	=	8 grams
Sugars	=	12 grams
1 pat butter	=	½ tablespoon
1 teaspoon fluid	=	about 5 grams
1 teaspoon dry	=	about 4 grams
1 grain	=	about 65 milligrams
1 minim	=	about 1 drop water

Abbreviations and Symbols Used in the Tables

avg	average		reg	regular
cal	calorie		sm	small
diam	diameter		svg	serving
enr	enriched		t	trace
g	gram		tbsp	tablespoon
IU	International Unit		tsp	teaspoon
lb	pound		w	with
lg	large		—	reliable data lacking
mcg	microgram		/	of; with
mg	milligram		"	inches
oz	ounce			

FORMS

FORM A
INDIVIDUAL ANALYSIS TABLE

Name	Age	Sex	Height	Current Weight	Desired Weight (see p. 175)	Level of Activity (see p. 173)	Individual Daily Total Calories

FORM B
WEEKLY MENU PLANNER AND CALORIE COUNTER

	Page	Menu	Calories Per Serving
Date:			
Brkft			
Lunch			
Dinner			
TOTAL			
Date:			
Brkft			
Lunch			
Dinner			
TOTAL			
Date:			
Brkft			
Lunch			
Dinner			
TOTAL			
Date:			
Brkft			
Lunch			
Dinner			
TOTAL			
Date:			
Brkft			
Lunch			
Dinner			
TOTAL			

FORM C
SUBSTITUTE RECORD

NAME	DATE	FOOD ITEM	CALORIES

BIBLIOGRAPHY

CAREY, RUTH L., UYHMEISTER, IRMA B. AND HUDSON, JENNIE S. *Commonsense Nutrition.* Omaha: Pacific Press, 1971.

CHANEY, MARGARET S. AND ROSS, MARGARET L. *Nutrition.* 8th ed. Boston: Houghton Mifflin Co., 1971.

CHURCH, C. F. AND CHURCH, H. N. *Food Value of Portions Commonly Used.* 11th ed. Philadelphia: J. B. Lippincott, 1970.

DAVIS, ADELLE. *Let's Cook It Right.* New York: The New American Library Inc., 1970.

DAVIS, ADELLE. *Let's Eat Right to Keep Fit.* New York: Harcourt, Brace, and World, Inc., 1954.

DEUTSCH, RONALD M. *The Family Guide to Better Food and Better Health.* Des Moines: Meredith Corp., 1971.

FREDERICKS, CARLTON AND BAILEY, HERBERT. *Food Facts and Fallacies.* New York: ARC Books, 1972.

GOODHART, ROBERT S. AND SHILS, MAURICE E. *Modern Nutrition in Health and Disease.* 5th ed. Philadelphia: Lea and Febiger, 1973.

GUTHRIE, HELEN A. *Introductory Nutrition.* 2nd ed. St. Louis: G. V. Mosby Co., 1971.

HAYES, ANNE. *Cooking for Health.* Quakertown: Humanitarian Society, 1969.

HUNTER, BEATRICE T. *The Natural Foods Cookbook.* New York: Pyramid Books, 1961.

LANGSETH-CHRISTENSON, LILLIAN. *The Down-To-Earth Natural Food Cookbook.* New York: Grosset & Dunlap, 1973.

LAPPE, FRANCES M. *Diet for a Small Planet.* New York: Ballantine Books, Inc., 1973.

LINDLAHR, VICTOR H. *You Are What You Eat.* Hollywood: Newcastle Publishing Company, 1971.

McDERMOTT, IRENE E., TRILLING, MABEL B. AND

NICOLAS, FLORENCE W. *Food for Better Living.* 3rd ed. Chicago: J. B. Lippincott Co., 1960.

MOYER, WILLIAM C. *Buying Guide for Fresh Fruits, Vegetables and Nuts.* 4th ed. Blue Goose, Inc. 1971.

NICHOLS, H. L., JR., *Cooking with Understanding.* Greenwich: North Castle Books, 1971.

Nutrition Search, *Nutrition Almanac.* 2nd ed. Minneapolis: John D. Kirschmann, 1973.

PATTI, CHARLES. *The Food Book.* New York: Fleet Press Corp., 1973.

Recommended Dietary Allowances. 7th ed. Washington, D.C.: National Academy of Sciences, 1968.

ROENEY, JEAN. *How to Shop for Food.* New York: Barnes and Noble Books, 1972.

ROSEN, MARGERY O. "Start with Healthy Cooking." *Family Health,* April, 1974.

TARR, YVONNE Y. *Natural Foods Dieting Book.* New York: Quadrangle Books, 1972.

U.S. Dept. of Agriculture. *Nutritive Value of Foods.* Home and Garden Bulletin No. 72. Washington: U.S. Gov't Print. Off., 1971.

University of Nottingham Seminar, Edited by MENDEL STEIN, *Vitamins.* Churchill Livingstone, Edinburgh and London, 1971.

WATT, B. K. AND MERILL, A. L. *Composition of Foods—Raw, Processed, Prepared.* U.S.D.A. Handbook No. 8. Washington: U.S. Gov't Print. Off., 1963.

WHITE, PHILIP L., Ed., *Let's Talk About Food,* 2nd ed. Chicago: American Medical Association, 1970.

WILSON, EVA D., FISCHER, KATHERINE H. AND FUGUE, MARY E. *Principles of Nutrition.* 2nd ed. New York: John Wiley & Sons, Inc., 1965.

INDEX

Dates:
    bars, lemon-glazed, 101
    and orange salad, 18
Desirable height and weight chart, 174, 175
Desserts, sweets:
    apple pie, 66–67
    apricot bar, 58
    banana-nut sundae, 117
    bananas and cream, 28
    berry gelatin, 37
    carrot cake, 92
    chocolate brownies, 156
    chocolate cake, 115
    chocolate chip cookies, 153
    chocolate velvet ice cream, 54
    corn pudding, 84
    creamy fruit parfait, 97
    fine fruit salad, 122
    Florida orange ice, 123–124
    fresh fruit salad, 146
    fresh pineapple boats, 73
    frozen green grapes, 78
    fruit cocktail, 51
    fruit cup, 65
    fruit paradise, 32
    fruit platter with sauce, 33–34
    gingerbread, 139
    lemon-glazed date bars, 101
    maple nut ice cream, 50
    nutritive composition of, 192–195
    orange sherbet, 150
    peach ice cream, 136
    peach puddingcake, 48
    peaches marinade, 104
    peanut puff cookies, 90
    vanilla ice cream, 41, 94
    wassail, 86
    yogurt, 25
    yogurt and pineapple, 74
    yogurt dessert, 25
Dressings, salad:
    Italian, 71
    Louis, 135
    nutritive composition of, 208–209
    spinach, 120
    tangy tossed green, 155
    Thousand Island, 48

Eggplant sauté, 90
Eggs:
    -cottage cheese salad, 137
    foo yung, 112–113
    poached, 167

    salad on lettuce, 139
    Spanish omelet, 123
Endive and mushroom salad, 132

Fats, oils:
    function of, 3
    nutritive composition of, 208–209
    sources of, 183
Fish, 87–105
    nutritive composition of, 183, 196–197
    storage and cooking of, 8
    (See also specific types)
Florida orange ice, 123–124
Flour, nutritive composition of, 186–191
Food composition (table), 185–219
    beverages, 186–187
    breads, flours, cereals, 186–191
    dairy products, 190–193
    desserts, sweets, 192–195
    fish, seafood, seaweed, 196–197
    fruits, fruit juices, 198–203
    grains, grain products, 186–191
    meat, poultry, 202–206
    nuts, nut products, seeds, 206–207
    oils, fats, shortening, 208–209
    salad dressings, sauces, 208–209
    soups, 208–211
    spices, herbs, 210–213
    vegetables, legumes, sprouts, vegetable juices,
        212–219
Franks, batter, 15
French bread, 31
French dip sandwiches, 140–141
French toast, 164
Frosting, cream cheese, 92
Fruit:
    cocktail, 51
    cup, 65
    nut, and rice casserole, 116
    nutritive composition of, 183, 198–203
    paradise, 32
    parfait, creamy, 97
    platter with sauce, 33–34
    salad, fine, 122
    salad, fresh, 146
    sauce, 94
    storage of, 7
Fruity milk, 63

Garbanzo stuffed cabbage, 117
Garden pilaf, 74
Gelatin, berry, 37
Georgia shake, 77

Catalog

If you are interested in a list of fine Paperback
books, covering a wide range of subjects
and interests, send your name and address,
requesting your free catalog, to:

McGraw-Hill Paperbacks
1221 Avenue of Americas
New York, N.Y. 10020